UNIVERSITY LIBRA
UW-STEVENS POI
W9-BIY-514

Political Behavior of the American Electorate

Political Behavior of the American Electorate

Eighth Edition

William H. Flanigan
University of Minnesota

Nancy H. Zingale
University of St. Thomas

A Division of Congressional Quarterly Inc.
Washington, D.C.

Copyright © 1994 Congressional Quarterly

All rights reserved. No part of this publication may be reproduced or transmitted in any form or by any means, electronic or mechanical, including photocopy, recording, or any information storage and retrieval system, without permission in writing from the publisher.

Cover design: Rich Pottern

Printed in the United States of America

Library of Congress Cataloging-in-Publication Data

Flanigan, William H.
Political behavior of the American electorate / William H. Flanigan, Nancy H. Zingale. -- 8th ed.
p. cm.
Includes bibliographical references and index.
ISBN 0-87187-797-X
1. Voting--United States. I. Zingale, Nancy H. II. Title.
JK1967.F38 1994 94-2163
324.973--dc20 CIP

JK
1967
.F38
1994

To
Amy K. Hill
and to the memory of
Ruth M. Flanigan
Edwin N. Flanigan
James S. Hill

Contents

chapter three

chapter four

chapter five

chapter six

c h a p t e r s e v e n

Political Communication and the Mass Media 142

c h a p t e r e i g h t

Vote Choice and Electoral Decisions 170

a p p e n d i x

Survey Research Methods 201

Index 211

Tables and Figures

Tables

Figures

Preface

THE ELECTION of 1992 may not have been a watershed event in American politics, but it was certainly one of the more unusual elections of recent years. Many of the truisms of American politics were thrown into doubt, and unexpected, even unprecedented, events abounded. An incumbent president, who had enjoyed approval ratings of around 90 percent just a year before, lost his bid for a second term, managing to win only a little over one-third of the popular vote. An independent candidate, with little organization and even less political experience, won 19 percent of the popular vote. Able to capitalize on voter disenchantment with the political parties and "politics as usual," he also spent unprecedented amounts of his own money, offering lengthy televised presentations to the public on economic and budgetary topics. And the winner, who triumphed with less than a majority of the popular vote, survived notable weaknesses and significant flaws previously thought to be fatal to a presidential campaign.

The first edition of this book was published in 1967. The plan of the book then, as now, was to present basic analysis and generalizations about the political behavior of Americans. What was unknowable at the time was that a decade of political trauma was beginning for the American polity. Not only would some basic changes in political life take place, but these changes would call into question some of the things political scientists thought they knew about the way Americans behave politically. The 1980s were a quieter time. Many of the trends that began or were accelerated by the crises of the late 1960s and early 1970s tapered off, but did not reverse, during the Reagan and Bush years. If nothing else, the election of 1992 demonstrated, once again, the capacity to jar the political system and disorient public opinion analysis. Nevertheless, as we consider the twenty-five years since that first edition, we are impressed with the overall continuity in the behavior of the electorate, even in the midst of significant changes in the political environment.

In this eighth edition we continue to focus attention on the major concepts and characteristics that shape Americans' responses to politics: Are Americans committed to upholding basic democratic values? Who votes and why? How does partisanship affect political behavior? How and why does partisanship change? How do economic and social characteristics influence individuals' politics? How much influence do the mass media have on our attitudes and political choices? How do party loyalties, candidates' personalities, and issues influence our choices among candidates? (Those familiar with previous editions will note that the organization of the book has changed slightly. The original concluding chapter has been expanded and moved to become a full introductory chapter, and "Vote Choice and Electoral Decisions," which originally preceded "Political Communication and the Mass Media," has been moved to provide the final chapter.)

Throughout the book we will place the answers to these and other questions in the context of the changes that have occurred in American political behavior over the past forty years. Wherever possible, we place these recent trends in the broader context of political change over the two hundred years of the Republic. Specifically, we are concerned with the decline in voter turnout, the drop in voter attachment to political parties, and the loss of trust in government that many citizens have expressed. These trends, and their implications for American democracy, have been the subject of much discussion by political analysts and commentators.

A second major focus of this book is to illustrate and document these trends in American political behavior with the best longitudinal data available. We rely heavily, although not exclusively, on data from the National Election Studies collected by the Center for Political Studies at the University of Michigan and distributed through the Inter-university Consortium for Political and Social Research (ICPSR). These surveys, covering a broad range of political topics and offering the best time series data available, have been conducted during the fall of every election year since 1952. Unless otherwise noted, the data here come from this extraordinarily rich series of studies. We hope that the numerous tables and figures contained in this book will be used not only for documenting the points made in the text but also for learning to read and interpret data. Even better, since the raw data are available for classroom use through the ICPSR, we hope to provide an impetus for obtaining high-quality data to answer questions prompted, but not answered, by this book.

Acknowledgments

THE FOLLOWING analysis and description of the American electorate depend heavily on the work of others. Until 1960 analysis of the research findings and data collected by social scientists was limited to an examination of published tables, but there have been significant changes since then. The major studies of American public opinion and voting behavior are now accessible to scholars throughout the world for further examination and analysis.

These developments in political analysis resulted from the cooperation of many individuals, but the efforts of two men associated with the Institute for Social Research at the University of Michigan deserve special mention. The late Angus Campbell first opened the archives of the Survey Research Center (SRC) to outside scholars. Warren Miller of the Center for Political Studies (CPS) directed the organization and expansion of these archival activities through the creation of the Inter-university Consortium for Political and Social Research (ICPSR). The ICPSR, composed of the CPS and over three hundred and seventy academic and research institutions, has made available to an extensive clientele not only the archives of the SRC and the CPS but thousands of other major data collections as well. Recognition of the benefits this work has provided for scholars in the field of political behavior has taken many forms. Most significantly, the National Science Foundation has begun continuous funding of the biennial National Election Studies.

This book is highly dependent on the ICPSR in two ways. First, our analyses are based primarily on the large quantities of material collected by the CPS and the ICPSR Historical Archive and distributed by the ICPSR. Second, several generations of the scholars whose work we cite have similarly benefited from the availability of these resources.

We are pleased to acknowledge our great debt to the individuals in both the ICPSR and the CPS who have contributed to the establishment of these resources and services. We must hasten to add that neither organization bears any responsibility for the analysis and interpretations presented here. Indeed, the hazard of their efforts in providing open archives is the sort of reinterpretation and reanalysis that follows. We can only hope that any weaknesses of this work will not reflect on the general worthiness and excellence of the ICPSR and the CPS.

We also wish to thank our editors at CQ Press—Brenda Carter, Shana Wagger, Kerry Kern, Tracy Villano, and Ann O'Malley—for their shepherding of the last two editions of this book to publication. It is a pleasure to work with such competent and pleasant people.

W. H. F.
N. H. Z.

chapter one

Political Culture and American Democracy

SUCCESSFUL DEMOCRACIES rest upon the consent of the governed and widespread public support. In representative democracies we look for regular, free elections to choose political leaders and, when necessary, to turn them out of office. A democratic system of government, at a minimum, affords its citizens the opportunity to organize, to speak freely, and to select its leaders.

Beyond this simple, widely agreed-upon view, which assumes a crucial role for the people in choosing their representatives and emphasizes the individual as an autonomous actor with inherent political rights, there is less consensus on what is required of citizens. On the one hand are visions of a well-informed electorate making decisions based on rational calculations of its own best interest or, possibly, a public good. On the other, some critics see a deluded public, manipulated by political elites to hold views and support policies that are in the interests of the elites rather than the people. Somewhere in between is the view that the electorate responds to generalized policy promises and symbolic issues in selecting its leaders, setting broad and rather vague outer limits on decision-makers. Specific policies, however, are negotiated between public officials and subsets of the attentive public who are unrepresentative of the general public, both in terms of their degree of interest in a particular policy and in the political resources available to them with which to exert influence. In the chapters that follow, you will have the opportunity to judge for yourself the level of information and capacity for rational decision-making that the American public displays.

With the collapse of communism in the Soviet Union and Eastern Europe, democracy appears to be in ascendancy. As nations of the former Soviet bloc attempt to institute democratic forms and procedures, we can ask what are the cultural requirements for instituting and sustaining a democratic system? In the United States, how widespread is support for democratic values and how are these values learned and transmitted from generation to generation? How confident are American citizens that their government is playing by democratic rules? How confident are they that a democratic system is the best route to satisfactory policy outcomes?

Elections are a basic component of a democratic political system. They are the formal mechanism by which we maintain or alter the existing political leadership. At occasional intervals, competitive elections give ordinary citizens the power to offer continued support to or rejection of their elected leaders. While the choices available to voters in a general election may not be numerous or even particularly dissimilar, democratic systems *must* provide for competition, usually by means of political parties, in presenting alternative candidates.

Representation is built on elections. To a degree, representation is disciplined by them as well. Elected officials carry out their representational duties in view of upcoming elections, which have the potential of removing them from office. Nevertheless, the day-to-day activities of representatives may be only slightly related to future electoral concerns, and most citizens rarely contact their elected representatives. Consequently, the average person is more actively involved in the electoral system as a voter than in the representational system.

Elections and representation operate within the context of political values and beliefs that form the political culture. The political culture provides the setting in which political processes operate. The political culture constrains electoral and representational activities but rarely determines election or legislative outcomes.

The political culture is a fundamental element of any democratic political system. The values and opinions of the people are the foundation of democracy. To a large extent the achievement of political goals in a democracy depends on the public. A critical look at American democracy includes assessment of the public's support for political institutions and its attitudes toward political leadership.

As much as any recent year, 1992 illustrated the possibility that Americans are becoming disenchanted with their political system and the way it operates. More generally, 1992 can be viewed in the context of several decades of changing attitudes about American government and politics. Most noteworthy has been a long-term decline in the level of trust Americans have for their political institutions as well as a decline in citizens' belief in their ability to influence governmental decisions.

In this chapter we will consider these and other basic orientations toward the American political system. The main focus will be on a broad pattern of beliefs that form part of the political culture and, secondarily, on the acquisition of these beliefs. We will examine the content of American political culture as a foundation for democracy. A distinction also will be made, where appropriate, between the beliefs of political leaders and those of the mass public, since a basic finding is that the beliefs of these two groups about the political system are quite dissimilar. The discussion of political culture will cover attitudes toward the role of individual participants in the system, and the implications of these attitudes for political action. Attention will of necessity focus on the values of the dominant national culture, though we must keep in mind that political subcultures exist that may support contrary values and attitudes.

Democratic Beliefs and Values

A major thrust of the analysis of democratic political systems, and the U.S. system in particular, has been the search for a fundamental, underlying set of widely supported values. Presumably, the commitment to these principles holds a democratic society together in the presence of conflict and provides support and legitimacy for the functioning of its political institutions. These beliefs and values are variously referred to as the "American creed," the "American consensus," or the "American ethos." [1]

Social and political theorists see obvious differences between the economic system and the political system. Most would say that the United States has, as an ideal, a democratic political system and a capitalist or free market economic system. Public attitudes are more likely to mix the two. Ordinary citizens may see freedom as a basic value and include various forms of economic and political activity under the term. And while freedom is highly valued in American culture, it is not an absolute. People in fact believe in all kinds of limitations on freedom. Similarly, the perceptions Americans hold of their country within the international community are a blend of political, economic, military, and other social elements. The public's view of "American power" is certainly as much economic as military.

When forced to make a choice between government intervention and a wholly free market, the American public is clearly in favor of strong government activity. In the 1992 National Election Study by the Center for Political Studies, by a ratio of 3 to 1, the public preferred government intervention to handle economic problems rather than depending solely upon free market operations. Still, Americans believe even more strongly in individualism. There is widespread support in all major social groups for the statement "people get ahead by their own hard work."

A distinction often is made between democratic *goals,* such as equality, individual freedom, and due process of law, and democratic *procedures,* such as majority rule and protection of the political rights of freedom of speech, press, and assembly. The distinction is an important one to make when the extent to which these ideals are supported in the political culture of a system is under consideration, for democratic goals can quite possibly be pursued through undemocratic means or democratic procedures can be used for antidemocratic ends. Likewise, mass support may exist for democratic goals but not for democratic procedures, or vice versa.

A widely held and perfectly plausible expectation is that the American public supports both these kinds of democratic values. At a highly abstract level this is true enough. American citizens overwhelmingly subscribe to the basic rules and goals of democracy when this commitment is kept vague and abstract. There is near unanimous belief in values such as freedom, justice, and equality. As individuals are asked about more and more precise applications of democratic principles, agreement disappears. Specifically, the American electorate cannot seem to reach widespread agreement on extending civil rights and liberties to individuals with unpopular political and social opinions or on extending social and economic equality to certain ethnic and racial minorities.

During recent decades there has been an increased willingness in the public to allow free speech on unpopular points of view and permit books with distasteful perspectives to remain in libraries. Numerous studies document this shift in attitudes occurring from the mid-1950s to the 1970s, and without exception they find a strong relationship between increased tolerance and higher levels of education.[2]

Several important qualifications are in order. First, the electorate's responses are attitudes that may have little meaning for it and are not measures of its behavior or of its attitudes under crisis or threat to democratic principles. Second, it may not be that people are more tolerant but that the focus of their intolerance has shifted. People now tolerate speeches by Marxists but object to those of fascists or racists.[3]

More broadly, the desire for censorship may have shifted from political speech to other forms of expression, such as art and music, particularly those involving sexual or sacrilegious themes.

Finally, it is essential to keep in mind the distinction between mass attitudes and those of the political, social, and economic leaders in American society who consistently support these democratic principles more strongly than the general public does. Support among leaders is usually so high that it is possible to conclude that the leaders in society defend and maintain democratic procedures. The leaders' consensus on democratic rights and values makes the weakness of the general public's support less crucial.

National studies by both Samuel Stouffer in the 1950s and Herbert McClosky in the 1960s support the view that leaders are stronger than the public in support of the "rules of the game." [4] The degree to which leaders support these "rules" in comparison with the public can be seen in Table 1-1. Political influentials—in this study delegates and alternates to the Democratic and Republican national conventions in 1956—are consistently more likely to agree with the rules of the game than is a sample of the electorate. It may not be reassuring to discover that 7 percent of the political influentials agreed that "the majority has the right to abolish minorities if it wants to" or that 13 percent agreed that "almost any unfairness or brutality may have to be justified when some great purpose is being carried out." But in both examples substantially *greater* percentages of the general electorate, 28 percent and 33 percent, respectively, supported these views.

In 1972 Jeane Kirkpatrick studied the attitudes of political leaders, focusing on delegates to the Democratic and Republican national conventions.[5] Although this study was concerned primarily with issues rather than principles, her findings suggest that the earlier pattern still existed in the 1970s. For example, Kirkpatrick found that among leaders, 17 percent endorsed abridging the rights of the accused to stop criminal activity, while in the public as a whole 46 percent supported stopping crime even at the risk of reducing rights.[6]

Presumably, leaders are recruited and educated in such a way that they come prepared with, or develop, agreement on democratic procedures. Leaders apparently make decisions that maintain democratic practices, even without widespread public support. A somewhat less comforting possibility is that the political elite is simply sophisticated enough to understand what the "correct" answer is to attitude questions dealing with democratic beliefs. The seemingly greater adherence to these values by the politically active would attest to the prominence

TABLE 1-1 Political Influentials Versus the Electorate: Responses to Items Expressing Belief in Democratic Values

Item	Percentage agreeing with item: Political influentials	Percentage agreeing with item: General electorate
There are times when it almost seems better for people to take the law into their own hands rather than wait for the machinery of government to act.	13	27
The majority has the right to abolish minorities if it wants to.	7	28
If congressional committees stuck strictly to the rules and gave every witness his rights, they would never succeed in exposing the many dangerous subversives they have turned up.	25	47
I don't mind a politician's methods if he manages to get the right things done.	26	42
Almost any unfairness or brutality may have to be justified when some great purpose is being carried out.	13	33
People ought to be allowed to vote even if they can't do so intelligently.	66	48
The true American way of life is disappearing so fast that we may have to use force to save it.	13	35
	$N = 3{,}020$	$N = 1{,}484$

SOURCE: Adapted from Herbert McClosky, "Consensus and Ideology in American Politics," *American Political Science Review* 58 (1964): 365, Table 1.

NOTE: Since respondents were forced to make a choice on each item, the number of omitted or "don't know" responses was, on the average, fewer than 1 percent and thus has little influence on the direction or magnitude of the results reported in this table.

of such norms in the mass political culture but would not necessarily suggest any great commitment to or willingness to abide by these values. Some of the least palatable aspects of the Watergate scandal suggest no great depth of appreciation of these principles on the part of some prominent members of the Nixon administration, and later revelations suggest the same about earlier liberal administrations, such as Kennedy's.

Reaction to the Supreme Court's decisions overturning laws that would punish flag burning illustrates several aspects of the role of political elites in supporting democratic values. Various political elites—

the Court itself and some congressional leaders—resisted the popular passion for punishing flag burners. At the same time, other political leaders saw an opportunity to exploit an issue that was playing well among the public. Finally, the relatively easy defeat of the proposed constitutional amendment to ban flag burning, once the issue became rephrased as "tampering with the Bill of Rights," demonstrates the generalized, if vague, support the public has for democratic values and the critical nature of elite leadership in these areas.

The widespread interest of political analysts in public opinion and democratic beliefs has been based partly on a somewhat mistaken impression. Stable democratic political systems have been assumed to rest on a nearly universal commitment to fundamental principles and their application, but the evidence on this point is inconclusive. Certainly, a democratic system cannot long survive widespread, intense hostility to democratic values, but positive belief in particular operating procedures among the public is probably unnecessary. Hostility to democratic procedures is fatal, whether among the leaders or the public, but support of these procedures may prove essential only among leaders. Perhaps the public need not agree on basic principles so long as it does not demand disruptive policies and procedures.

Pride in Nation

Feelings of strong national loyalty may or may not be narrowly political in content, but they are likely to provide support for the political system, whether the system is democratic or not. Patriotism may provide system support when other attitudes do not. When people are dissatisfied with public policies or the economy, for example, strong feelings of national loyalty may suppress hostile attitudes or disruptive behavior. Democratic as well as authoritarian leaders have used a foreign enemy or an external crisis to rally support and distract the public from troubles at home.

In response to questions in public opinion polls, Americans express a strong pride in their country: Ninety-six percent are proud to be an American; 89 percent agree they are very patriotic; 80 percent characterize their love of America as "very" or "extremely strong"; and 71 percent say their feelings about the flag are "very" or "extremely good."[7]

When people are asked about their pride in the United States, they tend to offer political factors as examples. In other countries people are much more likely to give nonpolitical reasons for their pride: their country's economy, culture, or physical beauty. They are not nearly so likely to say they are proud of their political system.[8] Americans not only give political reasons for their pride in the United States but also cite "freedom" or "liberty" as the aspect of their political system that makes them proud. Thus, not only is there strong patriotic pride in the nation, but a central democratic value is a prominent feature of that sentiment.

System Support

Overall, Americans are proud of their country and their democratic form of government. This translates into high levels of political system support. Eighty-five percent of the respondents to a national survey believe that "whatever its faults, the United States still has the best system of government in the world." Over half of the public "would not change anything" in the American political system.

As we noted above, vague principles may be widely endorsed while specific applications may be opposed. So it should not be surprising that respondents will agree to vague statements of system support and at the same time endorse contradictory specifics as well. Eighty percent of the public say the Constitution should not be amended.[9] However, majorities also believe that the Constitution should be amended to abolish the Electoral College, mandate a balanced budget, or adopt the Equal Rights Amendment. Almost certainly none of these answers tells us how people would behave if actually faced with choices on amending the Constitution.

In general, the public has considerable confidence in the *institutions* of government but not much confidence in the *individuals* charged with operating these institutions. Thus, there is virtually no popular support for abolishing the presidency or the Supreme Court or Congress, while there is simultaneous and widespread disenchantment with the way the nation's political leadership is performing in these major branches of government. Currently, less than one-third of the public has "great confidence" in those running the Supreme Court, the Congress, or presidency. This low level of confidence has existed for some twenty years and represents a noticeable drop from the levels of confidence characteristic of earlier years.

Another indicator of the changing public mood is found in a long series of inquiries about "trusting the government in Washington to do

FIGURE 1-1 Trust in Government, by Race, 1958-1992

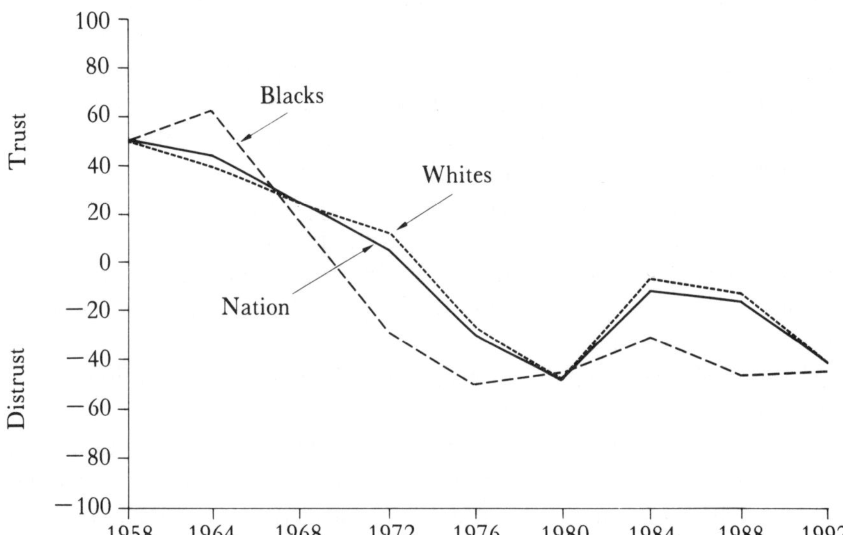

SOURCES: Arthur H. Miller, Thad A. Brown, and Alden S. Raine, "Social Conflict and Political Estrangement, 1958-1972" (Paper presented at the Midwest Political Science Association meeting, Chicago, 1973), Figure 2; Center for Political Studies National Election Studies.

the right thing." Thirty or forty years ago, trust was quite high, but that is not the case today. The steady decline in trust in government from 1958 to 1980 is illustrated in Figure 1-1. The only exception during this period was the increase in positive attitudes among blacks in 1964, occasioned by the early successes of the civil rights movement. The long-term decline in trust and confidence in government was accelerated by the Watergate-related disclosures in the early 1970s.

Even though the Watergate scandal and related matters had a disastrous impact on Richard Nixon's popularity, the general decline in respect for governmental institutions like the presidency began some time before. Curiously, this pattern of declining prestige extended to many nongovernmental institutions, such as the news media, schools, and the professions. Furthermore, the trend exists outside the United States in many of the developed nations of the world. Whatever the consequences of this trend, the causes are not limited to a few sensational political scandals.

The first term of the Reagan presidency witnessed a noticeable increase in trust, virtually all attributable to the changing attitudes of whites. This substantial upturn in trust appears related to the upbeat mood created by the Reagan administration and to a mild restoration of confidence in many public and private institutions in American society. This heightened trust did not survive Bush's administration, however. By 1992, levels of trust were again declining.

In the past, the youngest voters were typically the most trusting of government, a tendency one would expect, given their recent exposure to an educational process that tries to build support for the system. As late as the early 1960s, when most of the major socialization studies reported to date were undertaken, young people entered adulthood with strong affective feeling toward the government and a positive orientation toward themselves as participants in it.

A study of high school seniors and their parents, carried out in 1965 by M. Kent Jennings, showed that trust and confidence in government were fairly high among the students.[10] Learning, of course, continues into adulthood, and substantial modification of attitudes can occur through a variety of personal experiences with politics, new group membership, and the like.

If a group shares experiences, attitudes may be affected in a distinctive way. For example, attitudes of political support among adult black Americans increased temporarily in the early 1960s, concomitant with the growth of the civil rights movement (see Figure 1-1). The turbulent end of the 1960s had the opposite effect on the levels of trust among young people. When the students in the Jennings study were interviewed again in 1973, their level of trust had declined markedly and was accompanied by an increase in cynicism.[11] These changes were considerably greater than the changes in their parents' attitudes over the eight years, although the young people were still somewhat more supportive than their parents. A third interview of these individuals in 1982 showed a further drop in trust.

The 1972 National Election Study showed that the young people in the sample were the least trusting of government of any age group, a stark reversal of findings in earlier years when young people were generally the most trusting. It is possible that when dramatic changes occur, they are felt most intensely among those groups with the least firmly established attitudes. These patterns have fluctuated over the years, but since the 1970s young people have not been consistently more or less trusting than older people.

These general attitudes of distrust of and dissatisfaction with the government have a parallel in the declining confidence of individuals in their ability to participate effectively in the political process. A long trend in the individual's *sense of political efficacy,* that is, the individual's belief about his or her ability to influence government, is documented in Table 1-2. Between 1964 and 1968 more than 10 percent of the public shifted to feeling that they had little influence. Like trust in government, attitudes of political efficacy turned upward during the Reagan years and then down again during the Bush administration. This pattern is not nearly as dramatic as the changes in trust in government, which indicate that individuals have not lost as much confidence in themselves as they have in their leaders. It may be that the emergence in 1992 of independent presidential candidate Ross Perot gave some people a greater feeling of efficacy, accounting for the slight increase in that year. There always are differences among individuals in their sense of political efficacy, differences that are strongly related to education, general self-confidence, and experience with political participation. However, the decline in the overall level of feelings of efficacy at the same time that general levels of education were rising suggests that the decline is attributable to changes in the political environment, rather than to any changes in individual characteristics, such as skills or general self-confidence.

Citizen Roles and Political Participation

American citizens have a strongly developed sense of obligation to inform themselves, to participate in elections, and, to a lesser extent, to participate in other forms of political activity. About 90 percent of all adults believe it is the duty of good citizens to vote in elections, although obviously many of them do not act on that commitment at every election. Although Americans also believe in the importance of informing themselves about political and governmental affairs, they readily concede that in most cases they personally are not as well informed as they should be.

The most common form of political participation is exercising the right to vote. We will discuss voter turnout in Chapter 2, including the impact of declining levels of trust and political efficacy on citizens' willingness to participate. Interestingly, more intense forms of political activity, such as working on political campaigns, have not declined—although the levels of involvement have never been high. As can be seen

TABLE 1-2 Political Efficacy, 1952-1992

STATEMENT: "People like me don't have any say about what government does."

Responses	1952	1956	1960	1964	1968	1972	1976	1980	1984	1988	1992
Agree	31%	28%	27%	29%	41%	40%	41%	39%	33%	41%	36%
Disagree	68	71	72	70	58	59	56	59	66	58	63
Don't know, not ascertained	1	1	1	1	1	1	3	2	1	1	1
Total	100%	100%	100%	100%	100%	100%	100%	100%	100%	100%	100%
(*N*)	(1,799)	(1,762)	(1,954)	(1,571)	(1,337)	(2,705)	(2,403)	(1,408)	(1,978)	(1,775)	(2,257)

SOURCE: Survey Research Center; Center for Political Studies National Election Studies. Data provided by the Inter-university Consortium for Political and Social Research.

TABLE 1-3 Percentage of Population Involved in Campaign Activities in Presidential Election Years, 1952-1992

	1952	1956	1960	1964	1968	1972	1976	1980	1984	1988	1992
Do you belong to any political club or organization?	2	3	3	4	3	[a]	[a]	3	[a]	[a]	[a]
Did you give any money or buy tickets or anything to help the campaign for one of the parties or candidates?	4	10	11	11	12	10	9 8[b]	8 5[c]	7 5[c]	9 4[c] 26[b]	11 24[b]
Did you go to any political meetings, rallies, dinners or things like that?	7	7	8	8	14	9	6	8	4	7	8
Did you do any other work for one of the parties or candidates?	3	3	5	5	5	5	4	4	4	3	3
(*N*)	(1,614)	(1,772)	(3,021)	(1,571)	(1,558)	(2,705)	(2,872)	(1,614)	(1,989)	(2,040)	(2,257)

SOURCE: Survey Research Center; Center for Political Studies National Election Studies. Data provided by the Inter-university Consortium for Political and Social Research.

[a] Question was not asked in 1972, 1976, 1984, 1988, or 1992.
[b] Percentage mentioning a tax check-off contribution.
[c] Percentage giving to political groups during the campaign but not to parties or candidates.

in Table 1-3, the percent of the population involved in campaign activity did not change much during the period from 1952 to 1992. Even though there is considerable overlap among individuals in each category, the percentages do not represent the same set of individuals. For example, many individuals who contribute financially are not involved in the campaigns in any other way. More than half of the members of political clubs and organizations are not involved in any campaign activity. When all forms of campaign activity are counted, more than 10 percent of the electorate is involved in some way.

There are many forms of political activity that ordinary citizens engage in beyond campaigning in elections. Active, interested individuals with political concerns call and write public officials, become involved in interest groups dedicated to influencing public policy, circulate petitions, and even occasionally take to the streets to demonstrate. The general decline in positive feelings toward politics and government discussed above is not necessarily paralleled in the political feelings or behavior of the most active, concerned members of the public. If anything, while the public generally has become less interested in politics, a better informed, more concerned minority has become increasingly active in a wide range of political activities.

Childhood Socialization

Most social groups, particularly those with distinctive sets of norms and values, make some effort to teach these attitudes and expected behaviors to their new members. In most societies this process of socialization is focused primarily on the largest group of new members, children. Through the process of political socialization the political culture of a society is transmitted from one generation to the next, but this socialization is also an important mechanism through which change in the political culture can take place.

In societies in which most learning about politics takes place in the home, the prevailing political culture probably changes no faster than the attitudes of the adult population as a whole, in response to varied personal experiences and changing circumstances in the environment. In modern societies other agents of political socialization also are involved, particularly the educational system and, increasingly, the mass media. To the extent that these institutions instill a different set of values and norms in comparison with those held by the adult population as a whole, there is an opportunity for changing the political culture. In the Soviet

Union and the People's Republic of China, where the official ideology dominated both the schools and the mass communications system, massive changes in values took place within the span of a generation. (The fact that contrary attitudes survived this indoctrination attests to the multiplicity of agents of socialization, even in totalitarian states.) More diversity in views is permitted in the United States, but the prevalence of middle-class values among both teachers and the media guarantees that these orientations will continue to be widespread in the population as a whole.

Given the importance of the socialization process in the transmission of the fundamental beliefs and values of the political culture, it is surprising that the many recent socialization studies have not paid much attention to the development of attitudes supportive of democratic goals and procedures. Data collected by David Easton and Robert Hess show that children develop an affective attachment to the term *democracy* very early (by about the third grade), but the concept acquires meaning much more slowly.[12] The progress of this learning from the fourth grade to the eighth grade is shown for several concepts in Figure 1-2. Perhaps the most interesting aspect of this figure is the high level of disagreement among teachers over the correctness of including the right of dissent in the meaning of democracy. Other studies have shown that adolescents are somewhat more likely than their parents to endorse democratic values, but the process through which these ideals are learned and the extent to which children learn to apply them to concrete situations remain to be studied.

More emphasis has been placed on the development of the child's thinking about the institutions of government and about his or her own role as a citizen. The child's first view of government and governmental leaders casts them as all-powerful but benevolent, undoubtedly the result of the twin objectives of parents and teachers to instill an acceptance of authority and to shield young children from the harsher realities of political life. Gradually, the child acquires a more realistic and more cynical view of the world. Children also begin with a very personalized view of government; government means the president or, for some, the police officer. In time these images are replaced or supplemented with more abstract ideas about Congress and the election process.[13]

Throughout the socialization process, there are important differences in development associated with social class and intelligence as measured by IQ tests. Generally, this takes the form of learning and adopting the values of teachers more quickly, often with rather intrigu-

FIGURE 1-2 Children's and Teachers' Understanding of the Concept of Democracy

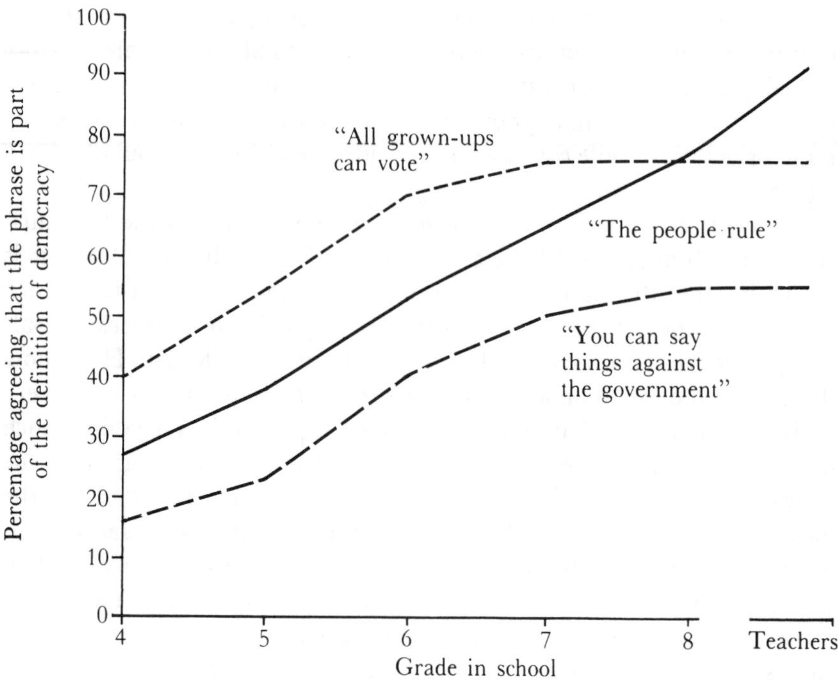

SOURCE: Adapted from Robert D. Hess and Judith V. Torney, *The Development of Political Attitudes in Children* (New York: Anchor Books, 1968), 75, Table 13.

ing results. Taking a partisan stance would be considered taboo in most American classrooms, but advocating nonpartisanship is not. An overwhelming majority of the teachers in the Easton and Hess sample thought it preferable to "vote for the person" than to join a political party. Children progressively adopt this view as they move through the elementary grades, and middle-class and high-IQ children do so at higher rates than others.[14] Some 87 percent of the teachers saw the United Nations as more influential than the United States in keeping world peace, and, by a margin of 2 to 1, teachers believe Congress has more to do with "running the country" than the president. Children learn these perceptions, inaccuracies and all, with the better students absorbing them faster.

During the elementary grades, children also develop a set of attitudes toward their own role as citizens. Initially, the emphasis is on obedience: The good citizen obeys the law, just as good children obey their parents. In the American socialization process, this is gradually replaced by a view of oneself as a more active participant in the political system: The good citizen is one who votes. Still later, the child adds to this the notion that the government can be influenced through the voting process. Data from *The Civic Culture* by Gabriel Almond and Sidney Verba suggest that the socialization process in the United States instills this set of attitudes in its citizens more successfully than in some other Western democracies.[15] Americans are more likely to view themselves as "participants" as opposed to "subjects" than are citizens of the United Kingdom, Germany, Italy, or Mexico. In all the countries studied, experiences with democratic decision-making, in the schools or in the family, were related to adult participation in politics and to the belief that the individual can influence government. Other studies have documented that, within the United States, children's attitudes toward their own possible effectiveness vis-à-vis government are related to social class; social class, in turn, is related to differences in the attitude toward authority within the home. Working-class parents are more likely to demand obedience and allow less input from children in the familial decision-making process than are middle-class parents. As a result, their children are less likely to see themselves as able to influence authority or to participate successfully in politics.

As with other attitudes, the development of confidence in one's own ability to influence government is related to social class and intelligence among children, just as it is related to social class and education in adults. Some other aspects of the view of the citizen's role that children develop in the later elementary years might conceivably hinder their effectiveness or willingness to participate in the real world of politics later on. The role of the individual in influencing government is stressed; the role of organized group activity in politics is downgraded. Similarly, children in the American culture develop a low tolerance for conflict, believing, for example, that it hurts the country when the political parties disagree.

Malaise

The expectations an individual develops about how the political process functions often are not satisfied in reality. When clear expectations are not met in the behavior of political leaders or in the experiences individuals have in the political process, disappointment, cynicism, or hostility may result. Americans come to hold rather high expectations for the political system and, consequently, are subject to considerable disenchantment with the performance of government and their own role in politics. Although no direct evidence on this point is available, nothing has been found to suggest that the value Americans place on the ideals of democracy, majority rule, or the importance of participation in politics has declined. Rather, events over the last thirty years have led to a larger perceived discrepancy between the specific American political institutions (and their incumbents) and the ideal.

These ideals, combined with the generally high expectations Americans hold for the political system, can lead to cynicism and mistrust of political leadership when scandals occur or policies appear not to work. We might think of this as "system malaise." But there is another form of disenchantment that operates at the individual level. The American ethos and the content of the political culture lead individuals to expect a wide range of conditions and values. They expect to enjoy freedom, justice, and equality; they expect to enjoy personal economic success; and they expect to be safe from violence.

If individuals find that what is happening to them is far different from these expectations, they may react with resentment. Many individuals, to be sure, respond to adversity in personal terms and do not view their problems from a collective or political perspective. Others, however, may engage in disruptive political activities. In a society such as the United States, the people who suffer economic hardship or are victims of social injustice are oftentimes minorities that are isolated by race, ethnicity, sexual preference, or some other identifiable characteristic. Under these circumstances such a group may develop a set of subcultural values that is quite different from the values of the dominant culture. The group may passively withdraw from political activity, or it may become actively disruptive of the system.

Disappointment and disenchantment may be equally widespread in society. If young people come to believe that their economic prospects are worse, not better, than were those of their parents at a similar age, or if large numbers of people come to fear that they are not safe at night from random violence, then the political reaction may be more systemwide. A growing hostility toward established political leaders and groups can make individuals throughout society susceptible to the appeals of antisystem leaders. To some extent individuals or small groups resocialize themselves, developing values that promote disruptive behavior.

Analysts are not decided on which attitudes reveal serious malaise in a society. Some overt forms of antisystem behavior—rioting, for instance—are readily recognizable. The 1992 rioting in Los Angeles in the wake of the Rodney King verdict illustrates that a disruptive, antisystem sentiment can emerge. However, there is little evidence of any sustained or widespread antisystem feeling in the United States.

Recent expressions of opinion indicate that Americans are worried about what is happening in society generally. For example, 80 percent of the public expressed the view in 1992 that the country was on the "wrong track." Seventy-two percent agreed with the statement that "things in the country are going badly." While ominous on the face of it, such views are quite variable and responsive to specific events. For example, in 1991, after the Persian Gulf War, only 34 percent of the respondents questioned thought the country was on the wrong track and 26 percent thought things were going badly. Furthermore, a little over a decade ago, when inflation was high and American hostages were held in Teheran, pessimistic views were just as widespread as in 1992.

National loyalty to and support for the political system can erode. Social malaise may undermine the system even though its causes may not be particularly political. Prolonged economic depression or high levels of violence in a society may diminish support. The processes of destabilization in stable democracies are not well understood because there is no example of internal destruction of an established democratic nation in modern times. Disruptive activities may result, however, from conditions that are short of destroying the system.

To a degree, a political system needs forceful criticism to solve problems and remain viable. So while political leaders may resent strong attacks on their policies, the role of critics who alert others in the society to the need for change is very important. If leaders respond appropriately, crisis may be avoided. American political culture encourages and needs both loyalty and dissent.

Maintaining a Democracy

Certainly, one of the more important aspects of political culture is its relevance to the maintenance of the political system. Belief in democratic ideals is essential to the preservation of a democratic system, both because such beliefs inhibit citizens from undemocratic actions and because the public will demand proper behavior on the part of political leaders.

In these terms, there is some uneasiness about public support for American democracy—and perhaps for any democratic regime. It is possible to view the United States as a democratic system that has survived without a strong democratic political culture because governmental policies have gained continual, widespread acceptance. If that satisfaction erodes, however, the public has no deep commitment to democratic values and processes that will inhibit support of antidemocratic leaders or disruptive activities. Democratic theory implies that the public should demand values and procedures embodying democratic principles. There is the hope or expectation that the public in a democratic society will insist on certain values and processes. More precisely, scholars argue that in the absence of insistence on particular values and procedures, democratic regimes will fail. Clearly, a mass public demanding democratic values and procedures is stronger support for a democratic regime. This does not mean, however, that a stronger form of support is necessary for a democratic system, although superficially it appears desirable. Quite possibly, strong support is nearly impossible to attain, and weak support is adequate, given other conditions.

In our view, a distinction should be made between the factors necessary for the establishment of democracy and those contributing to its maintenance. Stronger public support probably is required for the successful launching of a democracy than it is for maintaining an already established democracy. Possibly, preserving a regime simply requires that no substantial proportion of the society be actively hostile to the regime and engage in disruptive activities. In other words, absence of disruptive acts, not the presence of supportive attitudes, is crucial.

On the other hand, leaders' positive support for a political system is essential to its existence. If some leaders are willing to oppose the system, it is crucial that there be no substantial number of followers to which such leaders can appeal. The followers' attitudes, as opposed to their willingness to act themselves, may provide a base of support for antisystem behavior by leaders. In this sense, unanimous public support for democratic principles would be a more firm basis for a democratic system.

The increasing levels of dissatisfaction, accompanied by a lack of strong commitment to democratic values in the American public, appear to create some potential for public support of undemocratic leaders. As we shall see in subsequent chapters, many Americans feel an attachment to one or the other of the established political parties, an attachment that inhibits their embracing new political leaders. The parties and the public's attachment to them are often seen as preventing political change; they can also be seen as encouraging stability and preservation of a democratic system by lessening the likelihood of a demagogue's rise to power.

Notes

1. For a major effort to capture this fundamental aspect of political culture, see Herbert McClosky and John Zaller, *The American Ethos* (Cambridge, Mass.: Harvard University Press, 1984).
2. For the major study of the 1950s, see Samuel Stouffer, *Communism, Conformity and Civil Liberties* (Garden City, N.Y.: Doubleday, 1955); for more recent work, see C. Z. Nunn, H. J. Crockett, and J. A. Williams, *Tolerance for Nonconformity* (San Francisco: Jossey-Bass, 1978).
3. John L. Sullivan, James Piereson, and George E. Marcus, *Political Tolerance and American Democracy* (Chicago: University of Chicago Press, 1982).
4. Stouffer, *Communism, Conformity and Civil Liberties;* and Herbert McClosky, "Consensus and Ideology in American Politics," *American Political Science Review* 58 (June 1964): 361-382.
5. Jeane Kirkpatrick, *The New Presidential Elite* (New York: Russell Sage Foundation and the Twentieth Century Fund, 1976).
6. These data are recomputed from Kirkpatrick, *The New Presidential Elite,* Table 10.3, 302.
7. *The Public Perspective* 3 (May/June 1992): 7-9; Center for Political Studies National Election Studies, 1991, 1992.
8. Gabriel Almond and Sidney Verba, *The Civic Culture* (Princeton, N.J.: Princeton University Press, 1963). These patterns have been evident in cross-national public opinion polls ever since Almond and Verba first recorded them in 1963.
9. "Opinion Roundup," *Public Opinion* 2 (July 1979): 35, from a poll by the Gallup Organization in April and May 1979.
10. The findings of this study are most extensively reported in M. Kent Jennings and Richard G. Niemi, *The Political Character of Adolescence: The Influence of Families and Schools* (Princeton, N.J.: Princeton University Press, 1974); and *Generations and Politics* (Princeton, N.J.: Princeton University Press, 1981).
11. These observations are based on data provided with an instructional workbook by Paul A. Beck, Jere W. Bruner, and L. Douglas Dobson, *Political Socialization: Inheritance and Durability and Parental Political Views* (Washington, D.C.: American Political Science Association/Inter-university Consortium for Political and Social Research, 1974).
12. The results of this study have been reported in several articles and in Robert D. Hess and Judith V. Torney, *The Development of Political Attitudes in Children* (New York: Anchor Books, 1968); and David Easton and Jack Dennis, *Children in the Political System: Origins of Political Legitimacy* (New York: McGraw-Hill, 1969).
13. David Easton and Jack Dennis, "The Child's Image of Government," in *Socialization to Politics: A Reader,* ed. Jack Dennis (New York: John Wiley & Sons, 1973), 67.
14. Hess and Torney, *The Development of Political Attitudes in Children,* 186.
15. Almond and Verba, *The Civic Culture.*

Suggested Readings

Almond, Gabriel, and Sidney Verba. *The Civic Culture.* Princeton, N.J.: Princeton University Press, 1963. A classic study of political culture in five nations, including the United States.

Lipset, Seymour M., and William Schneider. *The Confidence Gap.* New York: Free Press, 1983. A wide-ranging survey of the public's attitudes toward American institutions.

McClosky, Herbert, and John Zaller. *The American Ethos.* Cambridge, Mass.: Harvard University Press, 1984. An analysis of the public's attitudes toward democracy and capitalism.

Sullivan, John L., James Piereson, and George E. Marcus. *Political Tolerance and American Democracy.* Chicago: University of Chicago Press, 1982. An innovative study of the public's tolerance of unpopular groups.

Verba, Sidney, and Norman Nie. *Participation in America: Political Democracy and Social Equality.* New York: Harper & Row, 1972. A survey of various forms of political participation and their determinants.

c h a p t e r   t w o

Suffrage and Turnout

IN 1992, for the first time in American history, over 100 million people voted in an election. Approximately 55 percent of the eligible electorate voted for president. The 1992 election reversed three decades of declining voter turnout from a high of over 60 percent in 1960 to a low near 50 percent in the 1980s. It is too soon to know whether this reversal will be sustained or represents a temporary deviation in a continuing downward trend.

The decline in the voting turnout rate since 1960 has occasioned a great deal of commentary and more than a little concern about the future of American democracy. The decline in turnout was paradoxical because it occurred at a time when the legal impediments to voting had been eliminated or eased and the education levels of American citizens were reaching all-time highs. Despite greater opportunities to vote, Americans seemed to be doing so less frequently. A favorite theme of editorial writers has focused on the declining turnout rate as a symbol of the growing disenchantment of voters with the political system. To have a sharp increase in turnout in a year punctuated by voter anger suggests a need to re-evaluate the factors that lie behind the decisions of millions of citizens to vote or not to vote.

In this chapter we will put these recent trends in voter turnout into a broader historical context. We will look at the factors that make some individuals more likely to vote than others and examine how changes in the political environment can affect whether people vote. In doing so we will come to some conclusions about what the decline in turnout, and its reversal in 1992, does and does not mean about the current state of the democratic process.

Extensions of Suffrage

Suffrage, or the *franchise*, means the right to vote. Originally, the U.S. Constitution gave the determination of who should have the right to vote entirely to the states. Later, various amendments were added to the Constitution that restricted the states' abilities to deny the right to vote on the basis of such characteristics as race, sex, or age. However, the basic constitutional provision that gives states the right to set the qualifications for voting remains, and over the years states have used such things as the ownership of property, literacy, or length of residency as criteria for granting or withholding the right to vote.

During the colonial period and the early years of the Republic, suffrage was commonly restricted to white males possessing varying amounts of property; thus, only a small proportion of the adult population was eligible to vote. The severity of the impact of property requirements varied from state to state, and their enforcement varied perhaps even more. Gradually, the required amount of property held or the amount of taxes paid to obtain suffrage was reduced. Sometimes these changes were hard-won reforms enacted by state legislatures or by state constitutional changes; at other times practical considerations led to substantial reforms. For example, delays in acquiring final title to land holdings in the western frontier areas during the 1800s made it impractical to establish property requirements for suffrage. Often during the very early years of American history, candidates in local elections would simply agree among themselves that all white males could vote rather than try to impose complicated restrictions on the electorate. Only in more settled communities could complex restrictions on suffrage be effectively enforced. In sections of the East, however, wealthy landlords sometimes supported the enfranchisement of their poorer tenants with the expectation of controlling their votes.[1]

After the eventual granting of suffrage to all white males, the next major change was the enfranchisement of black males by constitutional amendment following the Civil War. Even though this change was part of a set of issues so divisive that it had led to war, the numerical impact of adding black males was actually rather slight throughout the nation as a whole. However, unlike other changes in suffrage, this one had a geographical bias: The impact of enfranchising black males was felt almost entirely in the South. (Their subsequent disfranchisement in the South will be discussed below.) The next major constitutional extension of voting rights was suffrage for women in 1920. This created by far the most dramatic increase in the number of eligible voters, roughly doubling the size of the potential electorate. In the early 1970s, through a combination of federal statutory law and state laws followed by constitutional amendment, the definition of citizenship for purposes of voting was lowered to age eighteen, accomplishing another major extension of the suffrage.

These extensions of suffrage, which have not been easy or inevitable, may be explained by the existence of certain political forces. In stable political systems like the United States, the extension of suffrage will result from (1) a widely shared commitment to moral principles that entail further grants of suffrage, and (2) the expectation among political leaders that the newly franchised will support the political preferences of the leaders.

The political rhetoric of America carries strong themes of egalitarian democracy. Normally, young people who go through political and civic training in the educational system absorb ideals of individualism and equality. American nationalism, with the myths of the frontier and the melting pot, has justified these values. In part, the goals of American education are participation in and support of American democracy. Although seldom explicitly political in their indoctrination, American religious institutions have reinforced these themes in the political culture, while American literature and theater contribute to political education in these values. The result is that the commitment most Americans have to equality, individualism, and democracy has provided a basis for supporting extensions of voting rights.

But more than idealism contributed to the expansion of the electorate. In the two most dramatic extensions of suffrage, to blacks and to women, political leaders obviously expected the newly enfranchised to support certain policies. Republicans anticipated that black voters in the South after the Civil War would help to secure Republican domination of the southern states, and perhaps most southern states passed through a period during which at least some chance existed of combining the votes of blacks and poor whites into a governing majority. The intense prejudice of whites and the difficulty in maintaining the enfranchisement of blacks kept this strategy from working under most circumstances, but a significant element in Republican enthusiasm for black suffrage was the knowledge that Republican voters were being added to the rolls.

The same idealism that was behind the efforts to enfranchise blacks appears to have supported suffrage for women as well. Women were expected to clean up politics once they had the vote; they were seen optimistically as the cure for corruption in government, as unwavering opponents of alcohol, and as champions of virtue in the electorate.

Reformers of all sorts encouraged the enfranchisement of women as a means of promoting their own goals.

No doubt similar factors were at work in the most recent extension of suffrage to eighteen- to twenty-year-olds, but perhaps more important was the widespread feeling that a system calling upon young people to fight in the unpopular Vietnam War ought to extend to them the right to participate in the electoral process.

A unique aspect of the extension of suffrage in the United States was the addition of states in the frontier expansion across the continent. During the decades immediately preceding the Civil War, the politics of slavery dominated political decisions about additions of states, with accompanying expectations as to the policy impact of expansion. Here, too, the question of the expansion of the electorate was dominated largely by concern over the political persuasion of the newly enfranchised voters.

Restrictions on Suffrage

Under the provisions of the U.S. Constitution, the states set the qualifications for voters; the three extensions of suffrage by constitutional amendment did not alter this but rather prohibited the states from using certain criteria (race, sex, or age) to deny the right to vote. Since states retained the right to impose other restrictions, they have at times used these restrictions to prevent whole classes of people from voting. The most notorious of these efforts was the effective disfranchisement of blacks in the southern states during the late nineteenth and early twentieth centuries.

Several techniques for disfranchising blacks have been used during the past century in the South, and from time to time some of these techniques were applied in the North on a more limited basis to restrict the electoral participation of immigrants. The most common methods included white primaries, the poll tax, literacy tests, discriminatory administrative procedures, and intimidation. In some southern states only whites were allowed to vote in party primaries (the crucial election in one-party states), under the rationale that primaries to nominate candidates were internal functions of a private organization. The Supreme Court ruled such white primaries unconstitutional in 1944 on the grounds that the selection of candidates for election is a public function in which discrimination on the basis of race is prohibited. The now illegal poll tax, whereby each individual was charged a flat fee as a prerequisite for registration to vote, was used for years and no doubt disfranchised both poor blacks and poor whites. In some states the effect was cumulative, since poll taxes had to be paid for all previous years in which the individual had not voted. The poll tax eventually became unpopular with the white voters who had to pay it while the blacks, disfranchised by other means, did not. The literacy test gave local officials a device that could be administered in a selective way to permit registration of whites and practically prohibit the registration of blacks. The "standards of literacy" applied to blacks in some cases, for example, reading and interpreting the state constitution to the satisfaction of the white registrar made it impossible for even highly educated blacks to register, while whites might only be required to know how to sign their names. To remain effective over long periods of time, these and other similar administrative devices probably depended on intimidation or the use of violence against blacks. Detailed analysis by Jerrold Rusk and John Stucker of the impact of the poll tax and literacy test from 1876 to 1916 suggests that the poll tax was the more effective device and its efficacy was greatest where the tax rate was highest and its application most cumulative.[2]

A study of black registration in 1958 by Donald Matthews and James Prothro indicated that southern states using poll taxes and literacy tests still inhibited black voter registration after World War II.[3] The poll tax has since been outlawed by amendment to the U.S. Constitution, and the use of federal voting registrars in the South under the terms of the Voting Rights Act of 1965 has eliminated the worst excesses in the application of literacy tests. Registration rates in the South for whites and blacks were approximately equal by 1980, and turnout rates have concurrently increased to the point that there is now little difference in turnout between the North and South in presidential voting.

The outlawing of the poll tax through constitutional amendment and the suspension of literacy tests by the Voting Rights Act of 1965 and its extensions have eliminated two important restrictions on the right to vote. Other state restrictions on suffrage remain, although there is great variation from state to state. In many states, convicted felons cannot vote until they have served their entire sentence; in a few, a felony conviction entails a permanent forfeiture of voting rights. Residency requirements have been widely used and in the past were often highly restrictive; some states mandated up to two years of residence in the state before one was eligible to vote. Highly mobile segments of the population were thus often disfranchised intermittently as each move required a re-establishment of residence. In the 1970s the Middle Atlantic states, with their mobile populations and traditionally rigorous registration requirements, had as high a rate of unregistered citizens as did the states of the former Confederacy with their legacy of racial discrimination.

In 1972 the Supreme Court linked the imposition of a residency requirement to the length of time needed to prepare lists of registered voters before an election, suggesting that thirty days was sufficient to do this. Since then the Court has allowed state laws requiring fifty days to stand.

By the early 1990s the legal barriers to voting had been reduced, for the most part, to the requirement that voters be registered to vote in advance of an election. The inconvenience of administrative arrangements for voter registration and the frequent need to re-register have offered greater obstacles to voting than has the imposition of other eligibility standards. Some states have moved toward "same-day" registration in an effort to remove impediments to voting and increase electoral turnout. Even so, registration and associated residency requirements remain the most important legal restriction on voting today.

The Eligible Electorate

Since throughout American history different state and local election practices have existed, no single set of eligibility requirements can be used as a basis for deciding exactly who belonged to the electorate at any one time. For example, individual states had granted suffrage to blacks, women, and young voters, either in law or in practice, prior to these groups' nationwide enfranchisement. In some states, women had previously been allowed to vote in local and school elections but not in statewide or federal contests. Thus, there were many different electorates with different characteristics.

Although extensive data on the characteristics of the national electorate during the first century of the Republic are not available, some reasonable inferences can be drawn from suffrage laws and descriptive data.[4] The voters of 1789 can be described as white male adults who held some property. In the most permissive states, 80 percent or more of the white male adults were eligible to vote; in the most restrictive states, less than 10 percent were eligible. By 1850 property qualifications still existed in some states, but in many areas restrictions on white males had all but disappeared.

During the early years of the Republic, almost all voters resided in rural areas. The electorate has become steadily more urban since then, becoming predominantly city and town dwellers by the mid-twentieth century. The literacy rate of the electorate was high from the beginning, although the level of education was not. During the nineteenth century only a very small fraction of Americans (about 2 or 3 percent) graduated from high school, but the rate increased rapidly during the first half of the twentieth century to the point where now every year almost three-fourths of the seventeen-year-olds graduate from high school. When blacks were enfranchised after the Civil War, the overwhelming majority were illiterate, even though only about half of them had recently been slaves. The illiteracy rate among blacks has steadily declined and presently approaches the very low rate among whites.

After Reconstruction, blacks were disfranchised in state after state in the South, regardless of their literacy. By the early part of the twentieth century, some blacks enjoyed the vote in certain areas, and women had acquired the vote in various types of elections. White males, however, formed the bulk of the electorate. During this period, large numbers of immigrants joined the electorate. Despite the unfair social and economic aspects of the reception and treatment of immigrants, the political system accommodated millions of people from abroad without great stress. Indeed, political parties routinely recruited these newcomers to their ranks. Additional data probably would show that the number of naturalized citizens in the electorate never exceeded 25 percent and now represents a much smaller proportion of it.

In 1920 women were added to the electorate, and in the North the eligible electorate and the adult population were roughly equivalent. As late as 1950, large numbers of southern blacks were still effectively excluded from the electorate, but this has changed steadily since the early 1960s. The addition of younger voters in 1971 changed the eligible electorate once again.

Turnout in American Elections Historically

One of the most persistent complaints about the American electoral system in the twentieth century is its failure to achieve the high rates of voter turnout found in other countries and common in this country in the nineteenth century. Voter turnout in the United States was close to 80 percent prior to 1900 (see Figure 2-1); modern democracies around the world frequently record similarly high levels. Turnout in the United States during the twentieth century, in contrast, has exceeded 60 percent only in presidential elections, and in recent years the figure has been closer to 50 percent.

FIGURE 2-1 Estimated Turnout of Eligible Voters in Presidential Elections in the South, Non-South, and the Nation, 1860-1992

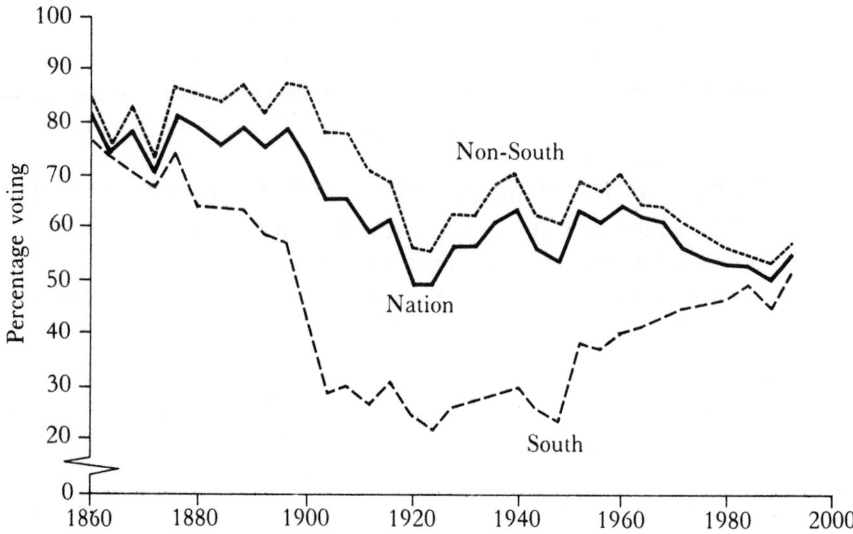

SOURCES: Robert Lane, *Political Life* (New York: Free Press, 1965), 20; Walter Dean Burnham, "The Changing Shape of the American Political Universe," *American Political Science Review* 59 (March 1965): 11, Figure 1; U.S. Bureau of the Census, *Historical Statistics of the United States, Colonial Times to 1970,* bicentennial ed. (Washington, D.C.: U.S. Government Printing Office, 1975), 1078-1080; U.S. Bureau of the Census, *Statistical Abstract of the United States, 1990,* 110th ed. (Washington, D.C.: U.S. Government Printing Office, 1989), 259; "Official Election Results," *Congressional Quarterly Weekly Report,* January 23, 1993, 190.

These unfavorable comparisons are somewhat misleading. The *voting turnout rate* is the percentage of the eligible population that actually votes in a particular election. This is ideally calculated as the number of votes cast divided by the total number of eligible adult citizens. The definition of "eligible adult" takes into account the historical changes in eligibility occasioned by the extension of suffrage to blacks, women, and eighteen-year-olds, but it does not take into account state restrictions on eligibility, such as registration requirements. As we have seen, these restrictions may be substantial. Thus, some of those included in the eligible population are not really able to vote; the turnout rate, when calculated in this manner, appears lower than it actually is. And, in some states historically, blacks, women, and eighteen-year-olds were given the right to vote before suffrage was extended to them by amendment to the U.S. Constitution; not including them in the denominator makes the turnout rate in earlier years appear higher that it actually was.

Even today in the United States, the calculation of voting turnout rate is difficult to make. We do not know the total number of ballots cast throughout the country; we only know the total vote for particular races. For example, we do not include the people who went to the polls but skipped the presidential race. Nor can we count the numbers who inadvertently invalidated their ballots. Even worse, we have no official count of citizens since the census no longer asks about citizenship. Thus, all noncitizens are counted as if they were eligible to vote. A recent analysis by Ruy Teixeira suggests an underestimate of about 4 percent in 1988.[5]

From Figure 2-1 it is apparent that some dramatic changes have occurred historically in the rate of voter turnout. Each major extension of suffrage—in 1868, 1920, and 1971—was marked by a drop in the proportion of the electorate voting. Perhaps this is not surprising, since the newly eligible voters might be expected to take some time to acquire the habit of exercising their right to vote. It should also be noted that the drop in the turnout rate occasioned by the extension of suffrage was, in each case, the continuation of a downward trend.

During the nineteenth century, national turnout appears to have been extremely high—always more than 70 percent. The decline in national turnout from shortly before 1900 to 1916 is in part attributable to the restriction of black voting in the South. This decline in voting in the South also resulted from the increasing one-party domination of the region. In many southern states the "real" election was the Democratic primary, with the Republicans offering only token opposition, or none at all, in the general election. Turnout was often extremely low in the general election—far lower than can be accounted for simply by the disfranchisement of blacks.

Explaining the voting record shown in Figure 2-1 for the northern states presents a more difficult problem. There was a substantial decline in turnout in the first two decades of the twentieth century, and turnout has never returned to its previous levels. The disfranchisement of blacks and whites in the South cannot account for northern nonvoting.

There are two quite different explanations for the decline in voting in the North that commenced in the late 1890s. A persuasive set of arguments has been made by E. E. Schattschneider and Walter Dean Burnham in their individual studies of this period.[6] They contend that a high level of party loyalty and political involvement during the last quarter of the nineteenth century caused high turnout and great partisan stability. Then, during the 1890s, electoral patterns shifted in such a way that the South became safely Democratic, and most of the rest of the nation came under the domination of the Republican party. Schattschneider's analysis emphasizes the extent to which this alignment enabled conservatives in both regions to dominate American politics for many years. According to this line of argument, one consequence of declining competition and greater conservatism throughout the electoral system was a loss of interest in politics accompanied by lower turnout and less partisan loyalty in the early twentieth century. Burnham emphasizes the disintegration of party voting with more ticket splitting and lower turnout in off-year elections.

Some elements of this account are undeniably accurate. Electoral patterns did change somewhat around the turn of the century, with many regions of the nation changing from competitive to one-party areas. Throughout areas previously characterized by high turnout, straight ticket voting, and stable voting patterns, turnout and partisan stability suffered greater fluctuations.

An alternative set of arguments gives these patterns a different interpretation.[7] The high rate of turnout in the nineteenth century may not have resulted from political involvement by an interested, well-informed electorate; on the contrary, it may have been possible only because of low levels of information and interest. During the last half of the nineteenth century, a largely uninformed electorate was aroused to vote by means of extreme and emotional political appeals. Presumably, in the absence of more general awareness of the political situation, these alarmist arguments produced firm commitments to vote. By and large, the parties manipulated the electorate—a manipulation possible because the electorate was not well informed.

Furthermore, this argument alleges that the party organizations "delivered" or "voted" substantial numbers of voters during this period. Thus, the remarkable stability of party voting may be a testimony to the corruption of the party organizations. The decline of stable party voting in the early twentieth century coincides with various attacks on political corruption and party machines. The resultant weakening of party machines and increased honesty in electoral activities could have reduced turnout. In fact, the apparent hostility of the electorate to the parties throughout this period seems inconsistent with strong party loyalty. A study by Jerrold Rusk shows dramatic changes in voting patterns associated with electoral reform laws, especially the introduction of the Australian ballot.[8] Prior to the introduction of electoral reforms, voting was often not secret; distinctively colored ballots prepared by the political parties and limited to one party were distributed to voters, marked, and openly placed in the ballot box. The Australian ballot provided for secret voting and an official ballot with all candidates' names appearing on it.

Another of the reforms instituted during the early twentieth century to combat corruption was the imposition of a system of voter registration. Besides limiting the opportunity for fraudulent voting, registration requirements created an additional barrier to the act of voting that had the effect of causing the least motivated potential voters to drop out of the electorate. Many states introduced permanent or semipermanent forms of registration; however, in others, like New York, where annual registration was required in many cities, the barrier to voting could be formidable.

After reaching an all-time low in the early 1920s, turnout in national elections increased steadily until 1940. There was a substantial drop in turnout during World War II and immediately thereafter, and since 1960 there has been a gradual decline. Great differences in turnout among the states are concealed within these national data. Rates of voting in the South, as shown in Figure 2-1, were consistently low until recently when they nearly converge with northern turnout. Regional differences in turnout in presidential voting have almost disappeared; state variation within regions, however, is still considerable.

High- and Low-Stimulus Elections

Elections vary in the amount of interest and attention they generate in the electorate. As can be seen in Figure 2-2, presidential elections draw high turnout, whereas off-year congressional elections are characterized by lower levels of turnout. Even in a presidential election year, fewer people vote in congressional elections than vote for president. The most dramatic decline in turnout is the 10 to 20 percent drop in voting experienced in off-year elections. Primaries and local elections elicit still lower turnout. Some of these differences can be accounted for by the lower visibility of these latter elections; when less information about an election is available to the voter, a lower level of interest is produced.

A number of elements would seem to influence the amount of interest in an election. The differences in level of interest from presidential elections to congressional elections to local elections can be viewed as a result of five factors:

FIGURE 2-2 Turnout of Eligible Voters in Presidential and Congressional Elections, 1868-1992

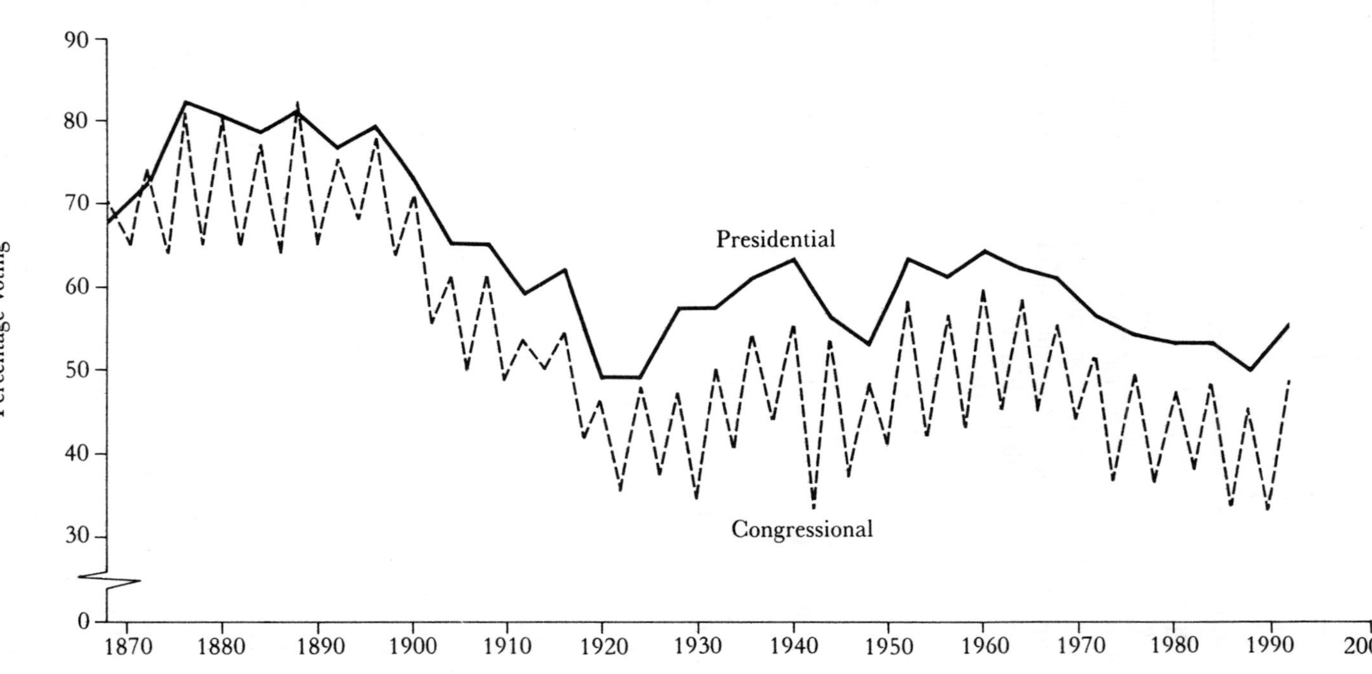

SOURCES: Historical Data Archive, Inter-university Consortium for Political and Social Research; U.S. Bureau of the Census, *Statistical Abstract of the United States, 1973,* 94th ed. (Washington, D.C.: U.S. Government Printing Office, 1973), 379; U.S. Bureau of the Census, *Statistical Abstract of the United States, 1990,* 110th ed. (Washington, D.C.: U.S. Government Printing Office, 1989), 258; "Election '92 Results," *Congressional Quarterly Weekly Report,* November 7, 1992, 3600-3607.

1. Differences in media coverage given the election.
2. Significance attached by voters to the office.
3. Importance of issues raised in the campaign.
4. Attractiveness of the candidates.
5. Competitiveness of the contest.

Variation in these factors leads to what Angus Campbell called "high-stimulus" and "low-stimulus" elections.[9]

Newspapers and television give far more coverage to the activities and speeches of presidential candidates than to those of congressional candidates. Even the most indifferent citizen comes to possess impressions and some information about presidential candidates and their campaigns. Such bombardment through the mass media awakens the relatively uninterested and often provides them with some reason for bothering to vote. This is not nearly so likely to happen in other election campaigns, where only the motivated citizens will become informed and concerned to any degree. Even so, a week or so after the election, a substantial proportion of the voters will not recall the name of the congressional candidate for whom they voted.

The factors of media coverage, the significance of the office, and the importance of the issues do a better job of explaining the differences in the levels of turnout in presidential elections versus other kinds of elections than they do among presidential elections themselves. None of these factors can account for the decline in turnout in presidential voting over the last three decades. Media coverage and campaigning through the media have increased; there is no evidence that the significance attached to the presidency has declined; and critical issues have been intensely debated, such as civil rights and the Vietnam War in 1968, the Vietnam War again in 1972, and the Iranian hostage crisis and inflation in 1980. Yet a steady erosion in turnout occurred through these years.

The lack of attractiveness of the presidential candidates has often been cited as a possible explanation, contrasting the enormously popular Dwight D. Eisenhower in 1952 and 1956 with the "lesser of two evils" contests of later years. In 1988 George Bush and Michael Dukakis illustrated the point as two relatively unattractive candidates ran in an election with the lowest turnout in three decades. However, the 1992 election challenged this conventional wisdom. None of the three major contenders, Bush, Bill Clinton, and Ross Perot, was viewed as especially attractive by the public, yet turnout increased to its highest level in some years.

Another factor often thought to raise the level of turnout in an election, perhaps by increasing the level of interest, is the degree of competition between the parties. Presumably, the closer and more uncertain the outcome, the more people will see their vote as potentially decisive. Undeniably, the virtual absence of party competition in the South during the period of black disfranchisement was associated with extremely low levels of turnout, even among white voters. Both turnout and competition in the South have increased since blacks joined the electorate. However, the elections of 1968, 1976, 1980, and 1988 suggest that the expectation of a close race does not invariably lead to heightened turnout, while the 1984 election shows that the expectation of a landslide does not necessarily depress turnout.

Another aspect of competitiveness probably has more relationship to the level of turnout. The decision to allow a race to remain uncontested or to offer only a "sacrificial lamb" can dramatically reduce turnout. In contrast, a hotly contested race with strenuous activity by party organizations is likely to get more voters to the polls on election day, even though the final outcome may not be particularly close.

Voters and Nonvoters

All but a small proportion of the eligible electorate vote at least occasionally, but individuals vary in the regularity with which they cast their ballots. Certainly, individual interest in politics is one factor creating such differences. In the last section, the level of interest in a campaign was treated as a characteristic of the political environment, generated by the importance of the office at stake, the amount of media coverage, and so on. But interest and involvement in politics are also characteristics of individuals, and individuals vary substantially in the attention they pay to politics, their involvement in politics, and the amount of information about candidates and issues they acquire. As one would expect, the probability of voting increases at each level of expressed interest and involvement in political campaigns. This relationship is illustrated in Figure 2-3: The highly interested, involved, and informed citizens (a combination of characteristics highly valued in the belief system of a democratic society) turn out to cast their ballots on election day, whereas the apathetic, uninvolved, and ill-informed stay at home.

Two deviant cases that run contrary to the expected pattern can also be seen in Figure 2-3. The first deviant condition, "alienation," describes voters characterized by high interest and low turnout. The

FIGURE 2-3 Relationship Between Electoral Participation and Interest, Involvement, and Information

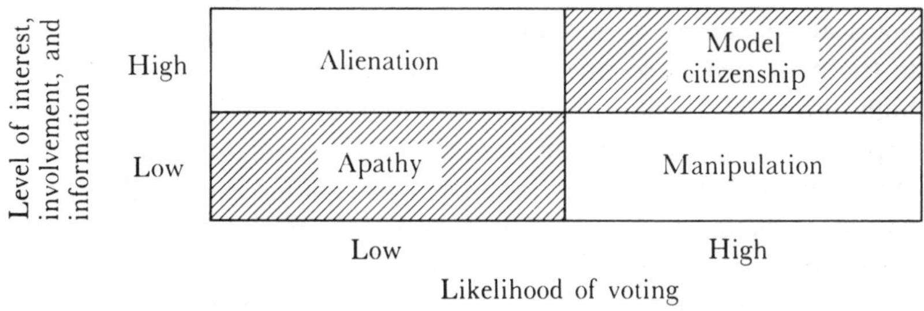

situation may be one of voluntary alienation in which individuals withdraw from political participation purposefully. Their high level of interest and information implies some reason for their withdrawal; they are dissatisfied with, or offended by, the political system. Nonvoluntary alienation refers to situations in which interested potential voters are prevented from participating. Both situations are dangerous to the political system because highly interested and informed citizens who do not participate have the potential for extremely disruptive activities. Alienation in this form is thought to be uncommon in American politics. In each presidential election since 1968 there has been speculation that large numbers of potential voters were dissatisfied with the candidates and would not cast a ballot for president. Even though the elections from 1968 to 1988 drew lower turnouts than those of 1960 or 1964, there is no reason to believe that a sizable proportion of the nonvoters was positively alienated. When nonvoters were asked in 1968 why they did not vote, only about 3 percent specifically mentioned unhappiness with the available choices. Similarly, a study focusing primarily on the causes of nonvoting in the 1976 election found voters and nonvoters to be quite similar in their levels of alienation and cynicism toward politics; for only 6 percent of the nonvoters was rejection of politics the main explanation of their nonvoting.[10] Studies have consistently shown no relationship between cynicism or alienation and nonvoting in elections. And 1992 was no exception. If anything, nonvoters in 1992 were somewhat more positive about the political system than voters.

The second deviant case, "manipulation," describes voters characterized by low interest and high turnout. It refers to a situation in which individuals with little information or interest become involved in voting. Presumably, this manipulation is achieved by getting individuals to vote either through coercion or by highly stimulating and arousing appeals. Coercive methods for ensuring turnout may range from police-state orders to fines for failure to vote. More common in the American political system are exceptionally moving or alarming appeals, bringing to the polls people so unsophisticated that they are easily moved. Very high levels of turnout can be inspired by emotional, inflammatory appeals; indeed, this is one possible explanation for the high turnout levels in the United States for many years after the Civil War. Campaigns were marked by extreme appeals, and, since education levels were low, it is reasonable to suspect that there were lower levels of interest, involvement, and information than during the campaigns of the twentieth century.

Even though interest in politics is strongly correlated with voting, about half of those who say they have "not much" interest do in fact vote in presidential elections, suggesting that still other factors are also at work. One of these is a sense of civic duty—the attitude that a good citizen has an obligation to vote, that it is important to vote, regardless of the expected impact on the outcome. Since such feelings are usually a prime focus of the political socialization carried on in the American educational system, turnout is the highest among those with the longest exposure to this system. Length of education is one of the best predictors of an individual's likelihood of voting.

Because education is so closely associated with relative affluence and social status, people who vote are usually slightly better off in socioeconomic terms than the population as a whole. This bias is likely to increase in low-stimulus elections, as greater numbers of occasional voters drop out of the electorate, leaving the field to the better educated and more affluent who rarely miss an election. In analyzing voting in presidential primaries, Barbara Norrander found voters in the 1988 Super Tuesday primaries to be older, better educated, and wealthier than their counterparts who did not vote. However, the common assumption that this leads to drastic political differences between primary voters and the general electorate is unfounded. In studying the 1980 presidential primaries, she discovered no substantial ideological or issue differences between primary voters and general election voters.[11]

Another important factor contributing to nonvoting is age; a relatively large proportion of young people pass up their first opportunities to vote. This situation has been magnified in presidential elections since 1972. The extension of the franchise to eighteen-year-olds enlarged the pool of eligible voters, yet in the 1980s, turnout gradually declined to

FIGURE 2-4 Percentage of the Electorate Reporting Having Voted in the 1992 Presidential Election, by Age

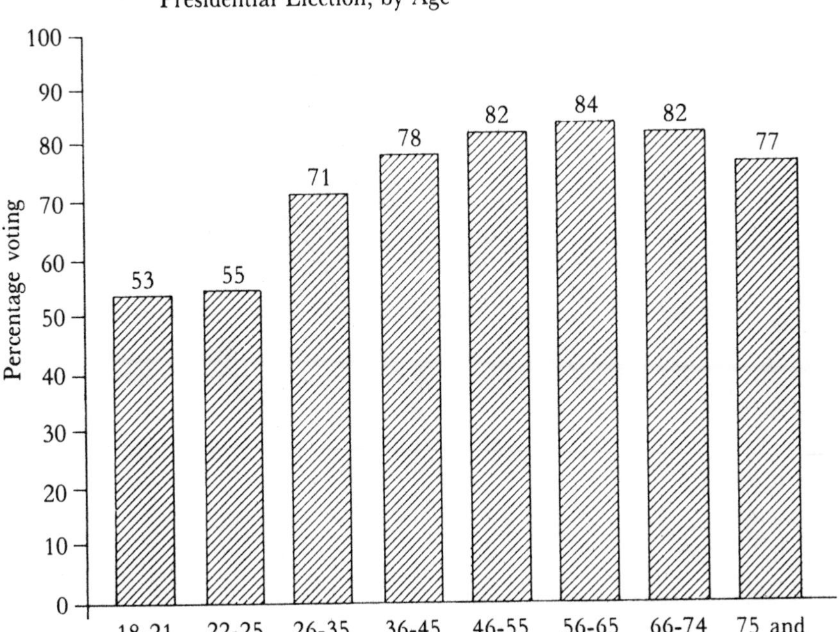

SOURCE: Center for Political Studies 1992 National Election Study. Data provided by the Inter-university Consortium for Political and Social Research.

its lowest point since 1948. Figure 2-4, based on survey data from the 1992 presidential election, shows that the likelihood of voting increases from young adulthood through middle age, with a subsequent downturn among the aged.* The tendency of young people not to vote is partially offset by their generally higher levels of education. While the turnout of middle-aged people is higher at each educational level than that of young adults, the gap narrows among the better educated (see Figure 2-5).

---

* The reported vote obtained in surveys, including surveys by the Bureau of the Census, is consistently higher than that of official statistics. Validation studies suggest that over 10 percent of the respondents claim to have voted when they did not. Bias in survey samples—that is, interviewing disproportionate numbers of voters—is also a factor contributing to the difference. See U.S. Bureau of the Census, Current Population Reports, Series P-23, No. 168, *Studies in the Measurement of Voter Turnout* (Washington, D.C.: U.S. Government Printing Office, 1990).

FIGURE 2-5 Turnout in the 1992 Presidential Election, by Age and Education

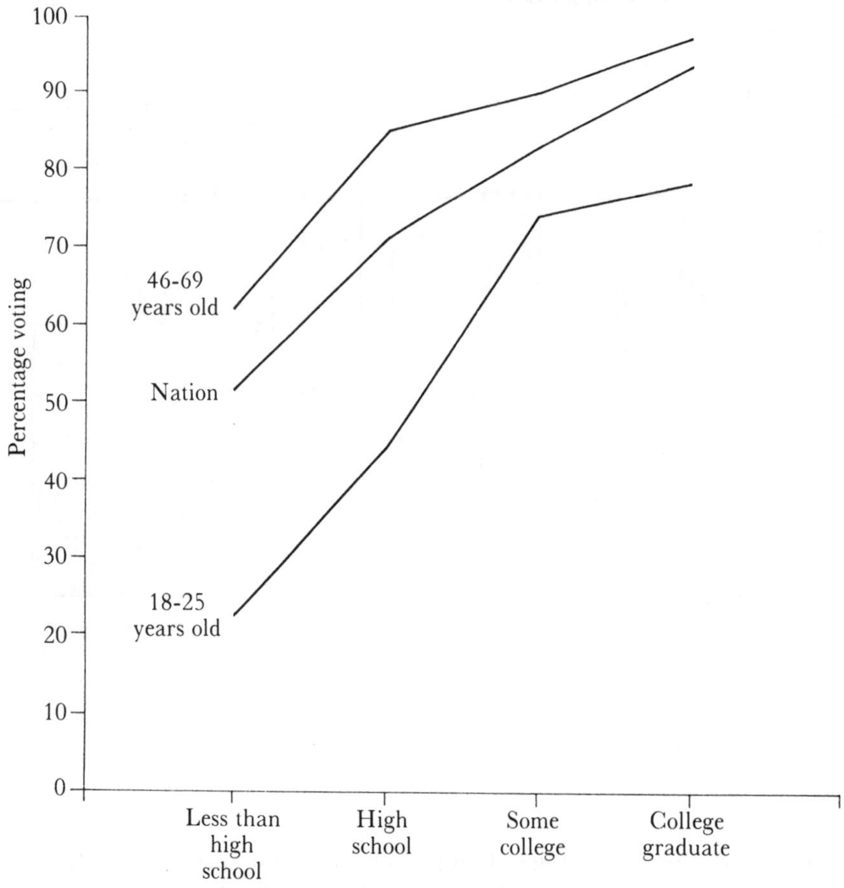

SOURCE: Center for Political Studies 1992 National Election Study. Data provided by the Inter-university Consortium for Political and Social Research.

Much of the nonvoting among young people may be attributed to the unsettled circumstances of this age group rather than to simple disinterest in politics, although young people are slightly less interested than older people of similar educational levels. Military service, being away at college, geographic mobility with the possible failure to meet residence requirements, and the additional hurdle of initial registration all create barriers to voting for the young that are less likely to affect older voters. Only about two-thirds of the people under twenty-five were registered to vote in 1992.

Another group that appears to be less socialized into political

TABLE 2-1 Turnout by Blacks, Hispanics, and Other Whites, 1992

	Hispanics	Blacks	Other whites	Total
Voted	61%	67%	78%	75%
Did not vote	39	33	22	25
Total	100%	100%	100%	100%
(N)	(170)	(290)	(1,735)	(2,256)

SOURCE: Center for Political Studies 1992 National Election Study. Data provided by the Inter-university Consortium for Political and Social Research.

activity is Hispanics. Taking age, education, and income into account, Hispanics are somewhat less likely to register and vote than other whites or blacks. In 1992, registration among Hispanics was 10 percent below the national average. Voter turnout among this group was comparably lower (see Table 2-1). (More drastic estimates of the difference between Hispanics and the rest of the population fail to take into account the large number of noncitizens in the Hispanic population.) Although there are many political differences within the Hispanic community, the various groups share the tendency for lower levels of participation in politics. Cultural and language barriers may explain these differences, but whatever the cause, this lack of political activity appears to be a failure of socialization into democratic participatory values.

By age thirty-five, most people have joined the voting population at least on an occasional basis. A small proportion of the middle-aged and older group remains outside the voting public. These habitual nonvoters, who have passed up several opportunities to vote, are less than 5 percent of the total electorate, according to current survey research estimates.* This group has been steadily decreasing in size, and the social forces that brought about this decrease will likely reduce it still further. In the past, this group of habitual nonvoters was disproportionately southern, black, and female. Restrictions against black suffrage, coupled with a traditional culture that worked against active participation of women in civic life, meant that as recently as 1952 in the South large proportions of blacks of both sexes, as well as white women, had never voted in a presidential election. The percentages of respondents in surveys from

* This "best estimate" of individuals outside the political system is unquestionably low. First, a disproportionately large number of people outside the political system would not even be included in the population of households from which the sample is drawn. Second, many of those in the sample who were never contacted or who refused to be interviewed would probably be classified as outside the political system.

1952 to 1980 who reported never having voted are shown in Figure 2-6. It is clear that dramatic changes have taken place in southern voting patterns during this time. By the late twentieth century, turnout patterns were quite similar in the North and South.

Registration as a Barrier to Voting

We have observed that registration requirements are the last major legal impediment to voting. Registration poses barriers to voting in several ways. In most parts of the country, an unregistered citizen must go to the courthouse several weeks before the election, during working hours, and fill out a form. This is not a horrendous burden, but it does take time and some ability to deal with a governmental bureaucracy. Regulations also typically cancel the registration of people who fail to vote in a few consecutive elections. In addition, residential mobility annually relocates millions of citizens in new precincts where they must re-register. All of these circumstances raise the costs of political involvement, costs that a significant number of citizens will choose not to assume. Furthermore, voter registration is not always purely an electoral matter: An unknown number of Americans prefer to remain off registration lists to avoid jury duty or bill collectors or a former spouse.

Nor surprisingly, individuals with little or no interest in politics lack the motivation to overcome registration barriers on their own. Once registered, however, most individuals take the further step and go to the polls on election day—a greater percentage in high-stimulus elections, like presidential elections, than low-stimulus elections. In 1992 less than 10 percent of those registered failed to vote.

Voter registration drives, in which volunteers go door to door or register voters at shopping malls and on college campuses, capture many politically uninvolved people. A certain proportion of these people will not have the interest or incentive to bear the further costs of getting to the polls on election day. As a result, political attitudes continue to distinguish registered voters from registered nonvoters.

Table 2-2 illustrates differences between the unregistered, registered nonvoters, and registered voters in terms of their level of interest in the election campaign and their partisanship. The registered nonvoters are in between the two larger groups and are somewhat more similar to the unregistered than to the registered voters. When it comes to personal characteristics, such as social class and education, registered nonvoters are also similar to the unregistered. So, even among the registered,

FIGURE 2-6 Percentage of Adults Who Have Never Voted, by Race and Sex for the South and Non-South, 1952-1980

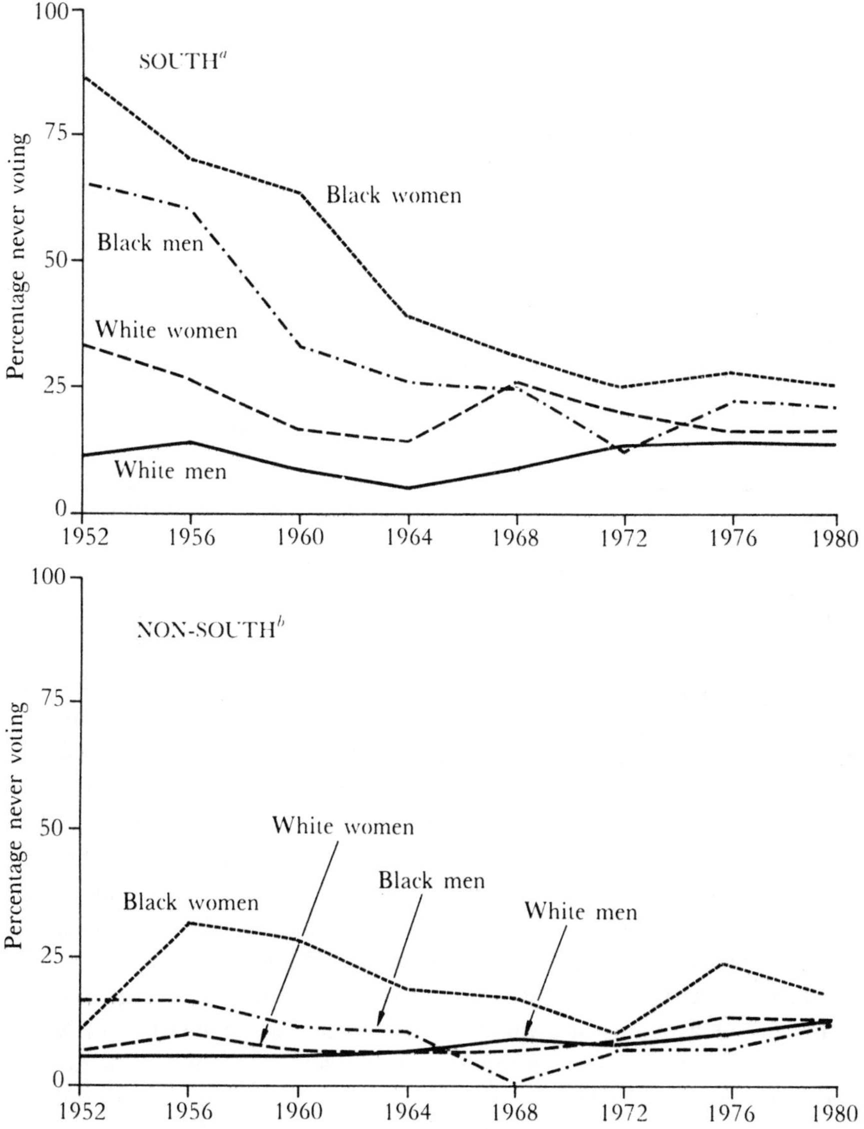

SOURCE: Survey Research Center; Center for Political Studies National Election Studies. Data provided by the Inter-university Consortium for Political and Social Research.

[a] The states included in the South are Alabama, Arkansas, Florida, Georgia, Kentucky, Louisiana, Maryland, Mississippi, North Carolina, Oklahoma, South Carolina, Tennessee, Texas, Virginia, and West Virginia.

[b] The states included in the non-South are the remainder.

TABLE 2-2 Interest and Partisanship of Registered Voters and Nonvoters and Unregistered Citizens, 1992

	Unregistered	Registered	
		Nonvoters	Voters
Very much interested	13%	21%	47%
Somewhat interested	46	50	43
Not interested at all	41	29	10
Total	100%	100%	100%
Strong Democrat	9%	16%	20%
Weak Democrat	18	17	17
Independent	51	43	35
Weak Republican	12	15	15
Strong Republican	5	8	13
Don't know, nothing	6	2	0
Total	101%	101%	100%
(N)	(392)	(155)	(1,695)

SOURCE: Center for Political Studies 1992 National Election Study. Data provided by the Inter-university Consortium for Political and Social Research.

political and social differences remain to a moderate degree between those who vote and those who do not.

Registration requirements thus present a considerable barrier to voting. It is an important (although not the only) reason why the United States has significantly lower turnout rates than other western democracies, where governments take responsibility for maintaining registration lists rather than placing the burden of registration on the individual.[12] In recent years, various plans have been introduced to reduce the difficulty in registration as a way to boost voter turnout. Some state governments have implemented "same day registration," whereby individuals can register at the polls on election day. Most notably, in 1993 Congress passed, and President Clinton signed, the "motor voter" bill, in which registration forms will be available at a variety of governmental agencies that citizens visit for other purposes. These include agencies where motor vehicles are registered and driver's licenses are obtained, though, owing to a Republican-sponsored amendment, not at unemployment and welfare offices. The purpose of the bill is clearly to make it easier for all citizens to exercise their right to vote, but Democratic support and Republican concerns point to a potential side effect. Since the unregistered tend to be poorer and less well-educated, Democrats, who traditionally represent such groups, hope (and Republicans fear) that reducing registration obstacles will increase the number of Democratic voters. As in the historical extensions of the suffrage, this effort to facilitate voter registration mixes philosophical concerns with political motivations.

Even though reducing registration requirements is a logical and fairly easy means to increase the turnout rate, we should not expect it to have an astounding effect. The best estimate of the impact of reducing registration barriers suggests it will increase turnout about 8 percentage points.[13] While obviously significant, the resulting turnout rate would still be substantially below that of other industrialized nations. Politically unmotivated individuals may still find it not worth their while to go to the polls to cast a ballot even though it was easy enough to get registered. Clearly, the overall decline in turnout during the last three decades, even as education levels increased and registration restrictions were relaxed, calls for further explanation.

Recent Changes in Turnout

How can we account for the overall decline in turnout over the last three decades? As we have seen, legal restrictions on voting have eased and education levels have increased; these circumstances should be expected to increase turnout, yet they have apparently been more than offset by other factors. One explanation has focused on the expansion of the electorate in 1971 to include eighteen-year-olds. Since young people are less likely to vote than older people, their inclusion in the electorate would be expected to decrease turnout, other things being equal. Apparently, however, this can account for only a small portion of the decline.

Another possibility, raised by political commentators in 1972, 1980, and 1984, is that "calling the election" early in the evening, before the polls close in some parts of the country, reduces turnout. Once potential voters learn that a television network has declared a winner in the race for president, the argument goes, they will no longer be interested in voting for president or any other office. The potential impact could have been even greater in 1980 than in other years because President Jimmy Carter conceded to Ronald Reagan before the polls closed in the West. In contrast, the 1976 election was so close that the winner was not known until early the following day (when the polls had closed in all fifty states), and there was no appreciable impact on turnout. The evidence on this matter is inconclusive, and there is no clear demonstration that these factors have influenced turnout in a significant way.[14] However, public concern about calling the election too early, together with congressional threats of regulation, led the networks to restrict their reporting voluntarily in 1988. The net result seemed to be a reduction in election night news coverage, with no increase in voter turnout. There was no early call of the presidential election in 1992, but no analyst has suggested that this was the reason for the increase in turnout.

A somewhat more sweeping form of this argument—and one harder to test—suggests that the style of media coverage of campaigns has turned elections into a "spectator sport" that voters watch with varying degrees of interest but feel no need to engage in. The prediction of the winners in polls, the focus in presidential debates on who won rather than on substance, the attention to the "horse race" aspects of the primary campaigns, and the networks' race to call the election first are all alleged factors in this withdrawal of the voter from active participation.

In a major study of nonvoting, Ruy Teixeira establishes two general explanations for the decline in turnout since 1960.[15] First, he cites a set of circumstances that he calls "social connectedness," that is, the extent to which individuals are socially integrated into their community. Older people, married people, those who attend church and are settled in the community are more socially connected than young, single, mobile people who do not belong to community organizations. Over the last few decades, the proportion of socially unconnected people has increased; Teixeira estimates that about one-third of the decline in turnout is associated with this decline in social connectedness.

The second factor is the extent of "political connectedness," that is, the degree to which people feel interested and involved in government and believe government is concerned and responsive to them. The decline in political connectedness over the last three decades is manifested in a loss of trust in government, a lower sense of political efficacy, a decline in interest in politics, and a diminished sense of civic duty, many of the same trends noted in Chapter 1. These changing attitudes toward government and politics account for over half of the decline in turnout, according to Teixeira's estimates.

So how do we account for the relatively sharp increase in voter turnout in 1992? Does it signify a reversal in these underlying trends, or was it a temporary and idiosyncratic departure from an ongoing pattern? Although it is too soon to answer this with any certainty, survey data suggest some possibilities.

There is little doubt that the presence of Ross Perot in the 1992 presidential race contributed to the higher turnout. An atypically high level of turnout emerged among those voters most attracted to Perot's candidacy: the young, the nonpartisan, and those disenchanted with government and political leadership. These groups, in fact, are the socially and politically disconnected whose increased numbers, Teixeira argues, have been responsible for the recent declines in turnout. Perhaps Perot's candidacy gave these voters an alternative that allowed them to connect with the political world, at least temporarily.

Beyond this, the campaigns of Perot, Clinton, and to a lesser degree Bush used new means for reaching the voters. Talk show appearances, Perot's infomercials, town meetings, and MTV's Rock the Vote initiative were all efforts to establish connections with the public in the age of cable television. Whether these innovations lead to a greater sense of involvement in politics probably depends, in the long run, on whether individuals enticed into voting in 1992 perceive any benefits from their involvement.

Throughout this discussion of turnout, we have implied the need for an explanation of nonvoting; we have assumed voting is "normal" or to be expected. However, this topic could be approached quite differently. The question could be asked, "Why do people bother to vote?" as if nonvoting were the natural pattern or expected behavior and voting required explanation. The answer that one vote can determine the outcome of an election and that most people vote anticipating that their vote may be crucial defies both reason and considerable evidence. One vote rarely decides an election, although many races are close, and no reasonable voter should expect to cast the deciding vote in an election.

There is, however, another sense in which "votes count" in an election, and that is as an expression of preference for a candidate or for a party, regardless of whether that candidate ultimately wins or loses. Elections are more than simply a mechanism for selecting public officials; they are also a means for communicating, albeit somewhat dimly, a set of attitudes to the government. For most Americans, voting remains the only means of influence regularly employed. Many see it as the only avenue open to ordinary citizens to make the government listen to their needs. The desire to be counted on one side of the fence or the other and the feeling that one ought to be so counted are perhaps the greatest spurs to voting. The recent decline in turnout suggests that fewer Americans are responding to these feelings.

Notes

1. Chilton Williamson, *American Suffrage from Property to Democracy: 1760-1860* (Princeton, N.J.: Princeton University Press, 1960), esp. 131-181.

2. Jerrold D. Rusk and John J. Stucker, "The Effect of the Southern System of Election Laws on Voting Participation," in *The History of American Electoral Behavior*, ed. Joel Silbey, Allan Bogue, and William Flanigan (Princeton, N.J.: Princeton University Press, 1978). For a treatment of these and many additional topics, see also J. Morgan Kousser, *The Shaping of Southern Politics* (New Haven, Conn.: Yale University Press, 1974).
3. Donald R. Matthews and James W. Prothro, "Political Factors and Negro Voter Registration in the South," *American Political Science Review* 57 (June 1963): 355-367.
4. U.S. Bureau of the Census, *Historical Statistics of the United States, Colonial Times to 1957; Continuation to 1962 and Revisions* (Washington, D.C.: U.S. Government Printing Office, 1965), 9, 65, 207.
5. Ruy A. Teixeira, *The Disappearing American Voter* (Washington, D.C.: The Brookings Institution, 1992), 10.
6. E. E. Schattschneider, *The Semisovereign People* (New York: Holt, Rinehart and Winston, 1960), esp. chap. 5; and Walter Dean Burnham, "The Changing Shape of the American Political Universe," *American Political Science Review* 59 (March 1965): 7-28.
7. The most general statement of this argument is found in Philip E. Converse, "Change in the American Electorate," in *The Human Meaning of Social Change*, ed. Angus Campbell and Philip E. Converse (New York: Russell Sage Foundation, 1972), 263-337. For an analysis that alters the estimates of turnout, see Ray M. Shortridge, "Estimating Voter Participation," in *Analyzing Electoral History*, ed. Jerome M. Clubb, William H. Flanigan, and Nancy H. Zingale (Beverly Hills, Calif.: Sage Publications, 1981), 137-152.
8. Jerrold D. Rusk, "The Effect of the Australian Ballot Reform on Split Ticket Voting: 1876-1908," *American Political Science Review* 64 (December 1970): 1220-1238.
9. Angus Campbell et al., eds., *Elections and the Political Order* (New York: John Wiley & Sons, 1966), 40-62.
10. Arthur T. Hadley, *The Empty Polling Booth* (Englewood Cliffs, N.J.: Prentice-Hall, 1978), 20, 41.
11. Barbara Norrander, *Super Tuesday: Regional Politics & Presidential Primaries* (Lexington: University of Kentucky Press, 1992); Norrander, "Ideological Representativeness of Presidential Primaries," *American Journal of Political Science* 33 (August 1989): 570-587.
12. G. Bingham Powell, Jr., "American Voter Turnout in Comparative Perspective," *American Political Science Review* 80 (March 1986): 17-44.
13. Teixeira, *The Disappearing American Voter,* chap. 4.
14. See Laurily K. Epstein and Gerald Strom, "Election Night Projections and West Coast Turnout," *American Politics Quarterly* 9 (October 1981): 479-491; and Raymond Wolfinger and Peter Linquiti, "Tuning In and Turning Out," *Public Opinion* (February-March 1981): 56-60.
15. Teixeira, *The Disappearing American Voter.*

Suggested Readings

Conway, M. Margaret. *Political Participation in the United States*, 2d ed. Washington, D.C.: CQ Press, 1991. A good introduction to the study of turnout and other forms of political participation.

Powell, G. Bingham, Jr. "American Voter Turnout in Comparative Perspective." *American Political Science Review* 80 (March 1986): 17-44. A careful analysis of the institutional and attitudinal factors that depress American turnout rates in comparison with those of other industrialized democracies.

Rusk, Jerrold D., and John J. Stucker. "The Effect of the Southern System of Election Laws on Voting Participation." In *The History of American Electoral Behavior*, ed. Joel Silbey, Allan Bogue, and William Flanigan. Princeton, N.J.: Princeton University Press, 1978. A sophisticated analysis of the disfranchisement of voters in the South in the nineteenth century.

Teixeira, Ruy A. *The Disappearing American Voter.* Washington, D.C.: The Brookings Institution, 1992. A sophisticated and thorough analysis of the factors that have contributed to the decline in turnout in the United States and a discussion of the impact of proposed reforms.

U.S. Bureau of the Census. *Voting and Registration in the Election of November 1992.* Series P-20, No. 466. Washington, D.C.: U.S. Government Printing Office, April 1993. A report of findings on turnout and registration based on a huge survey that allows complex analysis of many subgroups within the U.S. population.

chapter three

Partisanship

IN 1992 ROSS Perot's success in winning almost 20 percent of the presidential vote illustrated the public's increasing abandonment of the political parties. For many voters it was the politics of anger and disillusionment. Whatever else, 1992 ended the frequent speculation that the electoral victories of Ronald Reagan and George Bush paved the way for a fundamental restructuring—or realignment—of the party system in the Republicans' favor. Both these observations bear on the issue of *partisanship*—the sense of attachment or belonging that an individual feels for a political party. In this and the next two chapters we will explore the concept of partisanship and its implications for political behavior. In this chapter we will discuss the meaning of partisanship and how the partisanship of Americans has changed over the course of the country's political history. In Chapter 4 we will examine the impact of partisanship on the way people act politically and how partisanship changes over the lifetime of the individual and between generations. In Chapter 5 we will consider the social characteristics of partisans and independents.

Party Loyalty

For more than one hundred years the U.S. electorate has supported a two-party system in national politics. This remarkable stability is unknown in other democracies. Within this stable party system, however, voter support for Republicans and Democrats has fluctuated widely, and significant numbers of voters occasionally, as in 1992, abandon the traditional parties to support third-party or independent candidates. The aggregate vote totals for presidential elections, shown in Figure 3-1, reveal a wide range of party fortunes, even in elections close together in time. Some of the more dramatic fluctuations have involved the appearance of strong third-party candidates, such as Theodore Roosevelt in 1912, George Wallace in 1968, and Ross Perot in 1992. Perot's showing of 19 percent was the largest percentage won by a third-party candidate since 1912.

Despite these variations in election outcomes and despite the demonstrated capacity of American voters for highly selective and differentiated support for candidates offered them by the political parties, most voters have a basic and quite stable loyalty to one party or the other. This tendency of most individuals to be basically loyal to one political party makes the idea of partisanship, or *party identification* as it is often called, one of the most useful concepts for understanding the political behavior of individuals. After good survey data became available in the late 1940s, party identification assumed a central role in all voting behavior analysis.[1]

Party Identification

Party identification is a relatively uncomplicated measure determined by responses to the following questions:

> Generally speaking, do you usually think of yourself as a Republican, a Democrat, an independent, or what?
> (If R or D) Would you call yourself a strong (R), (D) or a not very strong (R), (D)?
> (If independent) Do you think of yourself as closer to the Republican party or to the Democratic party?

Leaving aside for the moment the people who do not or cannot respond to such questions, we have seven categories of participants in the electorate according to intensity of partisanship:

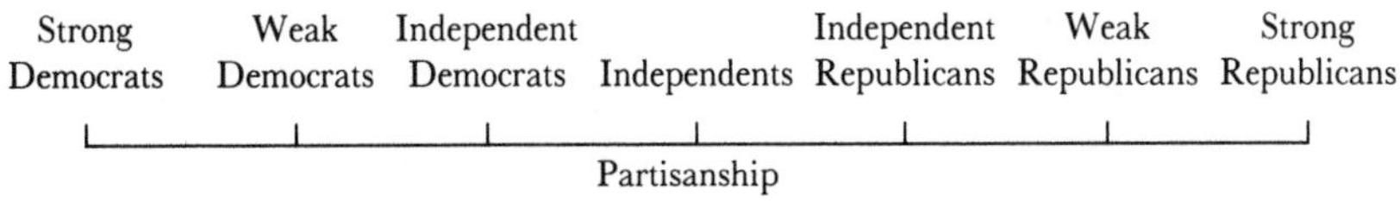

Because this self-identification measure of party loyalty is the best indicator of partisanship, political analysts commonly refer to partisanship and party identification interchangeably. Partisanship is the most important influence on political opinions and voting behavior. Many

FIGURE 3-1 Partisan Division of the Presidential Vote in the Nation, 1824-1992

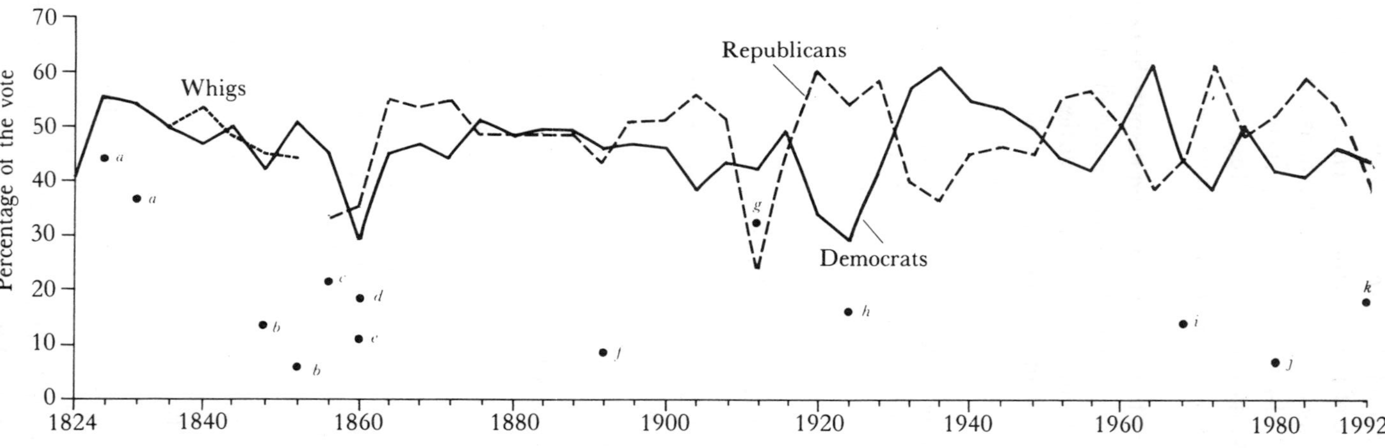

SOURCE: Historical Data Archive, Inter-university Consortium for Political and Social Research; "Official Election Results," *Congressional Quarterly Weekly Report*, January 23, 1993, 190.

NOTE: While presenting these data, we have not bothered to draw attention to the wide range of errors that may exist. There are errors in collecting and recording data, as well as errors in computation. The presidential election of 1960 provides an illustration of another form of uncertainty that enters into these data—choices made among alternative ways of presenting the data. It is customary to list the popular vote in such a way that Kennedy appears a narrow winner over Nixon in 1960. Actually, in order to reach this distribution of the total vote, it is necessary to exaggerate the Kennedy vote from Alabama, since on the slate of Democratic electors in Alabama there were uncommitted electors. Eventually six of the uncommitted electors voted for Harry Byrd; five electors voted for Kennedy. If the Kennedy popular vote in Alabama is reduced to a proportion, say 5/11 in this case, of the vote for Democratic electors and if only this reduced popular vote is added to his national total, Nixon, not Kennedy, has the larger popular vote total nationally in 1960. In percentages these are negligible changes, but symbolically such differences can become important. In these tables we have followed the usual practice of presenting the augmented Kennedy total.

Other parties gaining at least 5 percent of the vote: [a] National Republican, [b] Free Soil; [c] American; [d] Southern Democratic; [e] Constitutional Union; [f] People's; [g] Bull Moose; [h] Progressive; [i] American Independent; [j] Anderson Independent Candidacy; [k] Perot Independent Candidacy.

other influences are at work on voters in our society, and partisanship varies in its importance in different types of elections and in different time periods; nevertheless, no single factor compares in significance with partisanship.

Partisanship represents the feeling of sympathy for and loyalty to a political party that an individual acquires (probably) during childhood and holds (often) with increasing intensity throughout life. This self-image as a Democrat or a Republican is useful to the individual in a special way. For example, individuals who think of themselves as Republicans or Democrats respond to political information partially by using party identification to orient themselves, reacting to new information in such a way that it fits in with the ideals and feelings they already have. A Republican who hears a Republican party leader advocate a policy has a basis in party loyalty for supporting that policy, quite apart from other considerations. A Democrat may feel favorably inclined toward a candidate for office because that candidate bears the Democratic label. Partisanship orients individuals in their political environment, although it may also distort their picture of reality.

This underlying partisanship is also of interest to political analysts because it provides a base against which to measure deviations in particular elections. In other words, the individual voter's longstanding loyalty to one party means that, "other things being equal," or in the absence of disrupting forces, he or she can be expected to vote for that party. However, voters are responsive to a great variety of other influences that can either strengthen or weaken their tendency to vote for their usual party. Obvious variations occur from election to election in such factors as the attractiveness of the candidates, the impact of foreign and domestic policy issues, and purely local circumstances. These current factors, often called "short-term forces," may move voters away from their normal party choices.

These ideas can also be used in understanding the behavior of the electorate as a whole. If we added up the political predispositions of all the individuals in the electorate, we would have an "expected vote" or "normal vote." [2] This is the electoral outcome we would expect if all voters voted their party identification. Departures from this expected vote in actual elections represent the impact of short-term forces, such as issues or candidates.

In assessing the partisanship of the American electorate historically, we will not be able to add up individual party identifications to find an expected vote. Survey data of this type have only been available for the last forty years or so. Instead, we base our estimates on the only available data—election returns for aggregate units.[3] These data cannot, of course, reveal voting patterns of individuals; they do, however, allow one to make assessments of party loyalty and temporary deviations from party by collections of voters. Even though not exactly the same set of individuals turns out to vote in each election, we use the election returns over the years to indicate the collective partisanship of the electorate. From these data an estimate is made of the normal or expected vote for the Democratic and Republican parties. It is then possible to say, for example, that the electorate deviated from its normal voting pattern in favor of the Republican party in 1904 or that the voters departed somewhat from their normal Democratic loyalty in 1952.

Our estimates of the expected vote nationwide in presidential voting for the Democratic party from 1840 to the present and for the Republican party from 1872 to the present are shown in Figures 3-2a and 3-2b. The actual vote in these elections is also shown to indicate the amount of departure from underlying partisan patterns that occurred in each election.

Types of Electoral Change

As we have said, the utility of the concept of the expected vote lies, in part, in providing a base against which to measure and analyze departures from the expected pattern. One type of departure is usually referred to as *deviating change:* the temporary deviations from normal party loyalty attributable to the short-term forces of candidate images or issues.[4] The amount of deviating change in an election tells how well a candidate or party did relative to the party's normal performance. In these terms, the Eisenhower victories or the Nixon landslide appear even more dramatic because they represent big Republican margins during a time when the Democratic party held an advantage in party loyalists. These "deviating elections" involved substantial departures from the underlying strength of the two parties in the electorate.

These temporary deviating changes may be dramatic and reflect important electoral forces, but another type of change is of even greater interest. On rare occasions in American national politics, a permanent or *realigning change* in voting patterns occurs. In such instances the electorate departs from its expected voting pattern but does not thereafter return to the old pattern. On occasion these changes are large enough to alter the competitive balance between the parties, with significant conse-

FIGURE 3-2a Democratic Expected Vote in Presidential Elections, 1840-1992

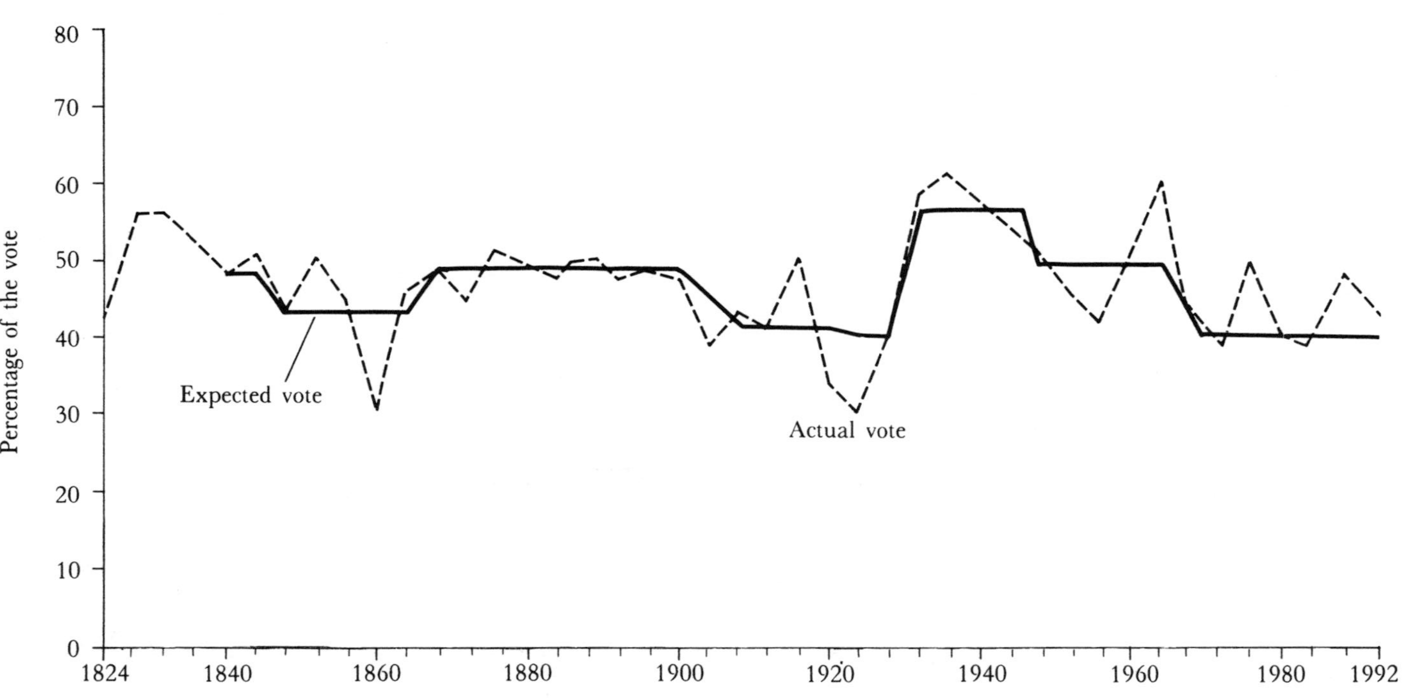

SOURCES: Jerome M. Clubb, William H. Flanigan, and Nancy H. Zingale, *Partisan Realignment* (Beverly Hills, Calif.: Sage Publications, 1980), 92-93, Table 3.1a; U.S. Bureau of the Census, *Statistical Abstract of the United States, 1990,* 110th ed. (Washington, D.C.: U.S. Government Printing Office, 1989); "Official Election Results," *Congressional Quarterly Weekly Report,* January 23, 1993, 190.

FIGURE 3-2b Republican Expected Vote in Presidential Elections, 1872-1992

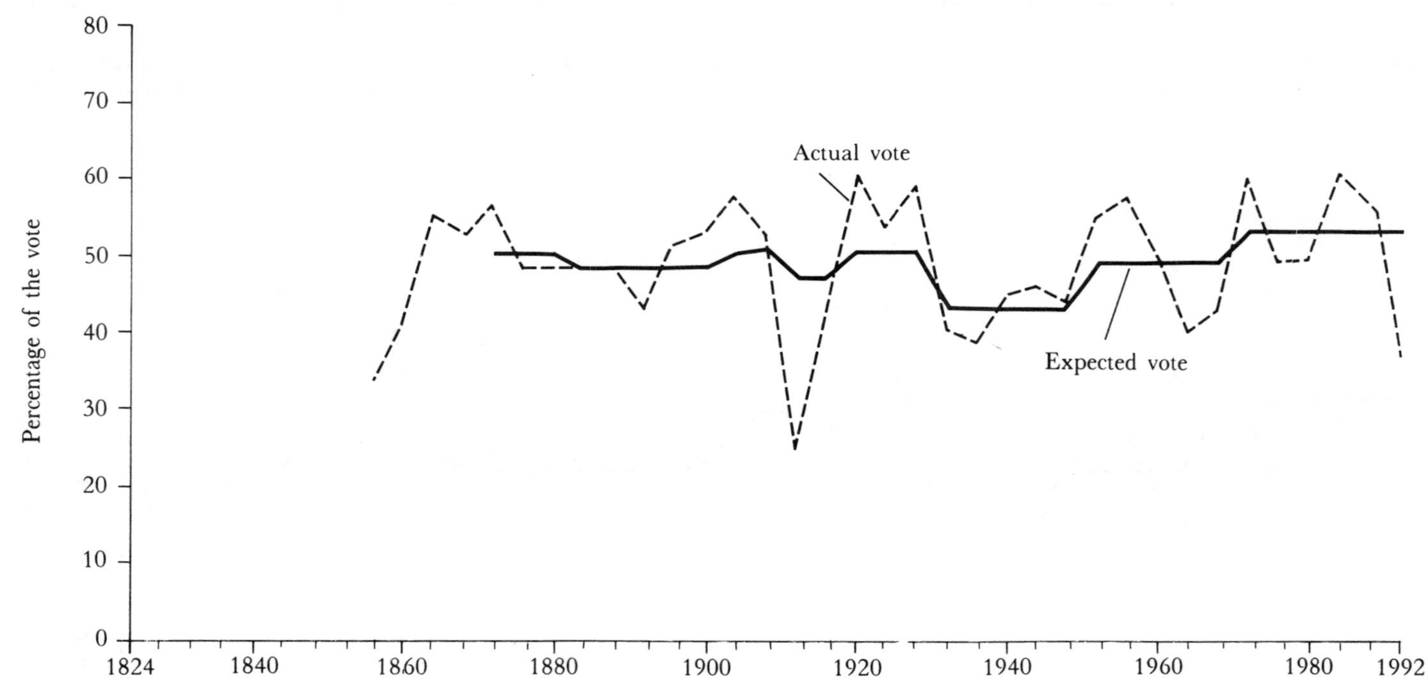

SOURCES: Jerome M. Clubb, William H. Flanigan, and Nancy H. Zingale, *Partisan Realignment* (Beverly Hills, Calif.: Sage Publications, 1980), 92-93, Table 3.1a; U.S. Bureau of the Census, *Statistical Abstract of the United States, 1990,* 110th ed. (Washington, D.C.: U.S. Government Printing Office, 1989); "Official Election Results," *Congressional Quarterly Weekly Report,* January 23, 1993, 190.

quences for the policy directions of the government. Such a period of change is usually referred to as a *partisan realignment*.[5]

Electoral analysts usually discuss three major realignments in American history: one accompanied the Civil War and the emergence of the Republican party, another followed the depression of 1893 and benefited the Republicans, and the most recent followed the depression of 1929 and led to Democratic party dominance. These abrupt changes in the expected votes of the parties can be seen in Figures 3-2a and 3-2b. Each realignment of partisan loyalties coincided with a major national crisis, leading to the supposition that a social or economic crisis is necessary to shake loose customary loyalties. But major crises and national traumas have not always led to disruptions of partisanship, suggesting that other political conditions must also be present in order for a crisis to produce a realignment. The nature of the realignment crisis has political significance, however, for it generally determines the lines along which the rearrangement in partisan loyalties will take place, as different segments of the electorate respond differently to the crisis and to attempts to solve it.

In general, realignments appear to happen in the following way. At a time of national crisis, the electorate rejects the party in power, giving a decisive victory to the other party, a victory that includes not only the presidency but also large majorities in both houses of Congress. Armed with this political mandate, the new party in office acts to meet the crisis, often with innovative policies that are sharp departures from the past. *If* the administration's policy initiatives are successful in solving the nation's problems (or at least are widely perceived as successful), then significant numbers of voters will become partisans of the new administration's party and continue voting for it in subsequent elections, thus causing a lasting change in the division of partisan strength in the electorate. If, on the other hand, the administration in power is *not* perceived as successful in handling the crisis, then in all likelihood the voters will reject that party in the next election, and its landslide victory in the previous election will be regarded, in retrospect, as a deviating election.

In a realignment it is very likely that the people who actually become partisans of the new majority party are the independents and previously uninvolved members of the electorate, not partisans of the other party. In other words, in a realignment few Democrats or Republicans switch parties; it appears more likely that independents drop their independent stance and become partisan. Thus, for a realignment to occur, a precondition may be a pool of people without partisan attachments who are "available" for realignment. This, in turn, suggests that there may be a longer sequence of events that forms a realignment cycle.

First there is the crisis that, if successfully handled, leads to a realignment. This initiates a period of electoral stability during which the parties take distinct stands on the issues that were at the heart of the crisis. Party loyalty is high during this period, both within the electorate and among the elected political leaders in government. However, as time passes, new problems arise and new issues gradually disrupt the old alignment and lead to greater electoral instability. During this period, often referred to as a *dealignment*, voters are much more susceptible to the personal appeals of candidates, to local issues, and to other elements that might lead to departures from underlying party loyalty. As the time since the last realignment lengthens, more and more new voters come into the electorate without attachments to the symbols and issues of the past that made their elders party loyalists. This group of voters without strong attachments to either party may provide the basis for a new realignment should a crisis arise and one or the other of the parties be perceived as successfully solving it.

Party Systems and Realignments

Political historians often divide American electoral history into five *party systems*—eras that are distinguished from each other by the different political parties that existed or by the different competitive relationships among the parties.[6] The transition from one party system to another has usually been marked by a realignment.

The first party system, which extended from the 1790s until about 1824, saw the relatively rapid formation of two parties, the Federalists and the Jeffersonian Republicans. The issue that divided these parties most clearly was their attitude toward the power of the central government. The commercial and financial interests supported the Federalist position of increasing the authority of the central government, whereas Jeffersonian Republicans distrusted the centralizing and, in their view, aristocratic tendencies of their rivals. These parties began as factions within the Congress, but before long they had gained organizations at the state and local level and had substantially broadened the base of political participation among the voting population. After 1815, competition between the two parties all but ceased as the Jeffersonian Republicans gained supremacy, moving the country into the Era of Good Feelings.

The second party system is usually dated from 1828, the year of the first presidential election with substantial popular participation, which marked the resurgence of party competition for the presidency. Emerging ultimately from this renewed competition were the Democrats and the Whigs, parties that competed fairly evenly for national power until the 1850s. Mass political participation increased and party organizations were strengthened as both parties sought electoral support from the common people. Although the Democratic party had come to prominence led by frontiersman Andrew Jackson, by the 1850s both Democrats and Whigs had adherents in all sections of the nation. Thus, when the issue of slavery broke full force upon the nation, the existing parties could not easily cope with the sectional differences they found within their ranks. As the Whigs and Democrats compromised or failed to act because of internal disagreements, a flurry of minor parties appeared to push the cause of abolitionism. One of these, the Republican party, eventually replaced the floundering Whigs as one of the two major parties that would dominate party systems thereafter.

The intense conflicts that preceded the Civil War led to the basic regional alignment of Democratic dominance in the South and Republican strength in the North that emerged from the war and that characterized the third party system. But the extreme intensity and durability of these partisan loyalties were also significantly dependent upon emotional attachments associated with the war. The strength of these partisan attachments after the Civil War was not lessened by the sharp competitiveness of the two parties throughout the system. Electoral forces were so evenly balanced that the Republican party could effectively control the presidency and Congress only by excluding the southern Democrats from participation in elections. Once Reconstruction relaxed enough to permit the full expression of Democratic strength, the nation was very narrowly divided, with the slightest deviation determining the outcome of elections.

The most dominant characteristic of the Civil War realignment was the regional division of party strongholds, but there was considerable Republican vote strength throughout much of the South and Democratic strength in most of the North. Especially in the North, states that regularly cast their electoral votes for Republican presidential candidates did so by very slim margins. Within each region persistent loyalty to the minority party was usually related to earlier opposition to the war. Seemingly, the intensity of feelings surrounding the war overwhelmed other issues, and the severity of the division over the war greatly inhibited the emergence of new issues along other lines. Thus, a significant feature of the Civil War realignment is its "freezing" of the party system.[7] Although later realignments have occurred and, indeed, a fourth and fifth party system can be identified, after the Civil War the same two parties have remained dominant. The subsequent realignments only changed the competitive position of these two parties relative to each other. While the choices were frozen following the Civil War, the relative strength of the parties was not. New parties have found it impossible to compete effectively (although they may affect electoral outcomes), and the remnants of the sectional realignment of the Civil War are still visible and occasionally potent in the political conflicts of today.

Toward the end of the nineteenth century, Civil War loyalties weakened enough to allow new parties, particularly the Populists in the Midwest and South, to make inroads into the votes of both major parties. Following the economic recession of 1893 for which the Democrats suffered politically, the Republican party began to improve its basic vote strength. In 1896 the formation of a coalition of Democrats and Populists and the unsuccessful presidential candidacy of their nominee, William Jennings Bryan, resulted in increased Republican strength in the East and a further strengthening of the secure position of the Democratic party in the South. Republican domination was solidified in the Midwest by the popularity of Theodore Roosevelt in the election of 1904. By the early twentieth century, competitive areas were confined to the Border States and a few Mountain States.

It is appropriate to view the realignment of 1896 and the fourth party system that followed as an adjustment of the Civil War alignment. Few areas shifted very far from the previous levels of voting; most individuals probably did not change their partisanship. The issue basis of this alignment was economic. The Republicans advocated development and modernization while opposing regulation of economic activity. The Democrats supported various policies intended to provide remedies for particular economic hardships. At a minimum these issues led the more prosperous, more modern areas in the North to shift toward the Republicans, and the more backward, more depressed areas in the South to shift toward the Democrats. These tendencies are based on normal vote patterns and should not obscure the considerable variation in the vote for president during these years, particularly in the elections of 1912 and 1916.

Following the onset of the Great Depression of 1929 under a Republican president, Democrat Franklin D. Roosevelt rode the reaction to economic hardship to a landslide victory in 1932. In his first administration, Roosevelt launched a program of economic recovery and public assistance called the New Deal. The Democrats emerged as the majority party, signaling the start of the fifth party system. The New Deal realignment resulted in far greater shifts than the prior realignment of 1896, since it shifted many of the northern states from Republican to Democratic status. This most recent realignment has more present-day interest than the others and is reflected most prominently in present voting patterns. Since the policies of the Democratic administration during the New Deal appealed more to the working class than to the middle class, more to poor farmers than to the prosperous, these groups responded differently to Democratic candidates. The New Deal and the electorate's response to Roosevelt's administration considerably sharpened the social class basis of party support. Especially for younger voters during these years, class politics was of greater salience than it had been before or has been since.

This realignment resulted in adjustments in previous loyalties, but it did not override them completely. The New Deal coalition was based on regional strength in the South, which was independent of social class, and further reinforced an already overwhelming dominance there. Perhaps the most incompatible elements in the New Deal coalition were southern middle-class whites, mainly conservative, and northern liberals, both white and black. Although the New Deal era established the basic pattern of partisanship that has led to the present alignment, changes have occurred in several major components of this pattern of party loyalties. Most notably, southern whites have drifted away from the Democratic party, particularly in presidential contests. To a degree, working-class whites in the North also have moved toward the Republican party on occasion, and middle-class voters have sometimes shifted toward the Democrats. A considerable shift in the expected presidential votes of both the Republican and Democratic parties took place in the late 1960s (see Figures 3-2a and 3-2b).

Survey data on party identification over the last forty-five years yield evidence of the New Deal alignment, as well as its recent deterioration (see Table 3-1). During these years, the Democrats have held an advantage over the Republicans, an advantage ranging from a high of 2 to 1 in 1964 to a low of 4 to 3 in 1988. This means, among other things, that in the nation as a whole the Democratic party has begun campaigns with more supporters than has the Republican party. Broadly speaking, the Democrats have tried to hold onto their following during a campaign, while the Republicans have attempted to win over a following.

TABLE 3-1 Party Identification of the Electorate, 1947-1992

	1947	1952	1954	1956	1958	1960	1962	1964	1966	1968
Democrats	46%	47%	47%	44%	47%	46%	47%	51%	45%	45%
Independents	21	22	22	24	19	23	23	22	28	29
Republicans	27	27	27	29	29	27	27	24	25	24
Nothing; don't know	7	4	4	3	5	4	3	2	2	2
Total	101%	100%	100%	100%	100%	100%	100%	99%	100%	100%
(*N*)	(1,287)	(1,799)	(1,139)	(1,762)	(1,269)	(1,954)	(1,317)	(1,571)	(1,291)	(1,557)

SOURCES: For 1947, National Opinion Research Center; for all other years, Survey Research Center, Center for Political Studies.

The advantage that the Democrats enjoyed nationwide was largely a result of having an overwhelming Democratic majority in the South, as shown in Table 3-2. Today, Democrats are still stronger in the South than in the North, but the proportion of Republicans in the South has increased to about the same level as in the North. In both the South and the North, independents hold the balance of power between Democrats and Republicans. Furthermore, the increasing tendency of southern Democrats to desert their party in presidential races means that those elections are far more competitive nationwide than the distribution of partisans would suggest.

The most interesting change reflected in these data is the increase beginning in 1966 in the proportion of independents. Supporters of George Wallace in the South represented part of this increase initially, but an even larger portion is comprised of young voters who are not choosing sides in politics as quickly as their elders did. This increase appears to have leveled off in the 1970s, and although the proportions have fluctuated, the number of independents remains at its highest point since the era of survey research began. This general loosening of party loyalties is widely suggested as the possible forerunner of a major realignment in partisanship.

The disintegration of the New Deal coalition should not be exaggerated, even though there has been erratic voting behavior in recent years. Deviations from Democratic loyalty have been most noticeable in presidential voting; the New Deal partisan realignment established in the 1930s remained intact longer in congressional voting. However, by the 1970s further shifts in the New Deal alignment became evident, as conservative Republicans began to show strength in races for other offices in many parts of the South. The Democratic vote for Congress in

1970	1972	1974	1976	1978	1980	1982	1984	1986	1988	1990	1992
44%	40%	38%	39%	39%	41%	44%	36%	40%	35%	39%	35%
31	35	36	36	38	35	30	34	33	36	35	38
24	23	22	23	21	22	24	28	26	28	24	25
1	2	4	2	3	2	2	2	2	2	2	2
100%	100%	100%	100%	101%	100%	100%	100%	101%	101%	100%	100%
(1,507)	(2,705)	(2,523)	(2,872)	(2,283)	(1,614)	(1,418)	(1,989)	(2,166)	(2,040)	(2,000)	(2,485)

the North and South since 1936 is plotted in Figure 3-3, illustrating the important role played by the South in Democratic victories through these years. The elections of the 1970s show the Democratic advantage in the South eroding; since that time, significantly more Republicans have been winning seats. It probably is no exaggeration to suggest that in the South only longstanding Democratic incumbents are safe from competition; as they step down, their seats will be contested by the Republicans. On the other hand, in some areas of the North moderate Republicans have been replaced by liberal Democrats, reflecting a weakness in long-established Republican support. The past several elections have revealed a degree of volatility in voting that suggests detachment from the partisan sympathies associated with the New Deal alignment.

Is Realignment Still Possible?

Despite speculation throughout the 1980s about a possible Republican realignment, the evidence seems clear that the American party system is in a period of continued dealignment. Some argue that the dealignment has gone so far, and the political parties have become so weak, that a traditional realignment is no longer possible.[8]

The 19 percent of the presidential vote that Perot gained in 1992, unprecedented for an independent or third-party candidate since the New Deal, demonstrates the lack of loyalty many voters feel to either the Democratic or Republican parties. Voter anger at incumbents, the parties, politicians, and government in general suggests voters are not likely to develop new loyalties quickly or enthusiastically embrace new policies and the policy makers who implement them.

TABLE 3-2 Party Identification of the Electorate for the Nation, the Non-South, and the South, 1952-1992

	THE NATION										
	1952	1956	1960	1964	1968	1972	1976	1980	1984	1988	1992
Strong Democrats	22%	21%	20%	27%	20%	15%	15%	18%	17%	17%	18%
Weak Democrats	25	23	24	25	25	26	25	23	20	18	17
Independents	22	23	22	22	29	35	36	34	34	36	38
Weak Republicans	14	14	14	13	14	13	14	14	15	14	14
Strong Republicans	13	15	15	11	10	10	9	8	13	14	11
Apolitical, other	4	4	5	2	2	2	2	2	2	2	2
Total	100%	100%	100%	100%	100%	101%	101%	99%	101%	101%	100%
(*N*)	(1,799)	(1,762)	(1,954)	(1,571)	(1,557)	(2,705)	(2,872)	(1,614)	(1,989)	(2,040)	(2,485)
	THE NON-SOUTH										
	1952	1956	1960	1964	1968	1972	1976	1980	1984	1988	1992
Strong Democrats	18%	17%	18%	23%	17%	13%	12%	15%	15%	16%	16%
Weak Democrats	22	19	20	23	24	22	22	22	18	16	17
Independents	26	26	25	25	28	37	38	37	33	36	39
Weak Republicans	16	16	16	16	17	16	17	14	17	16	15
Strong Republicans	17	18	17	12	12	12	10	9	14	15	12
Apolitical, other	2	2	4	1	1	1	2	2	2	2	1
Total	101%	98%	100%	100%	99%	101%	101%	99%	99%	101%	100%
(*N*)	(1,290)	(1,249)	(1,293)	(1,087)	(1,076)	(1,799)	(1,623)	(1,050)	(1,352)	(1,322)	(1,650)

	THE SOUTH										
	1952	1956	1960	1964	1968	1972	1976	1980	1984	1988	1992
Strong Democrats	31%	29%	23%	36%	26%	17%	19%	23%	19%	21%	21%
Weak Democrats	32	32	33	30	28	32	30	25	23	21	18
Independents	14	15	17	15	30	29	32	29	35	35	37
Weak Republicans	8	9	8	8	8	10	11	13	11	10	12
Strong Republicans	6	8	12	8	4	9	7	7	9	11	9
Apolitical, other	9	9	6	3	2	2	2	3	3	2	3
Total	100%	102%	99%	100%	98%	99%	101%	100%	100%	100%	100%
(*N*)	(509)	(513)	(661)	(484)	(481)	(906)	(780)	(564)	(596)	(718)	(835)

SOURCE: Survey Research Center; Center for Political Studies National Election Studies. Data provided by the Inter-university Consortium for Political and Social Research.

FIGURE 3-3 Democratic Vote for Congress, North and South, 1936-1992

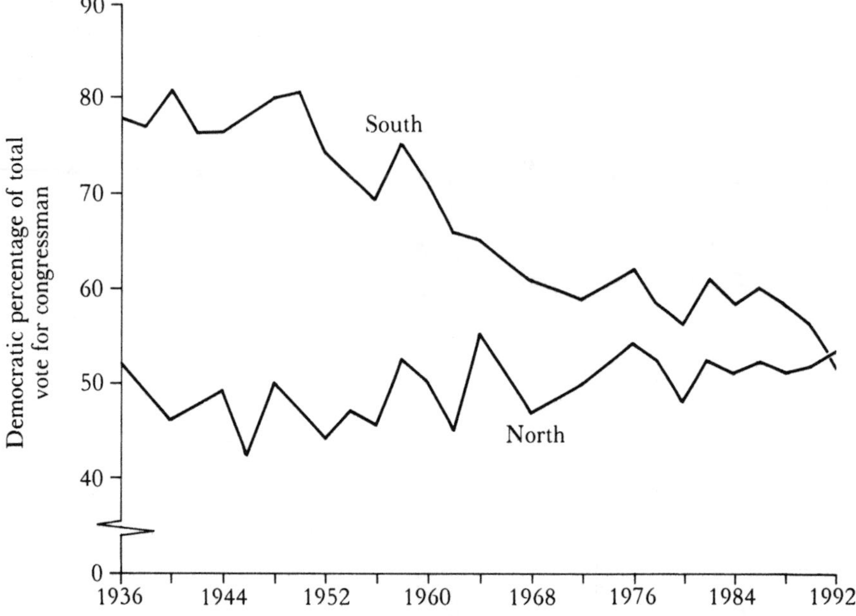

SOURCE: U.S. Bureau of the Census, *Statistical Abstract of the United States, 1993,* 113th ed. (Washington D.C.: U.S. Government Printing Office, 1992); "Election '92 Results," *Congressional Quarterly Weekly Report,* November 7, 1992, 3600-3607.

It is too soon to tell whether this continuing disenchantment with political parties signifies the parties' inability to ever recapture the loyalty of the voter, thereby rendering the concept of realignment obsolete. Clearly, however, it is not useful to see every modest shift in voter sentiment as forecasting a major reshaping of the American party system. The next realignment, if there is one, will also involve some rather fundamental changes in the attitudes of citizens toward political parties, political leaders, and government itself.

Notes

1. The most important work on party identification is in Angus Campbell, Philip E. Converse, Warren E. Miller, and Donald E. Stokes, *The American Voter*

(New York: John Wiley & Sons, 1960), 120-167. For a more recent treatment in comparative perspective, see Ian Budge, Ivor Crewe, and Dennis Farlie, eds., *Party Identification and Beyond* (New York: John Wiley & Sons, 1976), Part I.

2. For the most important statement of these ideas, see Philip E. Converse, "The Concept of a Normal Vote," in *Elections and the Political Order*, ed. Angus Campbell et al. (New York: John Wiley & Sons, 1966), 9-39.
3. This discussion and data presentation are based on our earlier work in William H. Flanigan and Nancy H. Zingale, "The Measurement of Electoral Change," *Political Methodology* 1 (Summer 1974): 49-82.
4. This and most discussions of the classification of elections are based on the work of V. O. Key and Angus Campbell. See V. O. Key, "A Theory of Critical Elections," *Journal of Politics* 17 (1955): 3-18; and Angus Campbell, "A Classification of Presidential Elections," in *Elections and the Political Order*, 63-77.
5. This and the following discussion draw heavily on Jerome M. Clubb, William H. Flanigan, and Nancy H. Zingale, *Partisan Realignment: Voters, Parties and Government in American History* (Boulder, Colo.: Westview Press, 1990).
6. See, for example, William N. Chambers and W. Dean Burnham, eds., *The American Party Systems: Stages of Political Development* (New York: Oxford University Press, 1975).
7. This concept was developed by S. M. Lipset and Stein Rokkan in their discussion of the development of the European party systems in *Party Systems and Voter Alignments* (New York: Free Press, 1967), 1-64.
8. Byron E. Shafer, *The End of Realignment? Interpreting American Electoral Eras* (Madison: University of Wisconsin Press, 1991).

Suggested Readings

Beck, Paul Allen. "The Dealignment Era in America." In *Electoral Change in Advanced Industrial Democracies: Realignment or Dealignment?* ed. Russell J. Dalton, Scott C. Flanagan, and Paul Allen Beck. Princeton, N.J.: Princeton University Press, 1984. A good survey of recent politics as an example of dealignment.

Burnham, W. Dean. *Critical Elections and the Mainsprings of American Politics.* New York: W. W. Norton, 1970. An early, important statement of the electoral realignment perspective.

Campbell, Angus, Philip E. Converse, Warren E. Miller, and Donald E. Stokes. *The American Voter.* New York: John Wiley & Sons, 1960. This is the classic study of public opinion and voting behavior in the United States.

Clubb, Jerome M., William H. Flanigan, and Nancy H. Zingale. *Partisan Realignment: Voters, Parties, and Government in American History.* Boulder, Colo.: Westview Press, 1990. A conceptualization of realignments that emphasizes both electoral behavior and political leadership.

Converse, Philip E. "The Concept of a Normal Vote." In *Elections and the Political Order*, ed. Angus Campbell, Philip E. Converse, Warren E. Miller, and Donald E. Stokes. New York: John Wiley & Sons, 1966. This chapter established the role of party identification as a baseline for the analysis of vote choice.

MacKuen, Michael B., Robert S. Erikson, and James A. Stimson. "Macropartisanship." *American Political Science Review* 83 (December 1989): 1125-1142. A sophisticated analysis of trends in aggregate party identification, arguing that the sizable amount of instability undermines the realignment perspective.

chapter four

Partisans and Partisan Change

AS WE DISCUSSED in Chapter 3, partisanship is a useful concept for tracing the dynamics of American political history. It is also crucial for understanding the political behavior of individuals. We begin this chapter by examining the impact of having—or not having—a party identification on the way people respond to politics. We then turn to the question of partisan change, looking first at change in individuals' partisanship over their lifetimes and then at changes across generations.

Voting Behavior

Recall that the standard party identification question, used in almost all political surveys, asks respondents whether they are Republicans, Democrats, or independents, and also whether they are "strong" or "not very strong" Republicans or Democrats. Not surprisingly, the likelihood of voting loyally for one party varies with the strength of individuals' partisanship. The defection rates of strong and weak (not very strong) partisans in each presidential election since 1952 are illustrated in Figure 4-1. Declining party loyalty is apparent with a decrease in the intensity of partisanship. Strong partisans consistently support the candidate of their party at higher rates than do weak partisans. (One should also note that in most years Republicans are more loyal to their party than Democrats, although this is partly accounted for by southern Democrats who regularly desert their party in presidential elections.) Obviously, differences in candidate appeal affect the propensity to defect. Very few Republicans defected from Dwight Eisenhower in the 1950s, Richard Nixon in 1972, or Ronald Reagan in 1984; many more deserted

FIGURE 4-1 Defection Rates, by Party Identifiers in Presidential Elections, 1952-1992

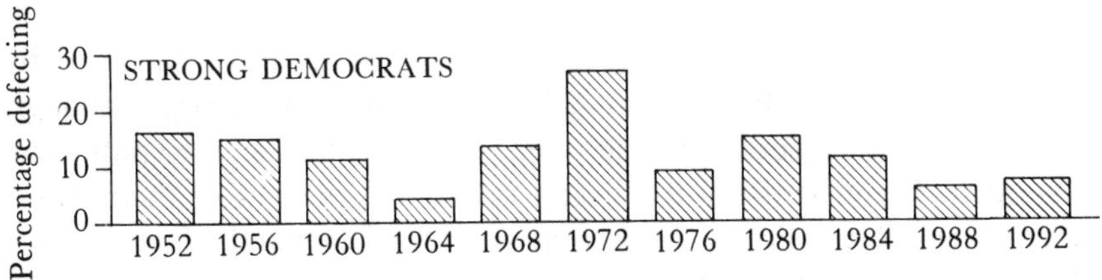

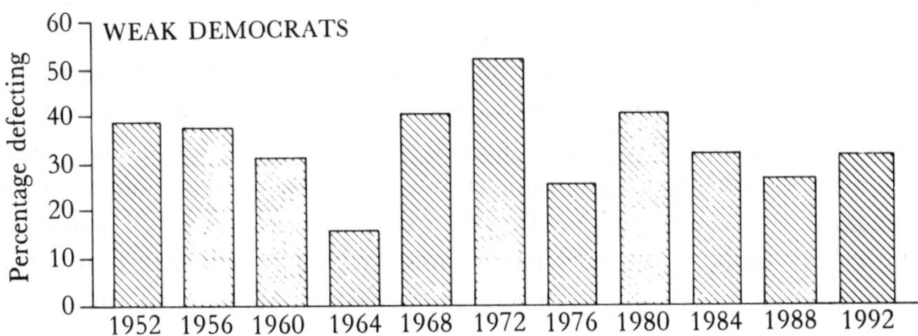

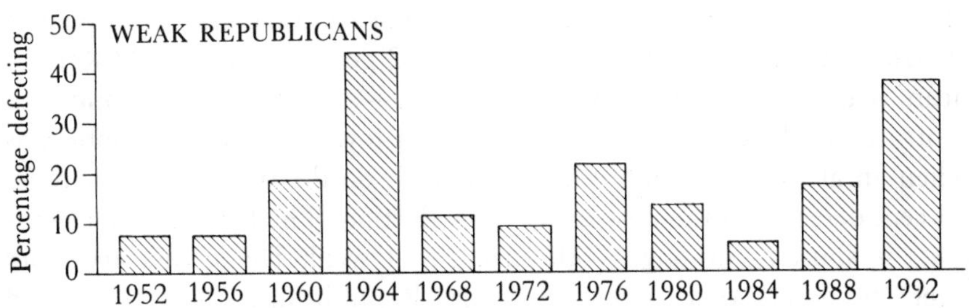

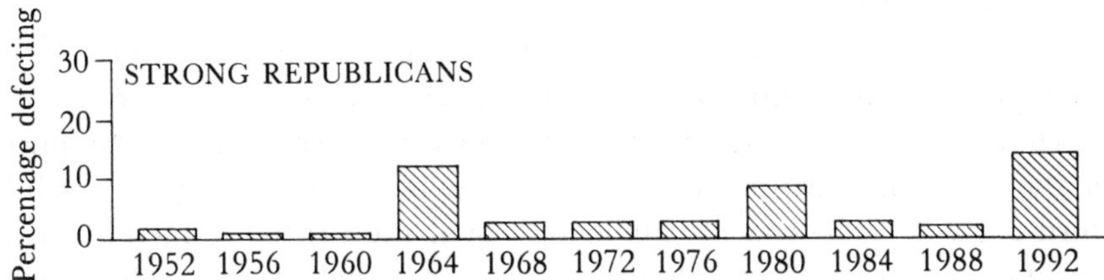

SOURCE: Survey Research Center; Center for Political Studies National Election Studies. Data provided by the Inter-university Consortium for Political and Social Research.

Barry Goldwater in 1964. Similarly, Democrats were very loyal to Lyndon Johnson in 1964 but abandoned George McGovern in large numbers in 1972.

Another potential cause of defection is attractive third-party candidates. In 1992 Ross Perot drew defectors from both parties, although more from the Republican side. Ten percent of strong Republicans defected to Perot, while Bill Clinton received 3 percent of their votes. Among weak Republicans, 25 percent voted for Perot and 14 percent for Clinton. The few strong Democrats who defected divided almost equally between Perot and George Bush, as did a greater number of weak Democrats who defected, giving Perot and Bush 17 and 14 percent of their votes, respectively. John Anderson in 1980 and George Wallace in 1968 similarly account for part of the upsurges in defections in those years. Historically, third-party candidates often have been viewed as "halfway houses" for partisans moving from one party to another. Not quite as dramatic for a partisan as defection to the opposition party, a vote for such a candidate may be a first step away from party loyalty. In any event, support for third parties and an increase in defection rates have generally been symptomatic of the loosening of party ties in a dealignment.

Although strong partisans vary in their loyalty from year to year depending on the candidates offered by their party, this tendency is much more pronounced among weak partisans. For example, the defection rate of strong Republicans varies from around 2 percent in a "good" Republican year to 10 percent in a "bad" year—a quite narrow range. In contrast, weak Republicans are almost as loyal as strong Republicans when an attractive Republican candidate is on the ticket, but nearly 50 percent defected in the disastrous 1964 election. The behavior of Democrats is similar, although both strong and weak Democrats are more likely to desert their party than are Republicans. Clearly, marked departures from the expected vote of a party are accomplished by wooing away the weaker partisans of the opposite party.

The tendency of both strong and weak partisans to vote according to their party identification becomes even more pronounced as one moves down the ticket to less visible and less publicized offices. This is a product of the dominant two-party system nationwide. Even highly successful third-party or independent candidates down the ticket are merely local disruptions that have virtually no impact on national patterns. The voting behavior of partisans in congressional races since 1952 differs from the presidential data in two significant ways (see Figure 4-2). First, differences between the party loyalty of strong and weak partisans are usually

FIGURE 4-2 Defection Rates, by Party Identifiers in Congressional Elections, 1952-1992

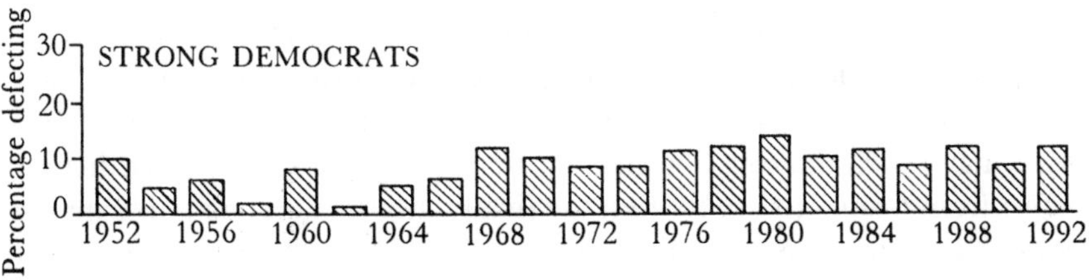

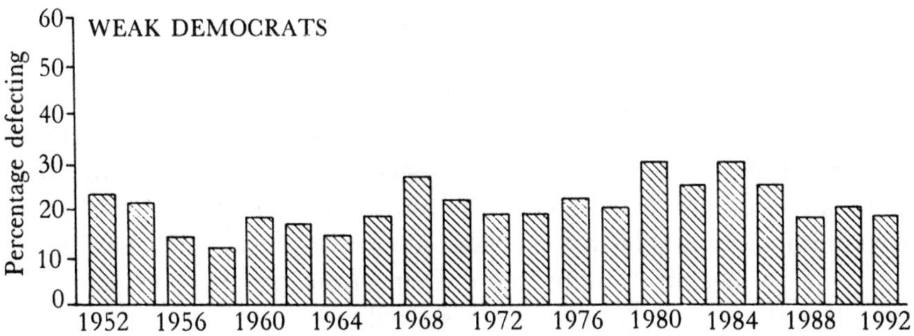

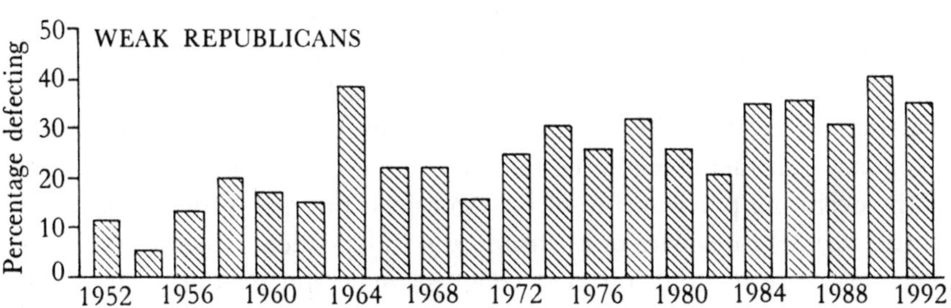

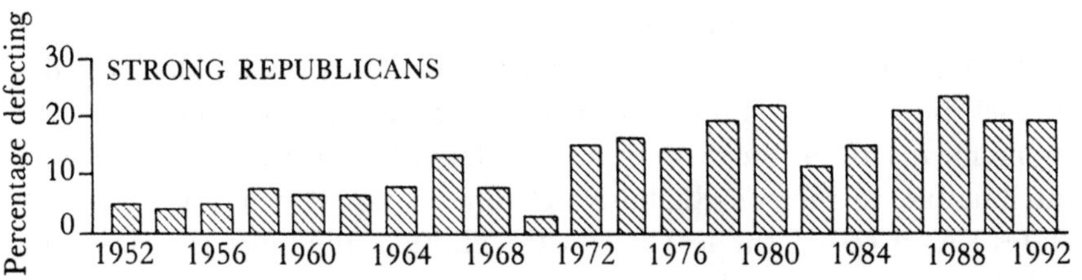

SOURCE: Survey Research Center; Center for Political Studies National Election Studies. Data provided by the Inter-university Consortium for Political and Social Research.

smaller. Second, the defection rate does not fluctuate from year to year nearly as much as in the presidential elections, particularly among weak partisans. Both these differences are attributable to the lower visibility of congressional races. In a presidential election, the flood of available information means that a particularly attractive candidate or a stirring issue may touch the consciousness of the weak partisans, causing them to defect from traditional party ties; the firmly attached, strong partisans are more likely to resist. In the less publicized congressional races, the information that might cause weak partisans to defect is less likely ever to reach them; in the absence of information about the candidates and issues, weak partisans vote their party identification.

In congressional voting, unlike presidential voting, Democrats are regularly more party loyal than are Republicans (see Figure 4-2). This is both cause and effect of the recent disjuncture of national politics, where Republicans are stronger in presidential politics and Democrats dominate in congressional politics. Throughout the 1970s and 1980s the Republicans were able to field more attractive presidential candidates than the Democrats, leading more Democratic partisans to defect in presidential races. In contrast, congressional races saw Republican partisans often defecting to vote for a long-term Democratic incumbent running against token Republican opposition.

The intensity of partisanship affects political behavior beyond its influence on the likelihood of voting for or defecting from a party's candidate. Strong partisans are also more likely to vote in all kinds of elections than are either weak partisans or independents. Indeed, one explanation sometimes offered for the decline in turnout in recent years is the declining partisanship of the American public.[1] The turnout rates of the various categories of partisans and independents for three types of elections—presidential, off-year congressional, and primary—are illustrated in Figure 4-3. The 1992 presidential primaries, despite all their accompanying publicity and frenetic campaigning, still had a lower average turnout than the 1990 off-year congressional election. Turnout declines in all categories as the presumed importance of the race decreases, but the rate is much steeper among the less partisan. (Part, but by no means all, of the drop in turnout for independents in primaries is attributable to their ineligibility to vote in party primaries in some states.) As a result, the less salient the election, the more the electorate will be dominated by the intense partisans, who are also less likely to defect from party ties in casting their ballots.

These ideas led Angus Campbell to suggest an intriguing theory of electoral change to explain the oft-observed phenomenon in American

FIGURE 4-3 Turnout by Partisans and Independents in Presidential, Congressional, and Primary Elections

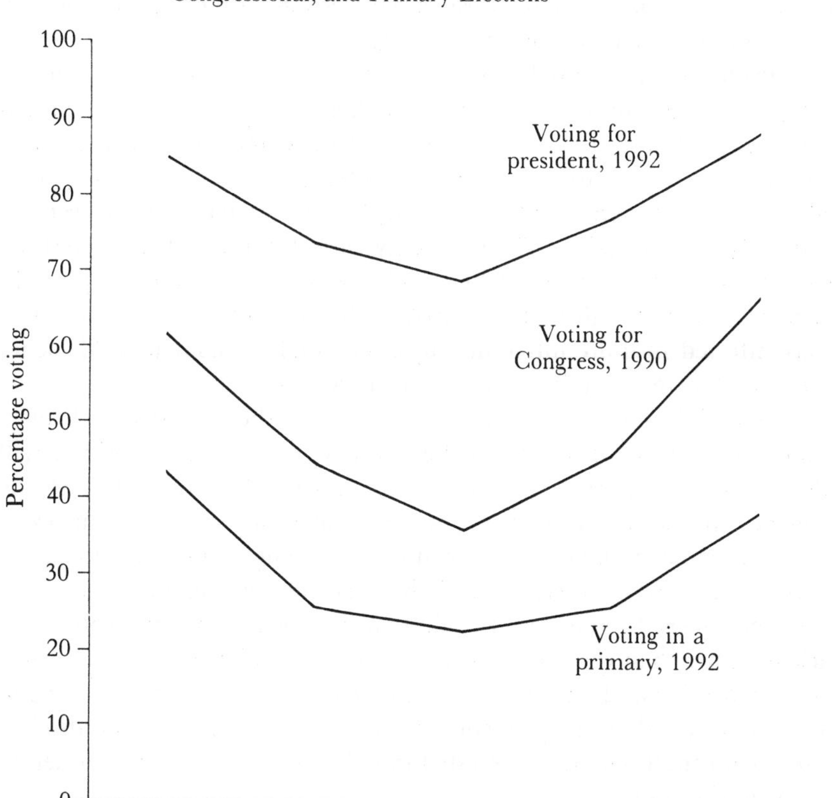

SOURCE: Center for Political Studies 1990 and 1992 National Election Study. Data provided by the Inter-university Consortium for Political and Social Research.

politics whereby the party winning the presidency is very likely to lose seats in the legislature in the next congressional election.[2] Because, the argument goes, presidential elections are usually accompanied by a high level of interest, large numbers of weak partisans and independents are drawn to the polls. Since these weak partisans and independents are more easily shifted from one party to another, they add disproportionately to the vote for one presidential candidate, usually the winner. In congressional elections these less committed voters do not turn out, while relatively large numbers of intense partisans do. These strong party identifiers are not so likely to shift their vote away from their party.

Consequently, support declines in off-year congressional elections for the party that won the previous presidential election with disproportionately large numbers of less interested voters.

Persuasive as Campbell's argument may be, it rests on some assumptions that indeed may be questionable. First, it assumes that high-stimulus elections will be landslides; that is, it assumes that the short-term forces bringing the less interested voter to the polls will work to the advantage of only one candidate. Even though this has usually been the case, it is not invariable. The extremely close 1960 presidential election, with its emphasis on the religion of Democratic candidate John F. Kennedy, was a high-turnout election, but different groups of voters were affected in quite different ways. The high turnout in 1992 benefited Clinton to a small degree, Perot much more so.

Second, Campbell's argument suggests that the less interested voters who come to the polls to vote for the attractive presidential candidate will also vote for that party's candidate in congressional elections. In fact, the evidence shows that in many cases weak partisans who defect in presidential elections return to their own party in congressional elections, or, in the case of Perot voters in 1992, have no congressional candidates on the same ticket to vote for. In addition, independents often split their tickets rather than vote for the congressional candidate of the same party as their presidential choice. To some extent, the argument also rests on the assumption that independents are not only less partisan, but also less informed, concerned, and interested in politics, a view that is frequently called into question.

Are Independents Apolitical?

Independents, who now account for more than one-third of the national electorate, are the most obvious source of additional votes for either party. While partisans, especially weak partisans, sometimes abandon their party, year after year independents are the largest bloc of uncommitted voters available to both parties. The independent's capacity for shifting back and forth between the major parties is shown in Table 4-1. Each party has, on occasion, successfully appealed to the independents, winning over a large majority to its side. In 1984 the independents voted almost 2 to 1 for Reagan over Walter Mondale, while Johnson held a similar advantage over Goldwater in 1964. The elections of 1976 (Jimmy Carter versus Gerald Ford) and 1960 (Kennedy versus Nixon) demonstrate the situation Republican presidential candidates faced for

TABLE 4-1 The Distribution of Votes for President by Independents, 1948-1992

	1948	1952	1956	1960	1964	1968	1972	1976	1980	1984	1988	1992
Democratic	57%	33%	27%	46%	66%	32%	33%	45%	26%	34%	46%	42%
Republican	43	67	73	54	34	47	65	55	56	66	53	30
Wallace [a]						21						
Schmitz [b]							2					
Anderson [c]									14			
Perot [d]												27
Other									4		2	
Total	100%	100%	100%	100%	100%	100%	100%	100%	100%	100%	101%	99%
(*N*)	—	(263)	(309)	(298)	(219)	(228)	(908)	(532)	(306)	(334)	(364)	(573)

SOURCE: Survey Research Center; Center for Political Studies National Election Studies. Data provided by the Inter-university Consortium for Political and Social Research.

[a] American Independent party candidate in 1968.
[b] American party candidate in 1972.
[c] Independent candidate in 1980.
[d] Independent candidate in 1992.

many years: they had to win a healthy majority of the independent vote even to stay in close contention. The fact that Bush won the presidency in 1988 while doing no better among independents than did Nixon and Ford in their earlier losses stems from the narrowing of the advantage the Democrats hold over the Republicans in the numbers of partisans in the electorate. Bush's loss of independent support in 1992 to both Clinton and Perot illustrates the dependence of either major-party candidate on the votes of independents.

Third-party or independent candidates find these unaffiliated voters a major source of votes. In 1992, 27 percent of the independents voted for Perot. Similarly, in 1968 more than 20 percent of the independents gave their votes to Wallace, and in 1980, 14 percent voted for Anderson. Put another way, more than half of Perot's and Anderson's votes came from independents. Furthermore, independents may shift dramatically in voting for president and remain quite stable in voting for Congress. As Figure 4-4 shows, independent voting for Congress has generally been more volatile in presidential election years than in off-year elections.

On what basis do independents switch their party preferences? Major voting studies contend that the popular image of political independents as intelligent, informed, dispassionate evaluators of candidates, parties, and issues is mistaken. Studies from the Bureau of Applied Social Research and the Survey Research Center have supported the view that partisans of both parties are better informed and more con-

FIGURE 4-4 Net Advantage for Republicans or Democrats in Presidential and Congressional Voting Among Independents, 1952-1992

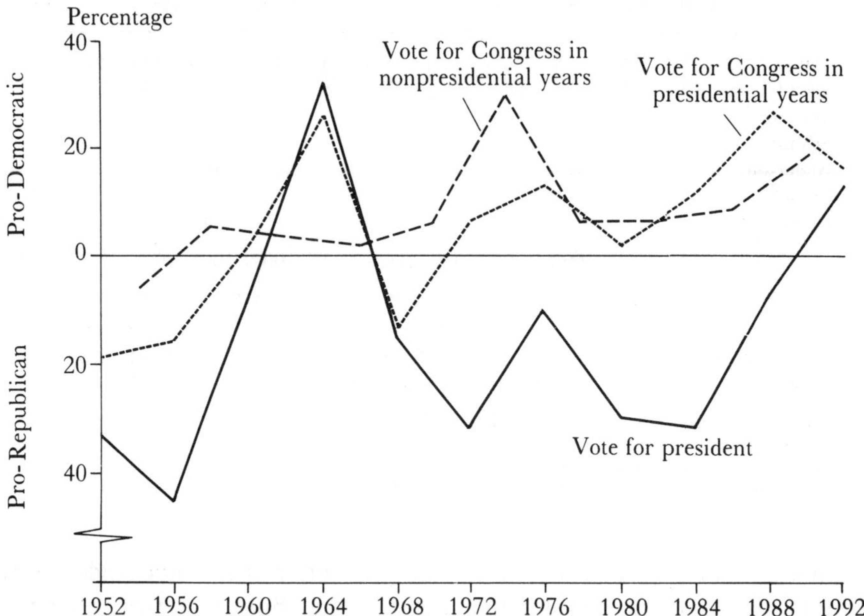

SOURCE: Survey Research Center; Center for Political Studies National Election Studies. Data provided by the Inter-university Consortium for Political and Social Research.

NOTE: The points in this figure represent the percentage of the vote given by independents to the Democrats minus the percentage they gave to the Republicans, i.e., the margin of difference between the two parties. For example, in 1978 the independent vote was 52 percent Democratic and 48 percent Republican. This appears as a 4 percent pro-Democratic percentage above the line.

cerned with politics than are the independents. This analysis has been reflected recently in the campaign strategies of both Democratic and Republican organizations. The view was widespread that the available voters—the voters that can be won over to either party—are an uninformed, apathetic group on whom intelligent, issue-oriented appeals and reasoned debate would be lost.

To pursue the analysis of independents, we need to make two distinctions that have not intruded on the discussion to this point. We will note these distinctions and then drop them because they complicate the analysis and are usually ignored.

TABLE 4-2 Party Identifiers, Self-Identified Independents, and People with No Preference, 1968-1992

	1968	1972	1976	1980	1984	1988	1992
Identify with a party	69%	64%	64%	64%	64%	63%	60%
Identify as independents	27	28	30	24	25	31	32
Have no preference	3	8	5	12	10	6	7
Don't know	a	0	a	0	0	0	1
Not ascertained	a	a	1	a	1	a	a
Total	99%	100%	100%	100%	100%	100%	100%
(*N*)	(1,557)	(2,702)	(1,320)	(1,614)	(1,989)	(2,040)	(2,485)

SOURCE: Survey Research Center; Center for Political Studies National Election Studies. Data provided by the Inter-university Consortium for Political and Social Research.

[a] Less than 0.5 percent.

First, there are important differences between nonpartisans who identify themselves as independents and those who lack any political identification. A sizable segment of the electorate answers the party identification question by saying that they aren't anything or that they don't know what they are. According to the coding conventions used by the Center for Political Studies, most of these nonidentifiers are included with the independents,[3] but there may be important conceptual distinctions between them and self-identified independents. These two types of nonpartisans are highlighted in the box in Table 4-2. Those in one set identify themselves as "independents"; the others do not think of themselves in terms of political labels. Since 1972 between one-sixth and one-third of the nonpartisans failed to identify themselves as independents. It is significant that the electorate is becoming more nonpartisan overall but not invariably more independent because these situations present different implications for the political parties. Self-identified independents think of themselves as having a political identity and are somewhat antiparty in orientation. The nonidentifying nonpartisans have a less clear self-image of themselves as political actors, but they are not particularly hostile to the political parties. They are less self-consciously political in many ways.

Second, within the large group of people who do not identify with a political party there are many people who say they "lean" toward either the Democratic or Republican party. These leaners comprise more than half of all nonpartisans, and they complicate analysis in a significant

FIGURE 4-5 Percentage of Turnout, High Interest, and Democratic Vote for President, by Partisanship, 1992

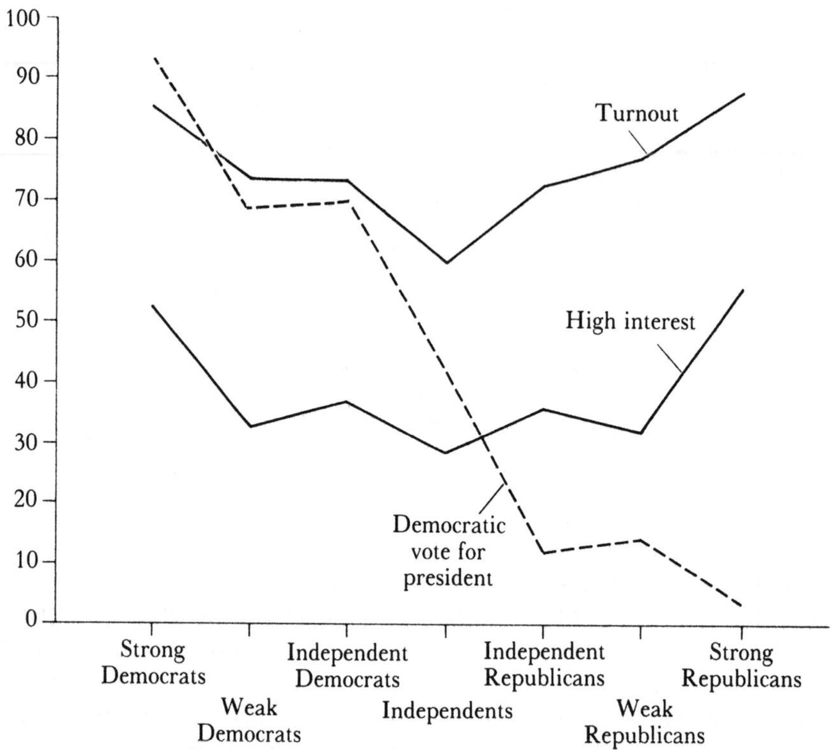

SOURCE: Center for Political Studies 1992 National Election Study. Data provided by the Inter-university Consortium for Political and Social Research.

way. On crucial attitudes and in important forms of political behavior, the leaning independents appear quite partisan. Independents who lean toward the Democratic party behave rather like weak Democratic partisans, and the same is true on the Republican side.[4] As can be seen in Figure 4-5, independent leaners are more interested in campaigns than are weak partisans, and they are generally as likely to vote and about as likely to be loyal to "their party" as are weak partisans.

How appropriate, then, is it to include all these "independents" in one category? On some characteristics like ideological self-identification and interest in public affairs there is much more variation within the three independent categories than between the several partisan categories. The differences between "leaners" and "pure" independents are often greater than the differences between Republican and Democratic partisans. Since the concept of "independent" embraces these three dissimilar groups, there is little wonder that some disagreement exists over what the true independent is like.

As a consequence of the inclusion of these various types of people under the label "independent," it is not surprising that it is difficult to make generalizations about the degree of political interest and information independents possess. Some independents have considerable interest in politics and others are quite apathetic. There are more informed, concerned voters among the leaning independents than among other nonpartisans, and the leaning independents are more likely to register and vote. When we question whether independents are attentive or apathetic toward politics, we must conclude that they are some of both.

To the student of contemporary American politics, these characteristics of the independent remain important because they determine the independent's susceptibility to political appeals. We and others have argued that the American electoral system is presently in a period of increased loosening of political ties, perhaps antecedent to a partisan realignment. The argument is that as larger and larger portions of the electorate either become independent or exhibit more independent behavior, these people form a pool of potential recruits for one of the parties, or a new party. Should someone like Perot or a leader of one of the existing parties be able to capture the imagination of this pool of available recruits on a lasting basis, it could lead to a significant change in the partisan division in the electorate.

Partisan Change

Partisanship can be thought of as a basic attitude that establishes a normal or expected vote, an estimate about how individuals or populations will vote, other things being equal. However, partisanship itself is not unchangeable. Individuals may change, not only their vote, but also their long-term party identification from one party to another. More important, over extended periods of time the partisan composition of the electorate may be altered as new voters of one political persuasion replace older voters of another. When the basic partisan division of the electorate changes, a partisan realignment occurs.

In the past the absence of survey data limited analysis of realignments, but during the current period we have the opportunity to study the individual processes of partisan change that underlie aggregate shifts in the partisan division of the electorate. These processes have been a matter of some controversy. One perspective holds that individual partisans are *converted* from one party to the other during a realignment. Other analysts, noting the psychological difficulty in changing long-held and deeply felt attachments, argue that such change probably comes about through *mobilization* rather than conversion. In other words, it is the independents or nonpolitical individuals, perhaps predominantly young voters just entering the electorate without strong partisan attachments, who fuel a realignment by joining the electorate overwhelmingly on the side of one party.

Some evidence on these points comes from the New Deal era. Although survey research was then in its infancy, some scholars have creatively used data from early surveys to try to answer these questions. Research by Kristi Andersen, reported in *The Changing American Voter*,[5] reveals high levels of nonvoting and nonpartisanship among young people and new citizens prior to the Great Depression. Those uninvolved, uncommitted potential participants entered the electorate in the 1930s disproportionately as Democrats. Andersen's findings on the electorate of the 1920s and 1930s support the view that realignments are based on the mobilization of new, independent voters rather than on the conversion of partisans. In contrast, Robert Erikson and Kent Tedin argue on the basis of early Gallup Poll data that much of the increase in the Democratic vote in the 1930s came from voters who had previously voted Republican.[6]

In this section we will examine the processes of partisan change in the contemporary period. Although we are in a better position to do so than we were for earlier eras, efforts are still hampered by a scarcity of panel data, that is, repeated interviews with the same individuals at different points in time. In most cases it will be necessary to infer individual changes from the behavior of similar types of individuals at different times.

Changes in Individuals Over a Lifetime

Two types of change in partisan identification can be distinguished, both of which have significant implications for political behavior. First, an individual may change from one party to another or to independent, or from independence to partisanship. Such change is of obvious importance if a large proportion of the electorate shifts in the same direction at about the same time. Second, an individual's partisanship may strengthen or weaken in intensity. A longstanding hypothesis states that the longer individuals identify with a party the stronger their partisanship will become.[7] In the electorate as a whole, these two types of change are not necessarily related to one another, so the occurrence of one form of change does not dictate or prevent the other. The recent increase in the number of independents at the expense of Democrats and Republicans does not necessarily mean that among the remaining partisans there has been no strengthening of loyalty with the lengthening of identification.

Analysts have attempted to explain partisan change by referring to three types of causal effects: (1) *period effects*, or the impact of a particular historical period that briefly affects partisanship across all age groups; (2) a *generation effect*, which affects the partisanship of a particular age group for the remainder of their political lives; and (3) a *life-cycle effect*, which produces changes associated with an individual's age. In current political behavior all three can be illustrated: a period effect that has resulted in an increasing independence in all age groups, a generation effect that keeps Democratic partisan loyalty high in the generation that entered the electorate during the New Deal, and a life-cycle effect that yields greater independence among the young than among their elders.

The difference between the 1950s, 1970s, and 1990s in the proportion of independents in various age groups is shown in Figure 4-6. The solid line represents the percentage of independents in each age group in 1972 and the broken line represents 1992. These two lines reflect a much higher rate of independence among the young when compared with 1952, the dotted line. The percentage of independents among older age groups in 1972, and in 1992 among those over seventy, is about the same as for voters of comparable age in 1952. However, in 1952 there were only slight differences associated with age, evidenced by the flatness of the dotted line. The youngest individuals were only a little more likely to be independent than the elderly and not nearly so likely to be independent as young people twenty and forty years later.

It is also possible to examine the change in particular age "cohorts" between 1952 and the later years using Figure 4-6.* The youngest cohort in 1952 was over forty years old in 1972 and reveals a substantially higher level of independence than it did when entering the electorate. By 1992 this cohort was over sixty years old and had become less

* In the absence of repeated observations of the same individuals over time, it is impossible to study many aspects of change. The use of age cohorts is an analytic technique that attempts to assess individual change through the use of surveys of different individuals over the years. Individuals of a certain age are isolated in an early survey, say thirty- to forty-year-olds in 1956, and they are compared with forty- to fifty-year-olds from a 1966 survey. This makes

(footnote continues)

independent once again. At each point along the lines, the vertical distance represents the changing percentage of independents in that age cohort. Most age cohorts became more independent during the early 1970s and somewhat less independent by 1992. To the extent that we can make the comparison, the cohorts are slightly more independent today than they were forty years ago.

Contrary to political folklore, there is little evidence that people become Republicans as they grow older, that is, that a life-cycle effect favors Republicans. It is true that older members of the electorate were, for some years, more likely to be Republicans than younger members. The generation of young people who came of age prior to the Great Depression contained large proportions of Republicans, an understandable situation given the advantage the Republicans enjoyed nationally at that time. Relatively few members of this generation have changed partisanship over the years, and these individuals constituted the older, more heavily Republican segment of the electorate. By the same token, the generation that entered the electorate during the New Deal was disproportionately Democratic. Since they also have remained stable in partisanship, older voters now look increasingly Democratic as this generation ages. For the next decade or so it will appear that the older the voters are, the more likely they are to be Democratic.

The tendency of individual partisanship to strengthen with age is the subject of some controversy.[8] During periods of stable party voting, there is likely to be increased partisanship the longer individuals identify with and vote for their party. On the other hand, when party voting is frequently disrupted, this reinforcement of partisanship may not occur. Even when the strength of partisanship does not increase with age, as appears to be the case in recent years, older partisans are less likely to abandon their party for an independent stance. This explains in part why older partisans were less likely to vote for an independent candidate in 1992 than were younger partisans. Nineteen percent of the Republican and Democratic partisans aged twenty-five and younger voted for Perot, while only 11 percent of partisans aged forty-five and older voted for him.

---

possible the comparison of an age cohort at two different times. This technique has been used in several studies of partisanship. See, for example, Paul R. Abramson, "Generational Change in American Electoral Behavior," *American Political Science Review* 68 (March 1974): 93-105; David Butler and Donald Stokes, *Political Change in Britain: Forces Shaping Electoral Choice* (New York: St. Martin's Press, 1969), esp. chaps. 3, 11; and Philip E. Converse, *The Dynamics of Party Support: Cohort-Analyzing Party Identification* (Beverly Hills, Calif.: Sage Publications, 1976).

FIGURE 4-6 Distribution of Independents by Age Cohorts, 1952, 1972, and 1992

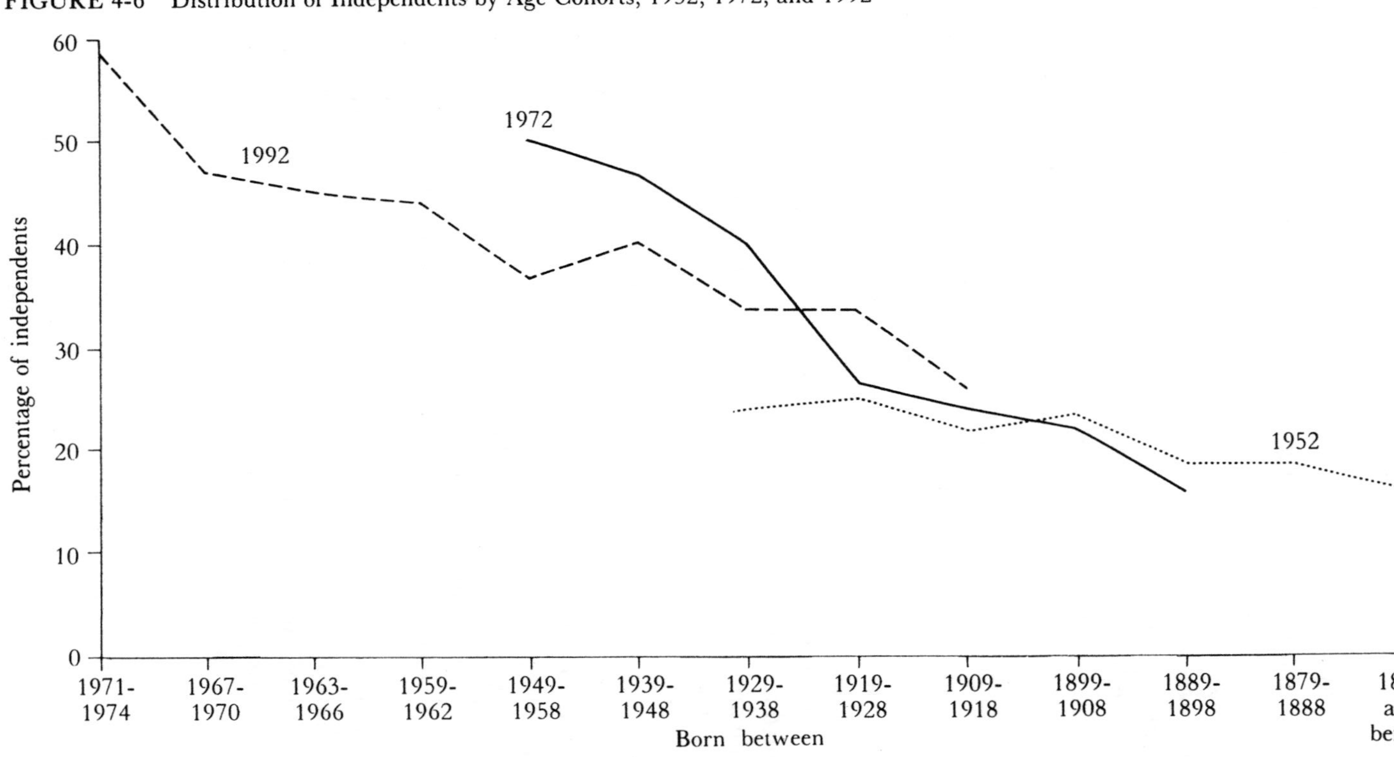

SOURCE: Center for Political Studies National Election Studies. Data provided by the Inter-university Consortium for Political and Social Research.

NOTE: The youngest cohort in each year includes only those old enough to vote. The last entry in 1952 and 1972 includes everyone seventy-five and older; the last entry in 1992 includes everyone seventy-one and older.

Gradual changes in individual partisanship have not been assessed satisfactorily for the entire public because the few election studies based on repeated interviews of the same individuals have covered at most four years. Nevertheless, the possibility that individuals change their partisanship over longer time periods is of considerable interest. In recent years speculation has focused on the possibility that the large number of young independents will become identified with one party or the other, thus creating a substantial shift in the overall partisan balance of the electorate, with or without a realigning crisis.

The best evidence on this point comes from a major study of political socialization conducted by M. Kent Jennings.[9] He surveyed a national sample of high school students and their parents in 1965, with follow-up interviews in 1973 and 1982. This provides a before-and-after picture of young people during the political traumas of the late 1960s and early 1970s, as well as a later snapshot after a more quiescent period. The interviews with the parents allow comparison with an older group experiencing the same political events.

As can be seen in Table 4-3 by looking at the percentages in the highlighted cells, the parental group was highly stable in their partisanship, with approximately three-fourths maintaining their party identification and only 3 or 4 percent switching from one party to the other from one interview to the next. About one in five switched into or out of the independent category. Between each time period, about equal numbers switched in each direction, so the aggregate or net change was nonexistent for the parents.

The young people were less stable in their partisanship, especially between 1965 and 1973 when substantial numbers of both Democratic and Republican identifiers shifted to an independent status. During the next interval from 1973 to 1982, these same young people were more stable in their loyalties, with about two-thirds maintaining the same party identification. This group, which was comprised of individuals roughly thirty-four years of age in 1982, remained much more independent than their parents, but the numbers of independents among them had not increased over this decade. As with their parents, very few young people (about one in twenty) switched from party to party during either time period.

Changes Across Generations

A shift in the partisan composition of the electorate owing to generational change is ordinarily a very gradual one, since political

TABLE 4-3 Stability and Change of Partisanship in Two Cohorts, High School Seniors and Their Parents

YOUNG PEOPLE

		1973					1982		
		Dem.	Ind.	Rep.			Dem.	Ind.	Rep.
	Dem.	24	14	3		Dem.	23	9	3
1965	Ind.	7	24	5	1973	Ind.	8	32	7
	Rep.	3	9	10		Rep.	2	4	13
	Total = 99%			N = 952		Total = 101%			N = 924

PARENTS

		1973					1982		
		Dem.	Ind.	Rep.			Dem.	Ind.	Rep.
	Dem.	39	5	3		Dem.	37	6	2
1965	Ind.	5	16	5	1973	Ind.	6	16	3
	Rep.	1	4	23		Rep.	2	4	24
	Total = 101%			N = 838		Total = 100%			N = 822

SOURCE: Adapted from M. Kent Jennings and Gregory B. Markus, "Partisan Orientations over the Long Haul," *American Political Science Review* 78, no. 4 (December 1984): 1004-1005, Tables 2 and 3.

NOTE: The highlighted cells (along the diagonal) represent those individuals who remained stable in their partisanship from one time period to the next. The off-diagonal cells represent individuals who changed their partisan identification.

attitudes, including partisanship, tend to be transmitted from parents to their children. Normally, more than two-thirds of the electorate identify with their parents' party if both parents had the same party identification. Certainly, the adoption of parents' partisanship by their children is consistent with the notion of family socialization. Children pick up the partisanship of their parents while quite young, but the parents' influence diminishes as the child comes into contact with other political and social influences during the teenage years. For most individuals the

FIGURE 4-7a Party Identification of High School Seniors and Their Parents in 1965

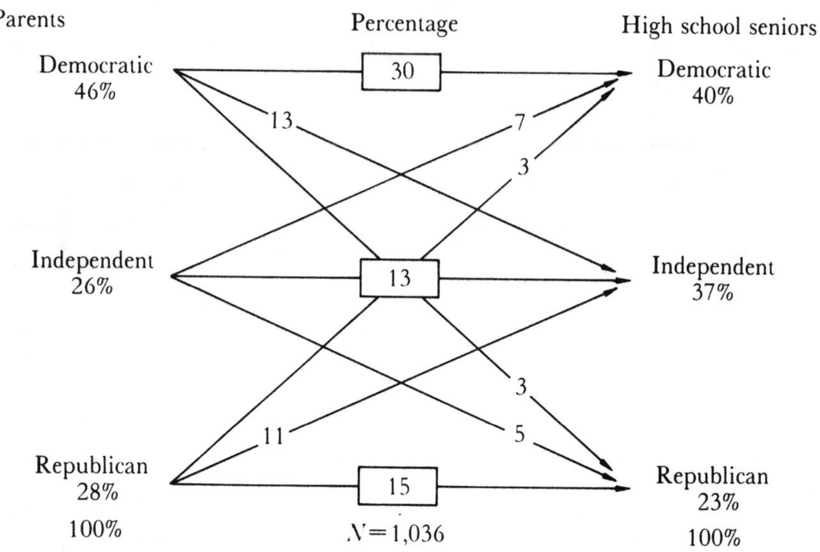

SOURCE: Adapted from Paul A. Beck, Jere W. Bruner, and L. Douglas Dobson, *Political Socialization* (Washington, D.C.: American Political Science Association, 1974), 22.

NOTE: On the left of the figure is the distribution of the parents' party identification and on the right is their children's. The numbers in the three boxes highlight the percentages of the children who had the same party identification as their parents. The numbers on the remaining arrows show various amounts of change from their parents' partisanship by the children. For example, 7 percent of the total number of children had independent parents but became Democrats.

political influence of their surroundings will be consistent with their family's political leanings, so the similarity between parents' and offspring's partisanship remains strong. On the other hand, people who remember their parents as having conflicting loyalties are more likely to be independents than either Democrats or Republicans. This is even more true of the children of parents without any partisan attachments. Thus, in each political generation a sizable number of voters lacks an inherited party loyalty.

The Jennings study also permits the examination of the process of generational change since it allows a comparison of party identification for parents and their children. As can be seen in Figure 4-7a, 58 percent of the seventeen-year-olds in 1965 had adopted the party identification of their parents. Of the high school seniors, 30 percent were Democratic

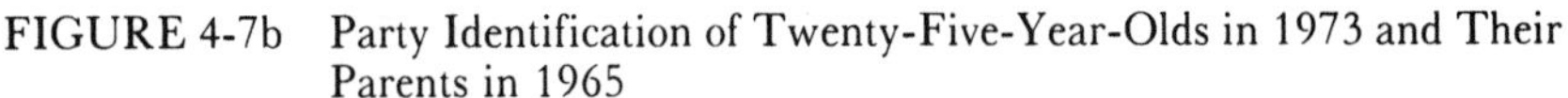

FIGURE 4-7b Party Identification of Twenty-Five-Year-Olds in 1973 and Their Parents in 1965

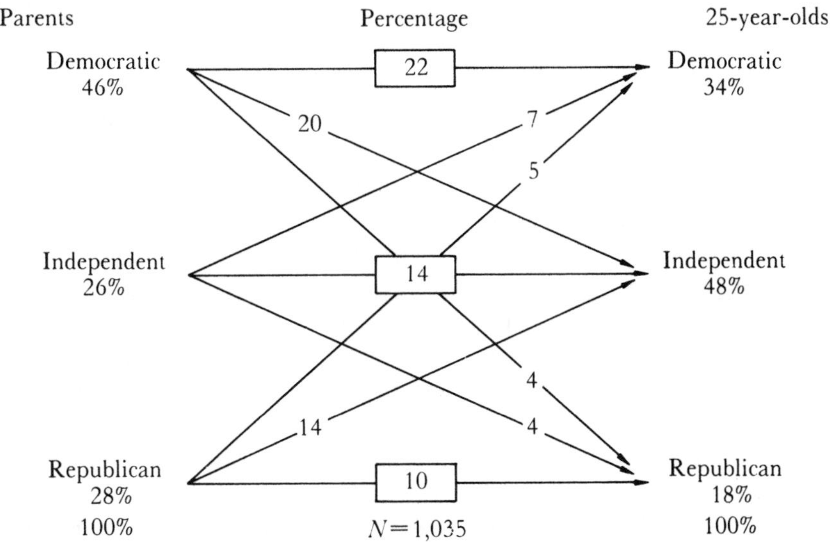

SOURCE: Adapted from Paul A. Beck, Jere W. Bruner, and L. Douglas Dobson, *Political Socialization* (Washington, D.C.: American Political Science Association, 1974).

and came from Democratic families. Another 10 percent of the seniors were Democratic but came from independent or Republican families. Although not explicitly shown in Figure 4-7a, Democrats had a somewhat higher transmission rate than either Republicans or independents. Despite this higher transmission rate, there were so many more Democratic parents that their children also contributed substantial numbers to the independent ranks.

As we saw before, the parents changed very little between 1965 and 1973, whereas the young people became markedly more independent. Thus, by 1973 less than half of the children shared their parents' party identification; only half of the children of Democratic parents were still Democrats, and only a little more than one-third of the Republican offspring were still Republicans (see Figure 4-7b). The increasing strength of the independents came from both parties. Between 1973 and 1982 (in data not shown here) there was no further erosion of the children's loyalty away from their parents' party. If anything, these young people drifted back to the party identification of their childhood.

These data from the Jennings study continue to show substantial transmission of parental political views, although not the high level of durability that earlier findings had suggested. It is reasonable to suppose that in more quiet times there would be greater continuity in the political views of parents and children.

This discussion of partisan change has relevance for understanding the process of electoral realignment. It suggests that changes in the party loyalty of the electorate observed during realignment are less the result of individuals changing from one party to another than of new voters, both young people and the previously uninvolved, who come into the electorate with a different distribution of party loyalties than did previous generations. Of particular interest, then, during the 1980s was the extent to which the youngest members of the electorate were abandoning independence and adopting a Republican partisanship in response to the policies and perceived successes of the Reagan administration.

During the 1980s the Republicans began to hold their own against the Democrats in attracting the youngest voters' loyalty. By 1992 the balance had shifted once again toward the Democrats, although more young people remain uncommitted independents than in previous years. More generally, the behavior of the youngest voters is of critical importance to the future strength of the political parties.

As we suggested in Chapter 3, there is ample evidence of dealignment in the electorate. The large number of independents and their shifting vote choices have guaranteed electoral volatility. The weak partisans also have contributed to this instability. As they grow older, however, independents come to identify with one party or the other. Thus, in the midst of dealignment, the political parties continue to attract a following. At the same time, this partisan following is much less loyal than it was decades ago after the New Deal realignment. The unanswered question for the American political parties is whether they can reclaim the level of loyalty from their supporters they once enjoyed. Obviously, the political parties have learned to survive without high levels of loyalty, but if we are approaching an American political system without party loyalty, we are on uncharted ground.

The political parties are as much victims of indifference as they are of hostility. Almost one-third of the electorate can think of nothing to say about the Democratic and Republican parties either positively or negatively. This indifference is even higher among independents. It is possible that if one or the other political party managed to perform well for a period of time, it would easily win over a large following.

Notes

1. Paul R. Abramson and John H. Aldrich, "The Decline of Electoral Participation in America," in *American Political Science Review* 76 (September 1982): 502-521.
2. Angus Campbell, "Surge and Decline: A Study of Electoral Change," in *Elections and the Political Order*, ed. Angus Campbell et al. (New York: John Wiley & Sons, 1966), 40-62.
3. Arthur H. Miller and Martin P. Wattenberg, "Measuring Party Identification: Independent or No Partisan Preference?" *American Journal of Political Science* 27 (February 1983): 106-121.
4. John Petrocik, "An Analysis of Intransitivities in the Index of Party Identification," *Political Methodology* 1 (Summer 1974): 31-47.
5. Norman H. Nie, Sidney Verba, and John R. Petrocik, *The Changing American Voter* (Cambridge, Mass.: Harvard University Press, 1976), chap. 5.
6. Robert S. Erikson and Kent L. Tedin, "The 1928-1936 Partisan Realignment: The Case for the Conversion Hypothesis," *American Political Science Review* 75 (December 1981): 951-962.
7. Philip E. Converse, *The Dynamics of Party Support: Cohort-Analyzing Party Identification* (Beverly Hills, Calif.: Sage Publications, 1976).
8. The main participants in this controversy are Philip Converse and Paul Abramson. See Converse, *The Dynamics of Party Support*; and Paul R. Abramson, "Developing Party Identification: A Further Examination of Life-Cycle, Generational, and Period Effects," *American Journal of Political Science* 23 (February 1979): 78-96.
9. The major findings of the first two waves of this study have been reported in M. Kent Jennings and Richard G. Niemi, *The Political Character of Adolescence: The Influence of Families and Schools* (Princeton, N.J.: Princeton University Press, 1974), and *Generations and Politics* (Princeton, N.J.: Princeton University Press, 1981); a report on partisanship using all three waves of interviews is contained in M. Kent Jennings and Gregory B. Markus, "Partisan Orientations over the Long Haul: Results from the Three-Wave Political Socialization Panel Study," *American Political Science Review* 78 (December 1984): 1000-1018.

Suggested Readings

Asher, Herbert B. *Presidential Elections and American Politics: Voters, Candidates, and Campaigns Since 1952*. Chicago: Dorsey Press, 1988. A comprehensive survey of the literature and findings on American electoral behavior.

Budge, Ian, Ivor Crewe, and Dennis Farlie. *Party Identification and Beyond.* New York: John Wiley & Sons, 1977. An excellent collection of articles on partisanship and other topics.

Jennings, M. Kent, and Gregory B. Markus. "Partisan Orientations over the Long Haul: Results from the Three-Wave Political Socialization Panel Study." *American Political Science Review* 78 (December 1984): 1000-1018. An analysis of partisan change and stability based on a fascinating study begun in 1965.

Keith, Bruce, David B. Magleby, Candice J. Nelson, Elizabeth Orr, Mark C. Westlye, and Raymond E. Wolfinger. *The Myth of the Independent Voter.* Berkeley, Calif.: University of California Press, 1992. An effort to reaffirm the importance of party identification in an era of increasing numbers of independents.

Nie, Norman, Sidney Verba, and John Petrocik. *The Changing American Voter.* Cambridge, Mass.: Harvard University Press, 1976. A major revisionist analysis of public opinion and voting behavior emphasizing the decline of partisanship.

Niemi, Richard G., and Herbert F. Weisberg. *Controversies in Voting Behavior.* Washington, D.C.: CQ Press, 1993. A collection of sophisticated articles on major topics in political behavior and public opinion.

Wattenberg, Martin P. *The Decline of American Political Parties: 1952-1988.* Cambridge, Mass.: Harvard University Press, 1990. A thorough analysis of the changing patterns of partisanship in recent decades.

chapter five

Social Characteristics of Partisans and Independents

TO THIS point the voting behavior and political partisanship of Americans have been discussed without examination of the forces behind these patterns. Attempts to explain American voting behavior have relied on social and economic factors to account for both stability and change in American politics. The major studies of the Survey Research Center and the Center for Political Studies have documented a wide range of relationships in the American electorate between social and economic characteristics and political behavior. Furthermore, many of the descriptions of voting patterns offered by American journalists and party strategists are based on social and economic factors. Analysis regularly attributes political trends to such things as a "farm revolt" or the "fixed-income groups"; frequently these explanations rely on so-called bloc voting, like "the black vote," "the Catholic vote," or "the union vote," implying that some social factor causes large numbers of people to vote the same way.

These explanations commonly focus on the association between social status and partisan choice. Typically, it is said that lower status people (working-class individuals, blue-collar workers), those with less education, those with low incomes, recently immigrated ethnic groups, racial minorities, and Catholics are more likely to vote Democratic. Conversely, higher status people (middle-class individuals, white-collar workers), the college educated, those with high incomes, whites of northern European stock, and Protestants are more likely to vote Republican. Although all these relationships exist and are important for understanding and interpreting American political behavior, one must be careful not to overstate the case, for any *single* social or economic characteristic is not likely to be a very good predictor of how an individual will behave politically. For example, even though those in white-collar occupations are more likely to be Republicans than are blue-collar workers, there are almost equal numbers of white-collar Democrats and white-collar Republicans.

The differences are similarly unimpressive for most other socioeconomic variables taken alone, mainly because the groups defined by each of these variables are, in the United States, quite heterogeneous with respect to other variables. For example, even though white-collar workers on the average are better off than blue-collar workers, both groups contain individuals of widely varying educational levels, religious affiliations, ethnic group membership, and even income levels. The same can be said about other social and economic variables. One exception is race. Because of the systematic discrimination against blacks in American culture, blacks form a much more homogeneous group socioeconomically, as well as a more politically self-conscious one, than most other groups in American society. It is not surprising, then, that their political behavior is also more homogeneous.

The ability to predict the political behavior of whites from their social and economic characteristics is increased if several variables are combined. In effect, more and more homogeneous groups are being created for analysis in this manner, and such groups are increasingly likely to behave in similar ways. The partisanship of selected socioeconomic groups in 1992 is displayed in Figure 5-1. Democratic identification tends to decline with increasing education among white Protestants and Catholics outside the South and among non-Hispanic whites in the South. A different pattern exists among white nonsoutherners without a religious affiliation: The better educated are distinctly more Democratic than the less well educated. Among blacks and Hispanics, groups that are too small to divide any further, the Democrats enjoy a marked advantage.

One factor that is often important in explaining political behavior and yet complicates simple social and economic interpretations is the nature of the community or the region in which the individual lives. Sometimes the culture and traditions of an area will reverse or reinforce the political tendencies of other social groupings to which the individual belongs; this may result in a pattern of behavior different from that of people with similar characteristics in other parts of the country. Unless the analyst controls for such contextual factors, finding common patterns in the group's behavior may be difficult.

In the past, the most obvious example of such a regional effect was the division between the South and the rest of the nation. Southern voters

FIGURE 5-1 Party Identification, by Region, Race/Ethnicity, Religion, and Education, 1992

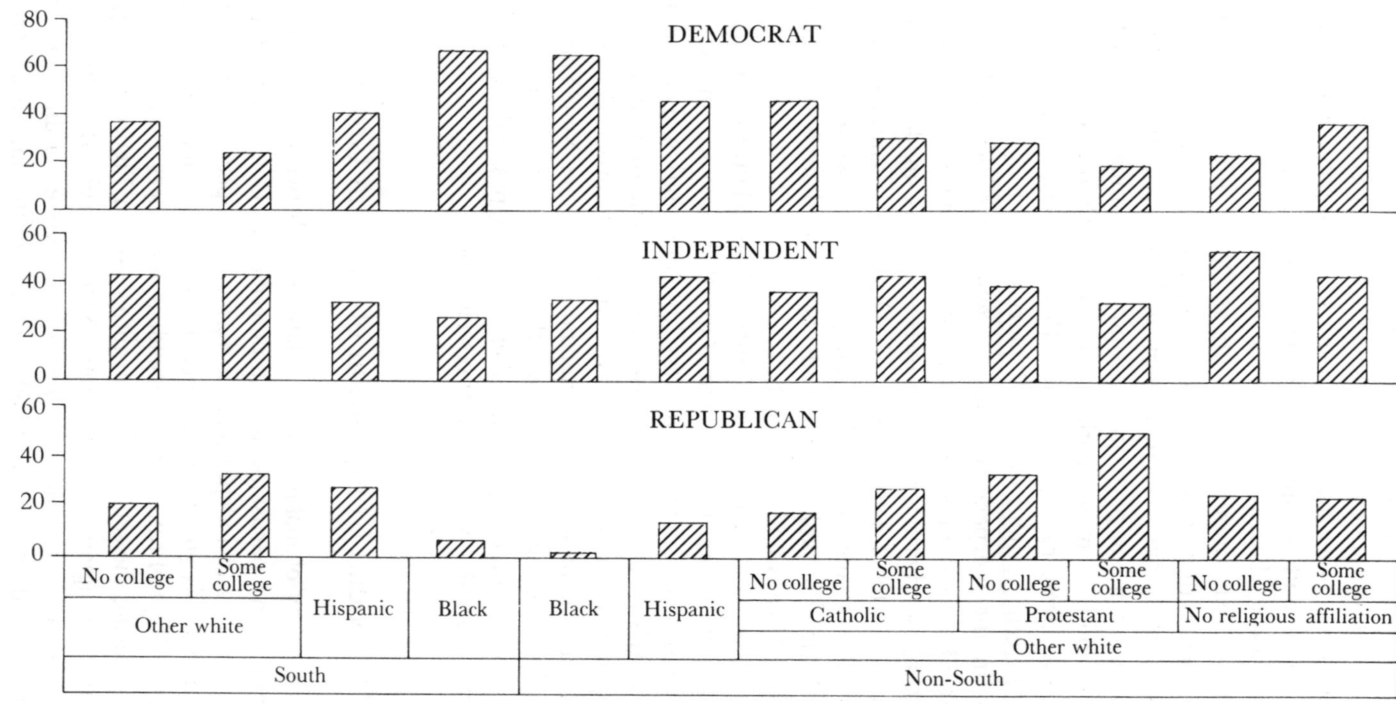

SOURCE: Center for Political Studies 1992 National Election Study. Data provided by the Inter-university Consortium for Political and Social Research.

became overwhelmingly Democratic after the Civil War, and for years this traditional attachment to the Democratic party virtually wiped out the impact of any other social or economic factor on political behavior. In the 1950s the southern middle class was about as Democratic as the southern working class, the highly educated about as Democratic as the less well educated, southern Protestants as Democratic as the relatively few Catholics in that region, and so on. This has changed dramatically in the last forty years. As can be seen in Figure 5-1, the relationship between education and partisanship is now very similar both inside and outside the South, as white southerners, particularly the better educated, have left the Democratic party. Since 1956 southern whites have gone from 63 percent Democratic to 32 percent. Most of the gains have appeared in the independent category, which has increased from 20 percent to 43 percent among southern whites. The proportion of Republicans among southern whites has increased more modestly, from 17 percent in 1956 to 26 percent in 1992. During this same period there was very little change in partisan support among whites outside the South, although the ranks of independents increased, drawing from both former Republicans and Democrats.

Controlling for region, as in Figure 5-1, is relatively simple. It is not such an easy matter to take community effects into account, however, since national surveys may contain very little information about community characteristics and very few cases from any one community. Nonetheless, community traditions may have substantial impact. For example, Italian-Americans in some New England and upstate New York cities traditionally have been Republican; their social group influence is strong, and yet it moves group members in the opposite direction from that taken by similar group influences elsewhere.

The Social Composition of Partisan Groups

Another way of looking at the relationship between socioeconomic characteristics and partisanship is to describe the Democratic and Republican parties and independents in terms of proportions of different kinds of individuals who make up their ranks. The social composition of Democratic, Republican, and independent identifiers is illustrated in Figure 5-2, using the same social categories used in Figure 5-1 (region, race/ethnicity, religion, and education). Note, however, that this way of looking at the data gives different results and answers a different set of questions. Instead of asking to what extent particular social groups support the Democratic or Republican parties, we can ask what proportion of all Democrats are black or Catholic. For example, looking at the partisanship of various social groups in Figure 5-1, we see that nonsouthern blacks are heavily Democratic (65 percent in 1992). If we calculate the proportion of all Democrats who are nonsouthern blacks, as in Figure 5-2, however, we find that nonsouthern blacks make up just 10 percent of the total group of Democrats. Because nonsouthern blacks make up a relatively small proportion of the population, their contribution to the total set of Democrats is also small, despite their lopsided preference for the Democratic party.

Studying the partisanship of various social groups has generally been regarded as the more interesting way of looking at the relationship between social characteristics and political behavior, largely because of the causal connection between partisanship and social characteristics. Thus, one is far more inclined to say that region, race and ethnicity, religion, or education "causes" an individual to select a particular political party than to say that political affiliation "causes" any of the others. Familiarity with the composition of the parties is useful, however, in understanding the campaign strategies and political appeals that the parties make to hold their supporters in line and sway the independents or opposition supporters to their side. For example, the fact that white southerners contribute about 20 percent of the total Democratic strength in the electorate and 25 percent of the Republican strength explains the serious competition between the parties for the vote of this group. Similarly, that blacks contribute 26 percent of the Democratic partisans but make up just 3 percent of the Republican partisans is a significant factor that both parties take into account.

The composition of the parties affects politics in another way. In a recent book on the evolution of the racial issue in the United States, Edward G. Carmines and James A. Stimson persuasively argue that the composition of the parties, particularly the party activists, influences the perceptions that less involved citizens hold about the philosophy and issue stands of the parties.[1] The fact that blacks are overwhelmingly Democratic while vocal racial conservatives are increasingly Republican allows the average voter to figure out which party is liberal and which is conservative on racial issues, even if race is never mentioned by candidates during the course of an election campaign.

As can be seen in Figure 5-2, the composition of the partisan identifiers is distinctively different; many groups make a sizable contribution to the Democratic following, yet relatively few social groups constitute a significant share of the Republican following. As a category,

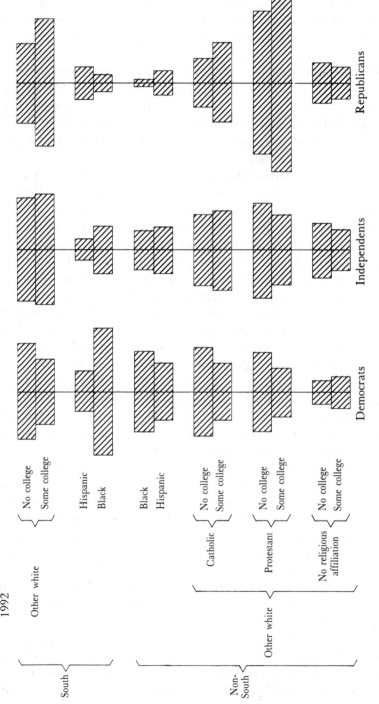

FIGURE 5-2 Social Composition of Democrats, Independents, and Republicans, by Region, Race/Ethnicity, Religion, and Education, 1992

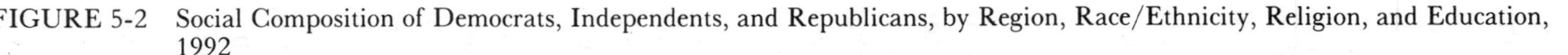

SOURCE: Center for Political Studies 1992 National Election Study. Data provided by the Inter-university Consortium for Political and Social Research.

Republicans are more homogeneous, consisting of relatively well-educated white Protestants from both the South and non-South.

Even though the Democrats are considerably more varied in social composition than the Republicans, the main conclusion to be drawn from an analysis of the partisan groupings is that they are basically heterogeneous. Both parties contain substantial proportions of differing religious groups and people with different educational levels; they both draw substantial portions of their votes from blue-collar as well as white-collar workers, from the young, the middle-aged, the old, and so on. Thus, with few exceptions, neither party can ignore any reasonably large social group. This, perhaps as much as any factor, forces the parties to take moderate and largely similar positions on most social issues.

Social Group Analysis

The impact of social groups on individual behavior is so commonly understood and accepted that it needs little elaboration, and the forms of group influence are too varied to discuss them all. Social analysis of political behavior has examined three main units: primary groups, secondary groups, and social classes. *Primary groups* are the face-to-face groups with which one associates, such as family, friends, and co-workers. *Secondary groups* are those organizations or collections of individuals with which one identifies, or is identified, that have some common interest or goal rather than personal contact as their major basis. *Social classes* are broad groupings based on position in society according to social status.

Primary Groups

Although investigations of the political behavior of primary groups are not numerous, all available evidence indicates that families and groups of friends are very likely to be politically homogeneous. Groups of co-workers appear somewhat more mixed politically. Presumably, the social forces in families and friendship groups are more intense and more likely to be based on, or to result in, political unanimity, but in most work situations people are thrown together without an opportunity to form groups based on common political values or any other shared traits. Friendship groups, even casual ones, may be formed so that individuals with much in common, including political views, naturally come together.

TABLE 5-1 Reported Partisan Preferences of Primary Groups by Respondent's Party Identification

	Respondent's party identification		
Primary group	Democrat	Independent	Republican
Reported party identification of spouse			
Democrat	75%	18%	14%
Independent	9	57	10
Republican	10	18	70
Don't know	6	8	6
Total	100%	101%	100%
(*N*)	(176)	(120)	(142)
Reported party identification of friends			
Democrat	66%	27%	19%
Independent	8	33	7
Republican	11	16	53
Don't know	15	23	19
Total	100%	99%	98%
(*N*)	(542)	(379)	(410)
Reported party identification of co-workers			
Democrat	65%	26%	23%
Independent	8	34	6
Republican	11	11	50
Don't know	16	29	20
Total	100%	100%	99%
(*N*)	(138)	(107)	(133)

SOURCE: General Social Survey, 1987. Data provided by the Inter-university Consortium for Political and Social Research.

NOTE: Respondents were asked to name three people with whom they discussed "important matters," after which their relationship with those mentioned was established. Reports only on those people with whom respondents talked about "political matters" on a regular basis.

Table 5-1 presents findings from a General Social Survey that illustrate the homogeneity of primary groups. Respondents were asked the political party of those people with whom they regularly discussed politics. The table shows that agreement on partisanship between spouses is highest, with 75 percent of the Democrats and 70 percent of the Republicans reporting that their spouses shared their party preference. Agreement was not quite so high with friends and co-workers but still reflects considerable likemindedness. Perhaps as important is the relatively low occurrence of mismatches of Democrats and Republicans in primary groups. The fact that significant percentages don't know the partisanship of friends and co-workers may reflect an avoidance of potential conflicts.

This discussion of primary groups has implications for the celebrated "gender gap" in the political preferences of men and women, a favorite topic of political commentators during the last decade. Women seemed to be less favorably inclined toward President Ronald Reagan, and toward Republicans in general, than were men. Table 5-2 presents the gender gap in partisanship in 1992. Although the gap exists, it is not large and would be reduced further if we introduced controls for race and socioeconomic variables. Given what we have said about the influence of primary groups, we should not be too surprised by the modest size of the gender gap. Men and women interact with each other in primary groups throughout society. They select friends and spouses from like-minded individuals; they respond, as family units, to similar social and economic forces. In the next chapter we will consider ways in which the views of men and women differ on certain issues, but given the general influence of primary groups, differences in overall political preferences are seldom large.

We have avoided use of the term *conformity* to describe this pattern of primary-group behavior because these group processes are more casual and more a matter of give-and-take than the term implies. Most people care very little about politics, and it plays a small part in their personal relations. In very few primary groups is politics of any consequence, so the things that happen in the group that lead to political homogeneity are of low salience. Individuals gradually create, evaluate, and revise their images of the world under the influence of social pressures. Many of these processes are face-to-face exchanges of information or reassurances that others share views or consider them plausible, realistic, and acceptable. Most individuals are not pressured by primary groups to conform or to change politically, at least not nearly as much as they are influenced by casual, impromptu expressions of similar ideas and values. Ordinarily, primary groups do not tolerate high levels of political tension and conflict. Also, very few people are subject to the social forces of only one or two primary groups, so conformity to group pressure would mean conformity to a large number of groups.

In addition to what happens within primary groups, another factor produces political similarity: the likelihood that primary-group members share the same social background and experiences outside the group. Members of any primary group are very apt to be socially, economically,

TABLE 5-2 Party Identification by Gender, 1992

	Men	Women
Strong Democrat	16%	20%
Weak Democrat	16	20
Independent	40	37
Weak Republican	15	14
Strong Republican	13	9
Total	100%	100%
(*N*)	(1,139)	(1,308)

SOURCE: Center for Political Studies 1992 National Election Study. Data provided by the Inter-university Consortium for Political and Social Research.

ethnically, and racially alike, and being alike in these ways means that the same general social influences are at work on them. Much happens outside the primary group to make it politically homogeneous.

Secondary Groups

Secondary groups form around some common interest and may or may not involve personal contact among members. This covers a range of groups in society, such as labor unions, religious or fraternal organizations, and professional groups. Secondary groups are presumably composed of overlapping primary groups whose pressures toward political homogeneity spill over, tending to make the members of secondary groups alike. In addition, members of secondary groups are likely to be subject to the same social forces outside the group. For example, members of a labor union are likely to be in the same income group, to live in the same type of neighborhood, and to have the same social and educational background, all of which would tend to make them alike politically.

A third factor at work is the role that a secondary group may play as a reference group. A group serves as a reference group for an individual who uses the group as a guide in forming opinions. For example, if union members, identifying with their labor union, perceive that a particular policy is good for the union, perhaps because the union leadership says that it is, and favor the policy because of this, the union is a political reference group for those individuals. In the same way, if a union member believes that other union members support a policy and supports the policy in part for this reason, then the union members serve as a reference group. Also, if a white-collar worker perceives that unions favor a policy, and he or she opposes it in part for that reason, then unions serve as a negative reference group.

The most sophisticated analysis of social groups and political behavior applied to national survey data appeared in *The American Voter* by Angus Campbell et al.[2] By controlling many outside social influences with matched groups, the authors demonstrated the degree to which an individual's political behavior is influenced by secondary-group membership among union members, blacks, Catholics, and Jews. They were able to show that union members, blacks, and Jews were considerably more Democratic than one would expect from the group members' other social characteristics, such as urban-rural residence, region, and occupational status. Even greater influence was present if the individual identified with the group. To establish the importance of identification with the group and belief in the legitimacy of the group's involvement in politics, the authors analyzed the presidential votes of union members, blacks, Catholics, and Jews. The increasing impact of identification with the group and of its perceived legitimacy was associated with an increasing Democratic vote. In other words, the stronger the belief in the legitimacy of the group's political involvement and the stronger the group identification, the greater the impact of group standards on vote choice.

Among the groups usually studied, blacks and Jews are the most distinctive politically. Jews have remained strongly Democratic in their partisanship over the years in spite of social and economic characteristics more typical of Republicans. And although Jews have at times not supported the Democratic ticket, Jewish partisanship in 1992 was almost identical to what it had been in the 1950s—66 percent Democratic, 30 percent independent, and 5 percent Republican. As we saw in Figure 5-1, blacks also are strongly Democratic in partisanship and typically vote 90 percent Democratic in presidential contests. The impact of group identification is most dramatically revealed by increased turnout and overwhelming support for black candidates, such as Jesse Jackson in the 1988 presidential primaries.

The behavior of union members in recent years, in contrast, illustrates a decline in group identification. Despite one-sided Democratic partisanship, union members have been quite volatile in voting for president. The election of 1984 represented a major failure of union leaders. They strongly committed themselves and their unions' resources to Walter Mondale but ultimately exercised little influence over the rank and file. Mondale only narrowly outpolled Reagan in union households.

In 1992 Bill Clinton was much more appealing to union members than either George Bush or Ross Perot, despite union leaders' general lack of enthusiasm.

The voting patterns of American religious groups usually are not particularly distinctive, or at least other factors are considered more important in determining vote choice. The 1960 presidential election provides a good example of how secondary groups become relevant in a particular election and temporarily have great influence on voting behavior. John F. Kennedy's Catholicism was a major issue throughout the campaign and of great importance to both Catholics and non-Catholics.

Researchers at the University of Michigan separated Protestant Democrats according to frequency of church attendance and compared each subgroup's defection from Kennedy by calculating the normal defection of the group as a whole.[3] Their findings are presented in Figure 5-3. Both inside and outside the South, Protestant Democrats who were more regular in church attendance were more likely to defect from the Democratic party. Among the nominal Protestants who never attended church, Kennedy's Catholicism exerted no such negative impact.

In recent years analysts have focused increased attention on religious groups in American society, especially within the highly varied Protestant category. In a probing analysis of religious groups spanning 1960 to 1992, David Leege has demonstrated the political distinctiveness of evangelical Protestants and Catholics in comparison with mainline Protestants.[4] Leege shows that for both evangelical Protestants and Catholics there are significant differences in political behavior associated with regularity of church attendance. Generally those who rarely attend church are quite similar to those unaffiliated with any religion. These differences are generally greatest on policy issues and political ideology rather than partisanship. We will return to their consideration in the next chapter. Here it is important to point out that it is this interaction with like-minded individuals, represented by church attendance, that likely creates and reinforces political distinctiveness.

Social factors, like religion or union membership, vary in their relative importance from election to election. After years of dormancy a social factor may temporarily become significant during a political campaign, like religion did in 1960, and subsequently recede in importance. This irregular rising and falling of issues, highlighting particular social groups at a given time, is a partial explanation for the political heterogeneity of American social groups. If the issues that dramatize a given social group become consistently salient, one would expect partisan

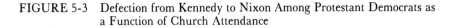

FIGURE 5-3 Defection from Kennedy to Nixon Among Protestant Democrats as a Function of Church Attendance

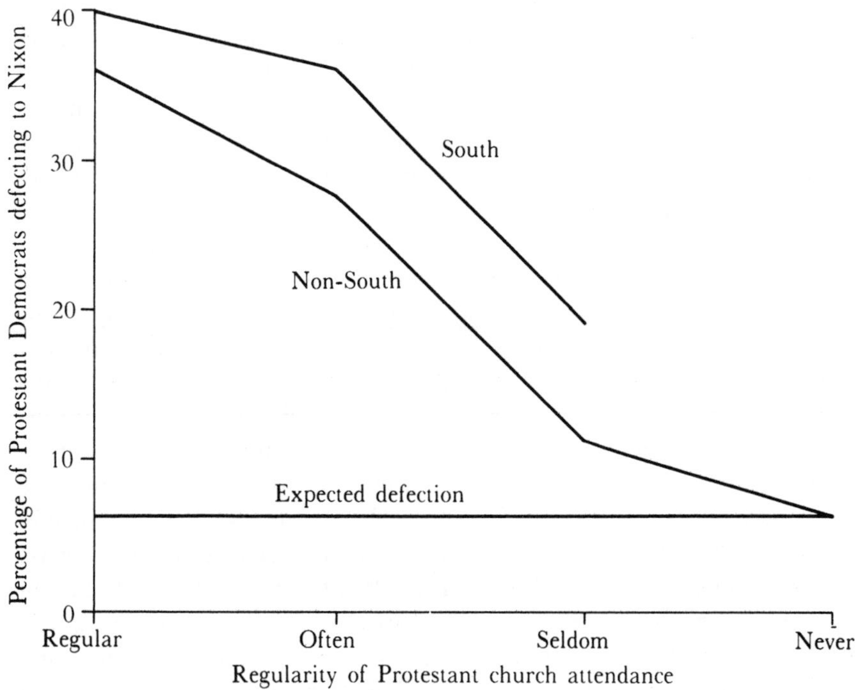

SOURCE: Angus Campbell, Philip E. Converse, Warren E. Miller, and Donald E. Stokes, eds., *Elections and the Political Order* (New York: John Wiley & Sons, 1966), 89, Figure 5.1.

NOTE: The number of Protestant Democrats who "never" attend church in the South is too small for inclusion.

realignment on the basis of membership or nonmembership in that group. But if the group is politically relevant for only one campaign or so, such major realignment does not occur. As specific issues are raised some partisan movement may occur, but on the whole the changing relevance of particular groups leads to political heterogeneity rather than to pure divisions.

Social Classes

The third major focus of analysis is social class. Some of the leading hypotheses of social and political theory link social classes and political behavior. Generally, analysis of social class assumes that differences exist in the economic and social interests of social classes, and that these conflicting interests will be translated into political forces. The critical variable in this view appears to be the importance of social class interests. In American society the importance of social class fluctuates but never becomes extremely high. The major political and sociological theories of social class have taken for granted the supreme importance of class interests, an assumption that seems unrealistic in American society. About one-third of all American adults say that they never think of themselves as members of a social class.

Given a choice between "middle class" and "working class," a majority of Americans are able to place themselves in a general social position, even to the point of including themselves in the "upper" or "lower" level of a class. Even though individual self-ratings are not perfectly congruent with the positions that social analysts would assign those individuals on the basis of characteristics like occupation, income, and education, a general social class structure is apparent. The political significance of social class varies from election to election in much the same way as that of secondary groups. In Figure 5-4 the relationship between self-identification as a member of the working or middle class and party identification is charted from 1952 through 1992 in the nation as a whole and in the South and non-South. The values on the graph line represent the strength of the relationship between social class and party, represented by Somer's d. If all working-class people identified with the Democratic party and all middle-class people were Republicans (with the independents split evenly between the two parties), the Somer's d would be + 1.0; if the reverse were true, it would be − 1.0. If there were no differences in the partisan preferences of middle- and working-class people, the coefficient would be 0.0. Because working-class people have been more likely to be Democratic than have middle-class people in each year since 1952, all the values in Figure 5-4 are positive.

A number of points can be made about the data presented. Although the strength of the relationship between social class and party has varied over the years, the national trend in the relationship is downward. In other words, since 1952 the differences in partisan preference between working- and middle-class people are getting smaller. In this context, 1976 and 1988 stand out as reversals of the trend. It is also clear from Figure 5-4 that the relationship between class and party has followed quite different patterns in and outside the South. Whereas the relationship has been declining outside the South, it has actually increased in the South. During the early 1950s middle- and working-class southerners were overwhelmingly Democratic; there were virtually no differences

FIGURE 5-4 The Relationship Between Social Class Identification and Party Identification, 1952-1992

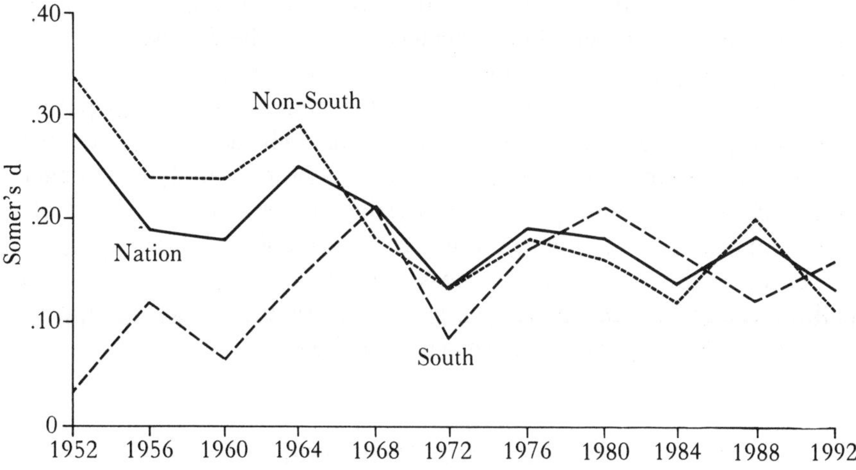

SOURCE: Survey Research Center, Center for Political Studies National Election Studies. Data provided by the Inter-university Consortium for Political and Social Research.

NOTE: The coefficients represented by points on the graph are Somer's d.

between them. Since that time a modest, class-based partisan alignment has emerged in the South. The middle class has become increasingly Republican, while the working class, particularly the black working class, remains quite solidly Democratic.

Another common expectation about the relationship between social class and partisanship has to do with upward and downward social mobility. To put it simply, the argument has been that upwardly mobile individuals abandon a Democratic identification and become Republicans, whereas the downwardly mobile abandon their Republican identification and become Democrats. Presumably the individual becomes an independent during the period of maximum social and political stress associated with this mobility. It has not been easy to assess mobility at a national level in the United States, so the surprisingly weak relationship usually found may result from inadequate measurement. In broad terms, most members of society are neither upwardly nor downwardly mobile, and the socially mobile seem no more apt to abandon their parents' party loyalty than the socially stable. There is, in fact, very little political difference between the upwardly and downwardly mobile, and this appears to hold for several measures of mobility.

Along with Canada, the United States is usually regarded as an extreme case among developed democracies for the insignificance of social class in political behavior; in most European democracies social class is of greater consequence.[5] Two factors may depress the apparent relationship between social class and voting behavior in the United States. Aggregating data for the entire population can hide stronger relationships in subgroups and in particular communities. Probably more important is the tendency of American political leaders not to emphasize highly divisive social class lines. Social class may serve as a political guide for some citizens on certain issues, but it does not appear to be extremely important in American politics.

Social Cross Pressures

One of the major ideas developed in the early voting studies by Paul Lazarsfeld, Bernard Berelson, and other researchers at the Bureau of Applied Social Research of Columbia University was the "cross-pressure hypothesis." [6] The cross-pressure hypothesis is simple in outline, but it can be confusing because it takes so many different forms. The hypothesis concerns the situation in which two (or more) forces or tendencies act on the individual, one in a Republican direction and the other in a Democratic direction. Sometimes this is stated as two factors predisposing a voter in a Republican or a Democratic direction. Usually the hypothesis is presented with two social dimensions, like occupation and religion, as in the diagram below.

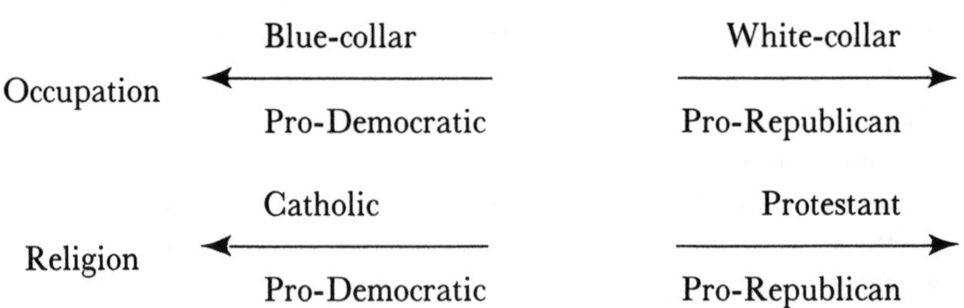

Some individuals are predisposed or pushed in a consistent way, such as white-collar Protestants, whose occupation and religion both predispose them in a Republican direction, or blue-collar Catholics predisposed in a Democratic direction.

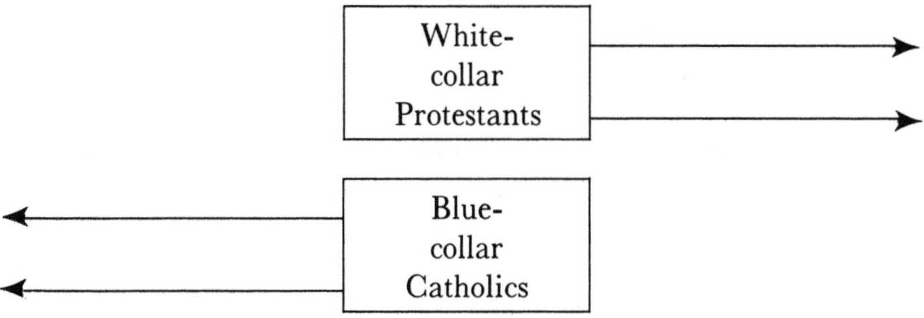

Some individuals are predisposed in both directions, or cross pressured.

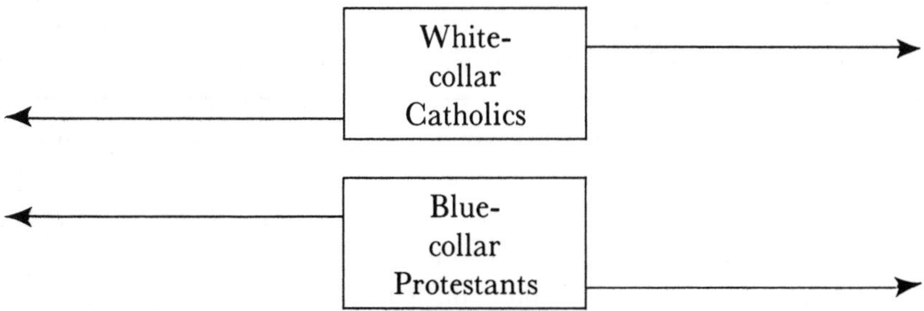

The cross-pressure hypothesis asserts that individuals under consistent pressure behave differently than individuals under cross pressure. The predictions under the hypothesis are:

Consistent Pressure	Cross Pressure
straight-ticket voting	split-ticket voting
early decision on vote	late decision on vote
high interest in politics	low interest in politics
high level of information	low level of information
consistent attitudes	conflicting attitudes

These expectations about voting behavior under cross pressure are actually specific applications of more general patterns investigated by sociologists and psychologists in a variety of ways. The responses to cross pressure predicted by the hypothesis are avoidance reactions—efforts to avoid or to minimize the anxiety produced by conflict.

The cross-pressure hypothesis also has some implications for empirical political theory. According to the cross-pressure hypothesis, many large social groups are expected to be stable politically; that is, they are consistently predisposed to be Republican or Democratic by the social forces working on them. Therefore, these social pressures lead to political stability among both Republicans and Democrats because they have politically consistent social backgrounds.

Between these politically consistent social groups there are cross-pressured groups predisposed toward both parties. According to the cross-pressure hypothesis, these groups are politically unstable, contributing the voters who switch from one party to another. This means that the available voters—the voters to whom the parties must appeal to win because they hold the balance of power in elections—are in a middle position between Democrats and Republicans. These arguments lead to a reassuring view of the American electorate. There is widespread political stability based on a relatively stable social system. Political flexibility and sensitivity are provided by groups between the partisans who are therefore politically moderate. As long as the stable partisan groups are roughly of the same size, stable competitive conditions are guaranteed. As long as social groups overlap somewhat, the necessary cross pressures will exist to produce the switching political moderates. It appears to be an electoral system that guarantees both competition and stability.

Nevertheless, there are some difficulties with this picture of the electoral system. For one thing, the social cross-pressure hypothesis is merely a tendency and not a perfect description of the impact of social forces on political behavior. The politically stable are more heterogeneous than the above account implies, and the politically flexible are not under dramatic social cross pressure, according to the best data available.

Discussion supporting the cross-pressure hypothesis is most extensive in the Elmira study, *Voting*, by Bernard Berelson, Paul Lazarsfeld, and William McPhee, which surveyed residents of Elmira, New York, from June through November 1948. They found that cross pressures affect the time when an individual decides how to vote. There was a slight tendency for cross pressures caused by religion and socioeconomic status to be associated with late decisions on voting. There were stronger relationships associated with conflicts in primary groups.

It is possible to conceptualize social cross pressure as leading to cross pressure on political attitudes, which in turn leads to the predicted patterns of behavior. Actually, attitudinal cross pressure is the only form of cross pressure that is strongly confirmed by national survey data. When attitudes toward the candidates and parties were measured by the Survey Research Center in 1952 and 1956, conflicting attitudes—those of an individual holding pro-Democratic and pro-Republican opinions—were associated with nonvoting, indecision, and indifference toward the election. These findings linking conflicting political attitudes with patterns of behavior have not always been confirmed in subsequent election studies, depending on exactly which attitudes are examined. Nevertheless, it remains reasonable to expect conflicting political attitudes to be associated with indecisiveness in voting behavior.

The American electoral system appears to operate in a way predicted by the cross-pressure hypothesis. There is partisan stability among both Republicans and Democrats, and the shifting of political fortunes is accomplished without intensity or extreme political appeals. One should, however, be skeptical of explaining these political patterns as a result of the social forces postulated by the cross-pressure hypothesis. Neither short-run partisan stability nor independent flexibility appears strongly associated with social-group predispositions.

Two conclusions can be drawn about social characteristics and voting behavior. On the one hand, social factors, such as race, religion, and occupation, as well as primary groups, have been shown to be related to partisanship. The long-term social and political patterns in the American electorate appear related. On the other hand, the short-term impact of social groups on voting behavior appears uneven and generally insignificant. Occasionally, social factors appear important nationally, as religion did in 1960, and under certain conditions social cross pressure may operate. However, social factors are not expected to show the same consistent, strong relationship with vote choice that was found in the case of partisanship.

Notes

1. Edward G. Carmines and James A. Stimson, *Issue Evolution: Race and the Transformation of American Politics* (Princeton, N.J.: Princeton University Press, 1989).
2. Angus Campbell, Philip E. Converse, Warren E. Miller, and Donald E. Stokes, *The American Voter* (New York: John Wiley & Sons, 1960), 295-332.
3. Philip E. Converse, Angus Campbell, Warren E. Miller, and Donald E. Stokes, "Stability and Change in 1960: A Reinstating Election," in *Elections and the Political Order*, ed. Angus Campbell, Philip E. Converse, Warren E. Miller, and Donald E. Stokes (New York: John Wiley & Sons, 1966), chap. 5.
4. David C. Leege, "The Decomposition of the Religious Vote: A Comparison of White, Non-Hispanic Catholics with Other Ethnoreligious Groups, 1960-1992" (Paper presented at the annual meeting of the American Political Science Association, Washington, D.C., 1993).
5. There are several important works on social class and political behavior. See Campbell et al., *The American Voter*, chap. 13. Students interested in this area of analysis should also see Robert Alford, *Party and Society* (Chicago: Rand McNally, 1963); and Richard Rose, ed., *Electoral Behavior* (New York: Free

Press, 1974). Perhaps the most significant work is David Butler and Donald E. Stokes, *Political Change in Britain: Forces Shaping Electoral Choice* (New York: St. Martin's Press, 1969).

6. Paul Lazarsfeld, Bernard Berelson, and Hazel Gaudet, *The People's Choice* (New York: Columbia University Press, 1944); and Bernard Berelson, Paul Lazarsfeld, and William McPhee, *Voting* (Chicago: University of Chicago Press, 1954).

Suggested Readings

Campbell, Angus, Philip E. Converse, Warren E. Miller, and Donald E. Stokes. *The American Voter*. New York: John Wiley & Sons, 1960. A classic study of the social psychological factors influencing political behavior.

Lazarsfeld, Paul, Bernard Berelson, and Hazel Gaudet. *The People's Choice*. New York: Columbia University Press, 1944. A classic study of Erie County, Ohio; the first making extensive use of survey research.

Leege, David C., and Lyman A. Kellstedt. *Rediscovering the Religious Factor in American Politics*. New York: M. E. Sharpe, 1993. A collection of articles exploring the impact of religious beliefs on political behavior.

Lipset, Seymour M., and Stein Rokkan. "Cleavage Structures, Party Systems and Voter Alignments: An Introduction." In *Party Systems and Voter Alignments*, ed. Seymour M. Lipset and Stein Rokkan. New York: Free Press, 1967. An important conceptual statement about the role of party and social cleavages in historical perspective.

Petrocik, John. *Party Coalitions: Realignments and Decline of the New Deal Party System*. Chicago: University of Chicago Press, 1981. An analysis of American politics that emphasizes social and economic characteristics.

c h a p t e r   s i x

Public Opinion and Ideology

PUBLIC OPINION—the collective attitudes of the public, or segments of the public, toward the issues of the day—is a significant aspect of American political behavior. Public opinion polls are an ever-present aspect of American journalism. We are constantly informed about what samples of Americans think on all manner of topics. The questions then arise: Are Americans informed, issue-oriented participants in the political process? Do they view problems and issues within a coherent ideological framework? What issues divide Democrats and Republicans? These questions address the nature and quality of American public opinion.

A *political ideology* is a set of fundamental beliefs or principles about politics and government: what the scope of government should be; how decisions should be made; what values should be pursued. In the United States the most prominent current ideological patterns are those captured by the terms *liberalism* and *conservatism*. Although these words are used in a variety of ways, generally liberalism endorses the idea of social change and advocates the involvement of government in effecting such change, whereas conservatism seeks to defend the status quo and prescribes a more limited role for governmental activity. Another common conception of the terms portrays liberalism as advocating equality and individual freedom and conservatism as endorsing a more structured, ordered society; however, these dimensions are not always joined in the political thinking of Americans. Also, some evidence indicates that since the election campaign of 1964 the terms have become increasingly associated with attitudes on racial integration. To complicate the matter further, public opinion data suggest that a segment of the American electorate uses these terms to signify a set of social attitudes or life style rather than any particular political beliefs.

Despite these ambiguities, most commentators on the American political scene, as well as its active participants, describe much of what happens in terms of liberalism or conservatism. Political history (and current news analysis) portrays situations in terms such as a "trend toward conservatism," "middle-of-the-road policies," and "rejection of liberalism." Furthermore, most political commentary regards the Democratic party as the liberal party and the Republican party as the conservative one, even though there is considerable ideological variation in both. Within each party, leaders and platforms are alleged to be relatively liberal or conservative. In the election of 1988 George Bush successfully pinned "the L word" on Democratic candidate Michael Dukakis. To prevent the same thing from happening in 1992, Bill Clinton proclaimed himself a new kind of Democrat, whose politics represented the center of the ideological spectrum.

Consideration of the ideological positions of the parties is complicated by the many dimensions of public policy: economic affairs; race relations; international affairs; and a variety of moral, social, and cultural concerns. These issue areas have many facets, and only a few themes dominate public attention at any one time. Not only does public attention to particular issues rise and fall, but the pattern of interrelationships among different sets of issues also changes over time.

Analysts of American political history draw special attention to those rare periods when a single issue dimension dominates the public's views of governmental policy. Periods such as the Civil War or the New Deal revealed deep divisions in the public, paralleled by a distinctiveness in the issue stands of the political parties. Electoral realignments of voters are forged by these unusually strong issue alignments, and during such times we would expect a close correspondence between attitudes on the relevant issues and partisanship.

At other times, highly salient issues may capture the attention of the public, but they are likely to cut across, rather than reinforce, other issue positions and party loyalties. If the parties do not take clearly differentiated stands on such issues and if party supporters are divided in their feelings toward the issues, party loyalty and the existing partisan alignment are undermined. In a complex political system like that of the United States, new, dissimilar issue divisions accumulate until a crisis causes one dimension to dominate and obscure other issues.

The most consistent and the most distinctive ideological difference between the parties emerged during the New Deal realignment. It focused on domestic economic issues, specifically on the question of what role the government should take in regulating the economy and providing social welfare benefits. These issues still underlie the division between the parties. Since the 1930s, the Democratic party has advocated more government activity, while the Republicans have preferred less. One of the reasons offered for the parties' general lack of ideological distinctiveness is the emergence of other issues that tend to cut across this economic dimension and do not divide the parties so clearly. One such area is race, though some argue that the parties have become increasingly polarized on this issue since 1964.[1] Another disruptive set of issues is what might be called "traditional values": the complex of issues involving abortion, sex education, gay rights, the role of women, and pornography.

In this chapter we will consider public opinion on several important issues and explore the relationship of social characteristics and partisanship to these opinions. We will look at the extent to which Americans have a political ideology representing a coherent set of fundamental beliefs or principles about politics that serves as a guide to current political issues, much as partisanship does. Finally, we will briefly consider the impact of public opinion on political leaders.

The Measurement of Public Opinion

The commercial opinion-polling organizations have spent fifty years asking Americans about their views on matters of public policy. Most of this investigation has taken one of two forms: (1) asking individuals whether they "approve or disapprove of" or "agree or disagree with" a statement of policy, or (2) asking individuals to pick their preference among two or more alternative statements of policy. This form of questioning seriously exaggerates the number of people who hold views on political issues. People can easily say "agree" or "disapprove" in response to a question, even if they know nothing at all about the topic. If given the opportunity, many people will volunteer the information that they hold no views on specific items of public policy. In 1964, for example, more than one-third of the American electorate had no opinion on U.S. involvement in Vietnam. In contrast, on the issue of abortion in the 1980s and early 1990s, fewer than 5 percent of all adults were without an opinion. More typically, in recent years approximately 10 percent of the electorate has had no opinion on major issues of public policy. Another 10 to 20 percent are unaware of what the government is doing in a policy area or where the parties and candidates stand on an issue. Philip Converse has shown that, in addition to these two categories of relatively uninformed individuals, a number of those individuals who appear to have an opinion may be regarded as responding to policy questions at random.[2]

There are several ways to explain this lack of opinion and information on topics of public policy. Generally, the same factors that explain nonvoting also account for the absence of opinions. Individuals with little interest in or concern with politics are least likely to have opinions on matters of public policy. Beyond this basic relationship, low socioeconomic status is associated with no opinion on issues; low income and little education create social circumstances in which individuals are less likely to have views and information on public policies.

Some issues of public policy, such as abortion or the death penalty, are relatively easy to understand; other issues may be much more difficult, requiring individuals to face complex considerations. Edward G. Carmines and James A. Stimson have argued that the public responds differently to "hard" issues that involve calculation of policy benefits and "easy" issues that call for symbolic, "gut responses."[3]

It is no simple matter to describe the distribution of opinions in the American electorate because no obvious, widely accepted method has been established to measure these opinions. Asking different questions in public opinion polls will elicit different answers. Even on the issue of abortion, on which most people have views, the distribution of opinions can be substantially altered by asking respondents whether they approve of "killing unborn children" as opposed to "letting women have control over their own bodies." Furthermore, there is no direct means to validate measures of opinions as there is with reports of voting behavior. Consequently, descriptions of public opinion must be taken as more uncertain, more tentative than conclusions drawn from the discussion of partisanship because independent indicators of opinions on public issues are rare.

Domestic Economic Issues

Ronald Reagan's landslide victory in 1980 and his administration's subsequent efforts at dismantling the social programs enacted by administrations of both parties in previous decades have been portrayed as a reversal of fifty years of economic liberalism. In policy terms this may well be the case. It is not true, however, that such a policy shift reflects any change in the American public's persistent willingness to support federal governmental programs intended to solve social problems. In economic matters Americans are more liberal than conservative. Increased government activity in domestic economic affairs or in welfare programs elicits no widespread, consistent public opposition. Over the years the main source of public opposition to federal government activities appears to be based on racial prejudice and not on economic considerations. To be sure, some individuals in the electorate oppose government economic activities for other reasons, but the ideological opponents of government activity are not numerous in the general public. In this respect, as in many others, the substantial number of political leaders who oppose "liberal" domestic economic programs is not a reflection of public opinion.

The distribution of attitudes toward spending for different governmental purposes is shown in Figure 6-1. These data were collected by the General Social Survey from 1973 to 1991. There is considerable variation in the belief that too much is being spent on welfare, with low points in the mid-1970s and since the mid-1980s. Attitudes favorable toward spending to protect the environment show a fairly dramatic increase in the latter half of the 1980s. The form of these questions—whether too much or too little is being spent on a problem—elicits answers that reflect both the attitude of the respondents and the current state of public policy. Thus, a period of cutbacks in public spending, such as the 1980s, would be expected to produce more responses of "too little" even if public attitudes about the ideal level of such spending had not changed.

When an examination is made of the relationship between social characteristics and issue stands on traditional economic issues (such as the choice between cutting or increasing spending on government services), one can expect to find dramatic differences among social groups. The pattern in Figure 6-2 is not too difficult to describe: The least economically secure, blacks and poorly educated southern whites, support government services most strongly. One group does not fit this interpretation: College-educated whites who have no religious affiliation are more supportive of spending for government services than any other white group in the nation.

Men and women do not respond to domestic economic issues in quite the same way. Generally the distribution of men's attitudes runs in a conservative direction and women's attitudes in a liberal direction. In the 1992 National Election Study, 38 percent of the men supported decreasing government services to reduce spending, while only 25 percent of the women agreed with that position. Controls for socioeconomic circumstances do not significantly alter these results, so we can conclude that men and women from the same social backgrounds have somewhat

FIGURE 6-1 Attitudes Toward Domestic Policies, 1973-1991

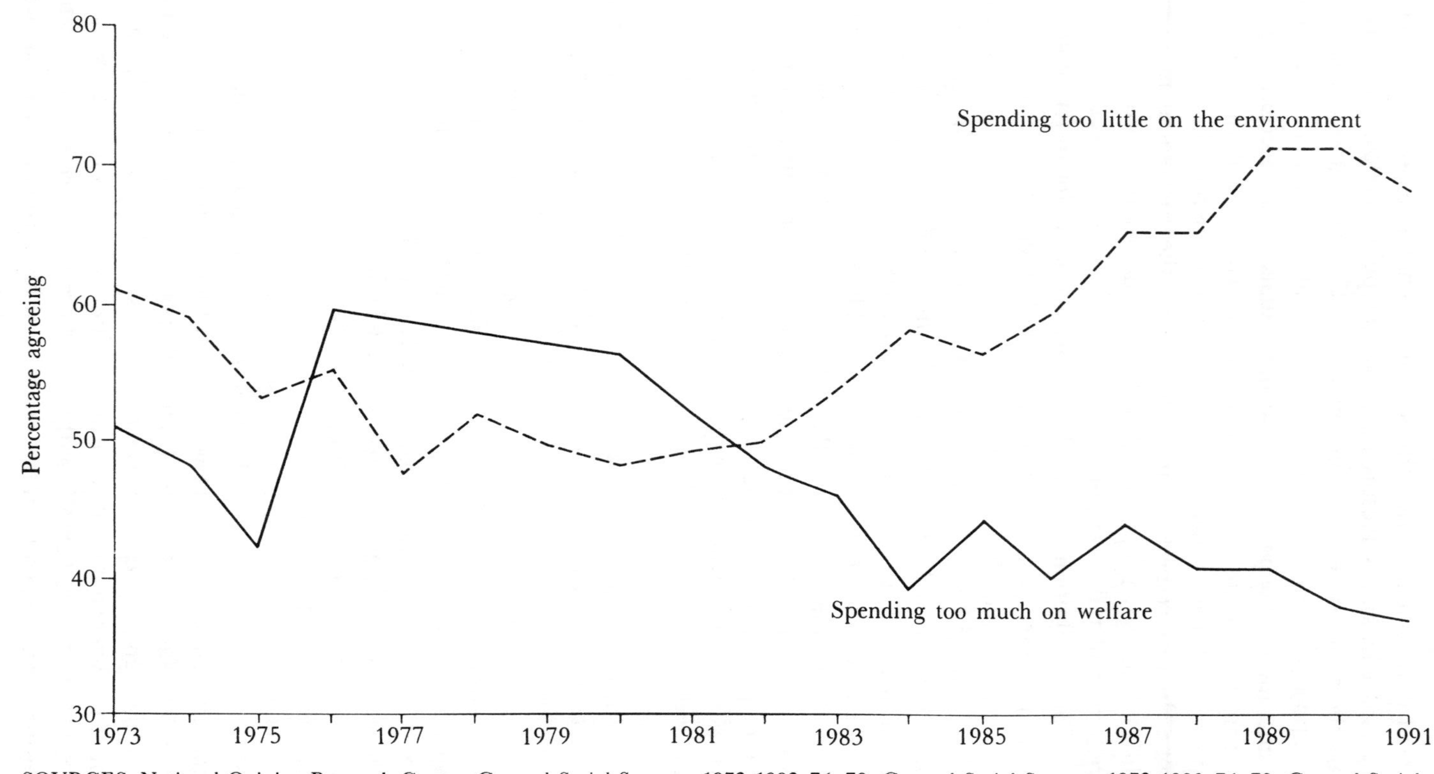

SOURCES: National Opinion Research Center, *General Social Surveys, 1972-1982*, 76, 79; *General Social Surveys, 1972-1983*, 76, 79; *General Social Surveys, 1972-1987*, 96, 98; *General Social Surveys, 1972-1991*, 105, 107.

FIGURE 6-2 Attitudes Toward Cutting Spending Versus Increasing Government Services, by Region, Race/Ethnicity, Religion, and Education, 1992

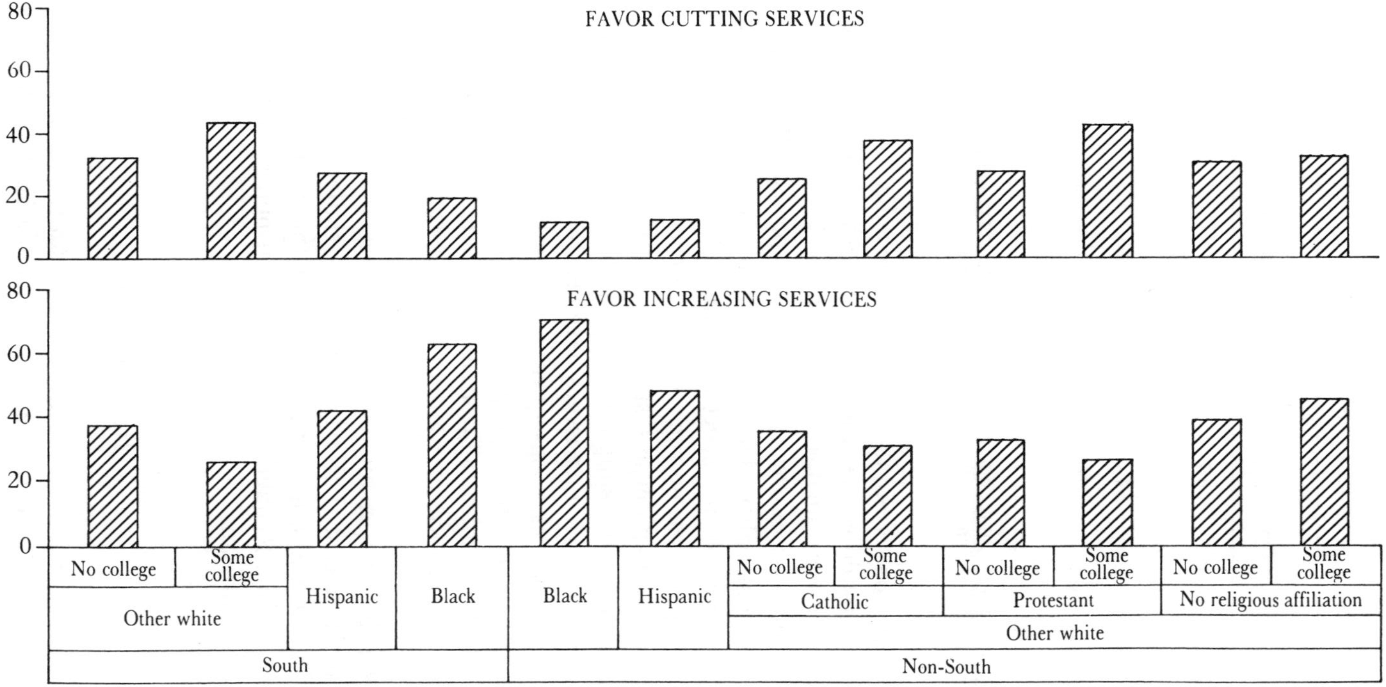

SOURCE: Center for Political Studies 1992 National Election Study. Data provided by the Inter-university Consortium for Political and Social Research.

TABLE 6-1 Attitudes Toward Cutting Spending Versus Increasing Government Services, by Partisanship, 1992

	Strong Democrats	Weak Democrats	Independents	Weak Republicans	Strong Republicans
Favors cutting spending	14%	19%	30%	49%	59%
Neutral	32	36	34	30	20
Favors increasing government services	54	45	37	21	21
Total	100%	100%	101%	100%	100%
(*N*)	(365)	(336)	(765)	(290)	(245)

SOURCE: Center for Political Studies 1992 National Election Study. Data provided by the Inter-university Consortium for Political and Social Research.

different views on certain domestic economic policies. However, this 12 percentage point difference was the maximum we found. On most issues the differences were small or nonexistent.

Favoring services over spending cuts represents the type of choice in governmental policy that characterized the New Deal. Thus, it would be reasonable to expect a dramatic difference between Democrats and Republicans on such an issue. Economic issues have divided Democrats and Republicans since the 1930s. During the last sixty years, partisans have supported or opposed economic policies quite consistently, whereas other issues have been of only temporary significance for the parties. Consequently, the relationship in Table 6-1 showing that Democrats disproportionately favor increased government services while Republicans favor cuts, is no surprise. Strong Democrats favor increased services over a reduction in spending by a margin of 54 percent to 14 percent; strong Republicans are just the opposite, favoring a reduction in spending over increased services by a margin of 59 percent to 21 percent. This basic pattern of relationship has existed for decades, but it is also important to observe that noticeable proportions of Democrats and Republicans hold opinions opposed by a majority of their fellow partisans.

Racial Issues

The most persistently volatile issues in American history have dealt with problems surrounding the treatment of blacks. After many years of little public attention to this problem, integration became a major focus of national and international attention in the 1950s. Two significant developments in the distribution of attitudes have been associated with this issue. First, during the past forty years southern blacks have become increasingly concerned with public policies affecting them and have changed from a largely apathetic, uninterested group to a concerned, involved, politically motivated group. Second, large numbers of southern whites have adjusted their opinions to accept the realities of the new legal and political position of blacks. White southerners still do not prefer integrated schools, but many have been willing to accept them. Support for school integration is high among blacks throughout the nation; at the same time, a majority of whites opposes federal government efforts to integrate the schools. Attitudes toward school integration are rather complex outside the South; whites living outside the South are more supportive of integration than are white southerners, but they are overwhelmingly opposed to busing. When a national sample of high school seniors from 1965 was reinterviewed in 1973, a sharp erosion in support for school integration was found among young, nonsouthern whites.[4] During the same period, southern whites changed relatively little; to a degree they became more supportive of integration. By 1982 when these respondents were interviewed again, nonsouthern white support for integration had eroded to the point that there was no difference between the South and non-South.

The general public is even more opposed to affirmative action efforts on behalf of blacks. Over two-thirds of all whites are strongly opposed to affirmative action. Well over one-third of all blacks are also opposed to such initiatives, and in the South close to half of the blacks oppose affirmative action.

In their book, *Issue Evolution*, Carmines and Stimson argue that an evolution of the racial issue since the early 1960s has led increasingly to the Democratic party being perceived as the liberal party on civil rights issues and the Republican party being perceived as the conservative party.[5] They see this distinction as the dominant perception of the parties in the eyes of the public. If this is so, it represents a fundamental redefinition of the issue alignment that has characterized the parties since the New Deal.

Prior to the 1960s, the Republican party was seen as more progressive, if anything, on civil rights than the Democrats, particularly in light of the strongly segregationist cast to the southern wing of the Democratic party. Carmines and Stimson show that a change occurred during the 1960s and 1970s, when the elites of the two parties—members of Congress, presidential candidates—as well as party activists became quite distinctive in their racial views. The Democratic party became dominated by northern liberals advocating stronger governmental action to ensure equal rights. At the same time the leadership of the Republican party became "racially conservative," that is, opposed to government intervention to ensure equal rights for minorities. As the elites and activists sorted themselves into distinct groups on the basis of their attitudes toward racial issues, the perceptions that the mass public held of the parties followed suit. Increasingly through the late 1960s and 1970s, Carmines and Stimson argue, the partisan choices of individual citizens fell in line with their attitudes on racial questions.

The role of race and racial issues in American politics is not always easy to trace, however. Because certain issues that are not explicitly stated in terms of race are nevertheless symbols of race in the minds of some people, candidates can make appeals based on racist attitudes without using racial language. For example, "law and order" may mean "keeping blacks in their place" to some, "welfare" may carry racial overtones, and so on.

On the whole, straightforward efforts to capture distinctive party images along racial lines do not succeed. Although more than half of the public in 1988 believed there were differences in what the parties stand for, only a small percentage characterized the differences in racial terms. Overwhelmingly, when people articulate differences between the parties it is in terms of symbols and issues associated with the New Deal realignment.

Social Issues

When presidential candidate Pat Buchanan issued a call for a "cultural war" at the Republican national convention in 1992, he reflected an emphasis on so-called traditional values that increasingly divide the two political parties. Issues such as abortion, pornography, gay rights, sex education, and prayer in the public schools have become prominent in recent years. While common wisdom positions Democrats on the liberal side and Republicans on the conservative side of these issues, significant numbers of political activists and leaders in both parties are not so easily placed. Indeed, E. J. Dionne has argued that a major reason why Americans are disenchanted with politics is that the parties insist on defining liberal and conservative in terms of the New Deal policy dimension, while the public is more interested in the traditional value dimension.[6] Although Buchanan's fiery convention speech is widely regarded as having hurt the image of the Republican party as it headed into the final stretch of the 1992 presidential campaign, there is no question that he appealed to a large, new constituency within the Republican party. At the same time, some longtime Republicans who are economic conservatives but support civil liberties and the right to privacy are wondering whether the Republican party is beginning to leave them out in the cold.

Certainly one of the most potent of these social issues is abortion. The 1973 Supreme Court decision in *Roe v. Wade* immediately generated a polarized response, turning election races in some areas into one-issue campaigns. Sixteen years later, *Webster v. Reproductive Health Services* had a similar effect when the Court appeared to invite state restrictions on the availability of abortion.

One of the difficulties in examining public opinion on the issue of abortion lies in the responses that different question wording elicits. Although responses to the same question are quite similar over time, different phrasing of questions will produce differing proportions of "pro-choice" or "pro-life" answers. In the following analysis, we use data from the National Election Studies (NES), which has used the same question in each biennial survey since the issue erupted.

The public's views on abortion are associated with several personal characteristics, most notably age, education, and religion. No matter what combination of characteristics is examined in the general public, invariably more than half of the people in the NES surveys support the right to abortion under at least some circumstances.* In simple terms, young people generally favor the right to abortion, the elderly are much more likely to oppose it, and the less well educated are less supportive of legal abortion than are the better educated. Given the frequent labeling of abortion as a "women's issue," it is worth noting that there is no difference in the views of women and men.

Perhaps surprisingly, given the Roman Catholic church's clear position in opposition to abortion, Catholics are no more inclined than

---

* These figures undoubtedly underestimate the proportion taking the pro-life position. The two response choices at the pro-life end of the continuum were: abortion should never be permitted, and abortion should be permitted only to save the life or health of the mother. The first is a more extreme position than many pro-life advocates would take; on the other hand, the second includes circumstances (health reasons) that have been explicitly rejected by pro-life advocates in and out of Congress. Thus, neither category is an entirely satisfactory indicator of pro-life sentiment. The most extreme pro-choice alternative offered is: By law, a woman should always be able to obtain an abortion as a matter of personal choice. We have used the most extreme category at either end of the continuum to indicate pro-life and pro-choice positions.

Protestants to oppose abortion. The real impact of religious differences is seen when the frequency of church attendance is taken into account. The net pro-choice minus pro-life percentages, taking into account age, religious preference, and frequency of church attendance, are shown in Figure 6-3. For each group, the percentage taking the most extreme pro-life position was subtracted from the percentage taking the most extreme pro-choice position. Thus, a positive number in Figure 6-3 indicates a preponderance of pro-choice supporters in a group; a negative number indicates a preponderance of pro-life supporters. Among both Catholics and Protestants, frequent churchgoers are less likely to support abortion than those who rarely or never attend. Furthermore, at most levels of church attendance, the young are more supportive of abortion rights than the old. The difference connected with age is rather slight among Protestants but quite dramatic among Catholics. In fact, young Catholics are just as pro-choice on the abortion issue as young Protestants.

The data in Figure 6-3 mask the different attitudes on abortion among Protestant groups. Table 6-2 divides mainline Protestants from evangelicals and compares them with Catholics and those with no religious affiliation, again controlling for frequency of church attendance. The evangelical Protestants who regularly attend church are even more pro-life than the Catholics who regularly attend. However, the mainline Protestants who regularly attend church are strongly pro-choice and roughly similar in this regard to the infrequent attenders of all faiths and those with no religious affiliation. Since most mainline Protestant churches take a position of individual moral responsibility on the question of abortion, the pro-choice stance of most of their adherents is not surprising.

Foreign Affairs

During the Cold War years, foreign policy, and the study of public opinion about foreign policy, focused on relations between the United States and the Soviet Union. Questions centered on the relative strength of the two countries, the likelihood of nuclear conflict between them, and the preference for negotiation or military strength as a strategy for keeping the peace. With the breakup of the Soviet Union, the focus of foreign policy has shifted away from superpower military relations toward involvement, or noninvolvement, in trouble spots around the world. While the American public has kept abreast of these developments, most attitudes on international affairs have remained quite stable.

FIGURE 6-3 Attitudes Toward Abortion Among Young and Old Catholics and Protestants, by Frequency of Church Attendance, 1992

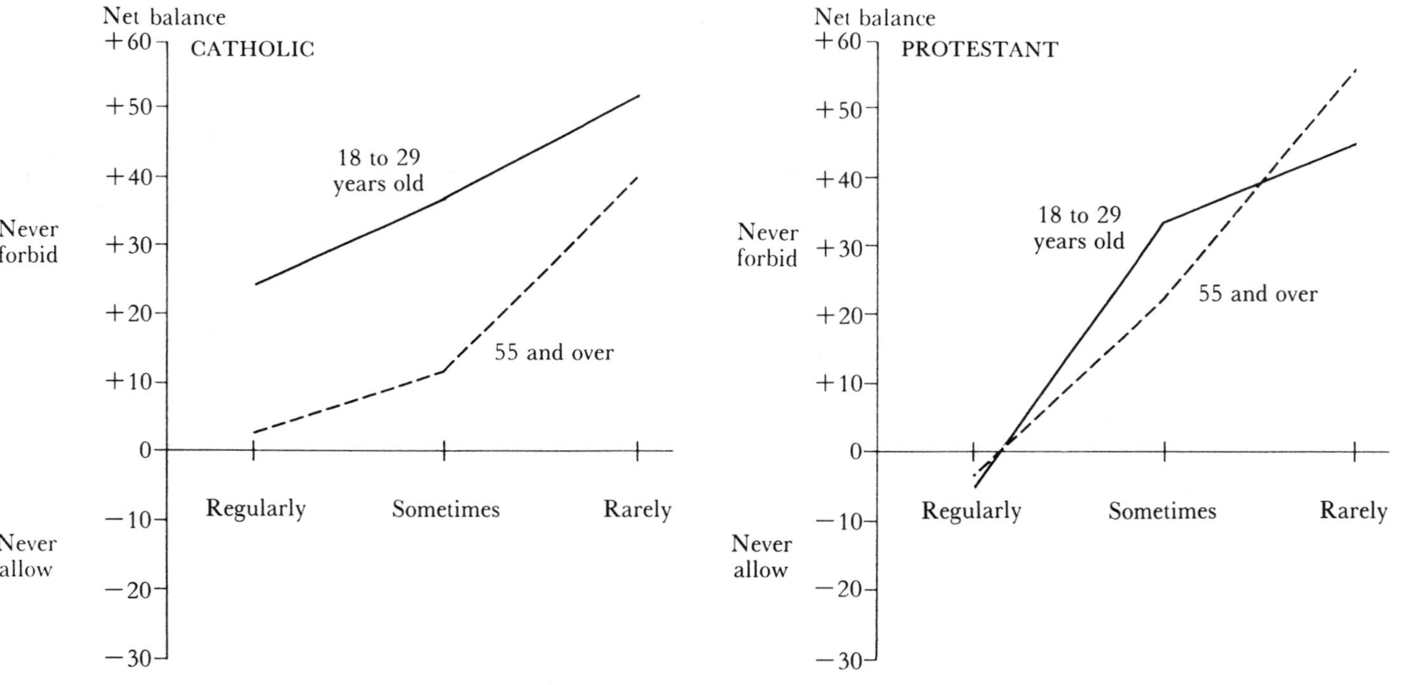

SOURCE: Center for Political Studies 1992 National Election Study. Data provided by the Inter-university Consortium for Political and Social Research.

NOTE: Percentage "never forbid" minus "never allow" calculated over the total in each category.

TABLE 6-2 Views on Abortion, by Religion and Frequency of Church Attendance, 1992

	Mainline Protestants		Evangelical Protestants		Catholics		
	Frequent	Infrequent	Frequent	Infrequent	Frequent	Infrequent	No affiliation
Pro-life	6%	1%	19%	8%	16%	3%	3%
Pro-life, with exceptions	21	23	45	26	34	25	15
Pro-choice, with limitations	21	14	14	13	17	11	11
Pro-choice	49	59	20	50	30	58	67
Other/don't know	3	3	3	2	4	3	5
Total	100%	100%	101%	99%	101%	100%	101%
(*N*)	(221)	(90)	(484)	(100)	(349)	(106)	(346)

SOURCE: Center for Political Studies 1992 National Election Study. Data provided by the Inter-university Consortium for Political and Social Research.

As Figure 6-4 shows, public opinion on two items of expenditure, foreign aid and the military, has not reacted in the least to dramatic events abroad.

Issues of foreign affairs vary greatly in salience, particularly in response to involvement of the nation in a military conflict. For brief periods, episodes such as the hostage crisis in Iran or the Persian Gulf conflict are extremely dramatic events that capture the public's attention. Ultimately, however, this effect may not last.

In analyzing the public's attitudes toward international events, we need to distinguish between brief conflicts and longer lasting wars. There is a truism now in American politics that says the American public will support—usually enthusiastically—brief military involvement in a foreign conflict that seems to be successful (and they will forget it quickly if it is not successful). If, however, combat drags on, support will diminish, especially if there are significant U.S. casualties. Usually the Vietnam experience is cited as evidence of the failure of support for prolonged conflicts, but the Korean War more than forty years ago was a similar case in point. In this section we will use public opinion on Vietnam during the 1960s and early 1970s and a panel study of attitudes toward the Persian Gulf War in the early 1990s to illustrate these patterns.

For more than a decade the most enduring issue of American foreign policy was concern over military policies in Vietnam.[7] Perhaps the most significant feature of public opinion concerning the Vietnam War was the sluggish pace with which awareness of the seriousness of American involvement developed and the slowness with which criticism and disenchantment with the course of the war in Vietnam increased. Although American military advisors had been in Vietnam since the mid-1950s, more than one-third of the electorate in 1964 had no opinion on questions about Vietnam. However, by 1968 only one in ten had no opinion. The general public was much slower than opinion elites to respond to the issue.

One question the Survey Research Center consistently asked its national sample during this time was whether we did the right thing in getting involved in Vietnam or whether we should have stayed out. Over the course of the war, the percentage of the electorate responding that the United States should have stayed out of Vietnam rose from 24 percent in 1964 to 57 percent in 1972. To a slight degree Republicans were more likely to hold this view than Democrats prior to 1968, when the war was still "Johnson's war"; after the Republican victory in the 1968 election, Democrats became somewhat more likely than Republicans to view the

FIGURE 6-4 Attitudes Toward Foreign Aid and Increased Spending for the Military, 1973-1991

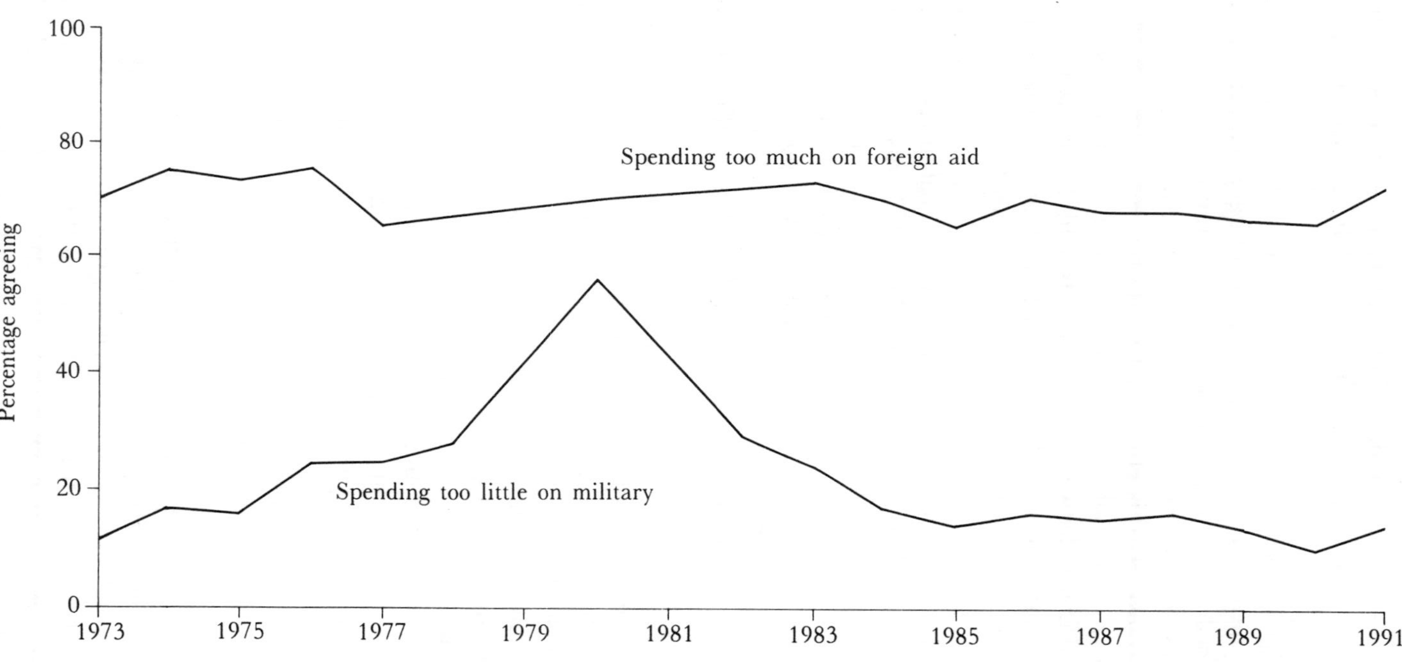

SOURCES: National Opinion Research Center, *General Social Surveys, 1972-1982 Cumulative Codebook, 78; General Social Surveys, 1972-1987*, 97; *General Social Surveys, 1972-1991*, 107.

FIGURE 6-5 Attitudes Toward U.S. Involvement in Vietnam, 1964-1972

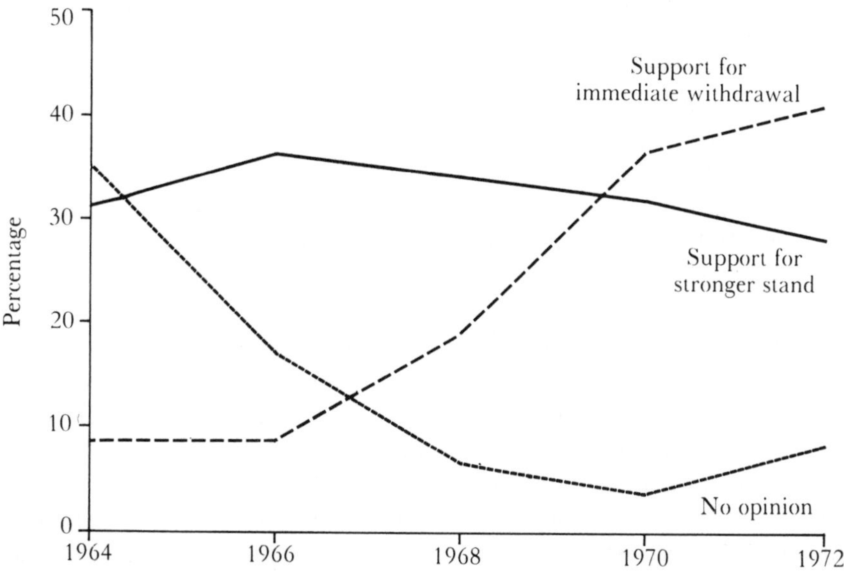

SOURCE: Survey Research Center; Center for Political Studies National Election Studies. Data provided by the Inter-university Consortium for Political and Social Research.

war as a mistake. This set of responses should not be interpreted as especially "dovish." Some people believed it had been a mistake to get involved, but once we were there, they believed we should win at all costs.

A better indication of hawk-dove sentiment is given by the responses to a second question, shown in Figure 6-5, asking whether the United States should pull out immediately or take a stronger stand, even if it meant invading North Vietnam. Not shown in the figure are the large but declining proportions of respondents who favored the existing policy of the administration over either alternative. Support for a stronger stand remained stable after 1964, with about one-third of the electorate favoring an escalation of the war. In earlier years, popular support for prompt withdrawal was low, less than 10 percent; by 1968 it had grown to 20 percent and increased more rapidly after that. By 1970 support for withdrawal was more than 30 percent; by 1972 it was more than 40 percent. Clearly, as the war dragged on, support for military involvement declined dramatically.

Attitudes toward the war in Vietnam evolved over several years. By contrast, opinions changed quickly about U.S. involvement in the Persian Gulf. Deployment of American military forces to Saudi Arabia began in the late summer of 1990, in response to Iraq's invasion of Kuwait. By the late fall, as deployment of U.S. troops continued, the public was somewhat divided in its support of this policy (Table 6-3). Fifty-nine percent of the public believed this was the correct policy to pursue, while 39 percent believed it was not. When asked whether "the United States was becoming stronger in the world," only 26 percent of the respondents said yes.

These views shifted fairly dramatically after the brief war with Iraq in early 1991. When the same people were interviewed again in June 1991 following the war, 81 percent felt the war had been the right thing to do, and only 18 percent thought the United States should have stayed out. Presumably as a result of this perceived success, 61 percent of the public believed the United States had become stronger in the world.

Political analysts have long noted a "rally-round-the-flag" phenomenon that occurs at times of international crisis.[8] Presidents invariably get a boost in popularity ratings in the polls in the midst of an international incident, even when the actions of the administration are not particularly successful. John F. Kennedy got such a boost after the disastrous Bay of Pigs invasion of Cuba in 1961, as did Jimmy Carter—temporarily—when hostages were taken at the American Embassy in Iran in 1979. And as Table 6-3 shows, public approval of President Bush's handling of the Gulf War was extremely high during and immediately following the conflict, representing a substantial increase over his earlier ratings. Not only the president benefits from a brief, apparently successful military encounter. During the Persian Gulf War, many individuals became well known and highly esteemed, at least for a short while: Generals Colin Powell and Norman Schwarzkopf became famous and highly respected; previously unknown television news reporters became widely recognized; leaders in Washington (such as Secretary of Defense Dick Cheney, who received high approval ratings) enjoyed much broader recognition; and even members of Congress improved their public images.

Not all of this enthusiasm survived the passage of time. By the fall of 1992 when the same respondents were interviewed for a third time, the belief that the United States was stronger was back to where it had been before the war, and approval of the president's handling of the war had fallen almost 20 percent, although it was still quite high. Only a little over half of the public thought anything good had come from the Gulf War. As with the Vietnam War, it would be a mistake to view these reservations as "dovish." Most of the people who were disen-

TABLE 6-3 Public Opinion Before and After the Persian Gulf War

	Fall 1990, before the Persian Gulf War	June 1991, after the Persian Gulf War	Fall 1992, a year and a half after the Persian Gulf War
The United States did the right thing to send the military to the Persian Gulf	59%	81%	74%
The United States should have stayed out of the Gulf	39%	18%	20%
The United States has become stronger in the world	26%	61%	27%
It was worth it to fight the Persian Gulf War		65%	52%
Approval of President Bush's handling of the Persian Gulf War	59%	85%	67%

SOURCE: Center for Political Studies National Election Studies, 1990, 1991, 1992. Data provided by the Inter-university Consortium for Political and Social Research.

chanted with the war believed the fighting should have continued until Saddam Hussein was driven from power.

Most people were supportive of U.S. involvement in the Gulf War from the fall of 1990 to the fall of 1992, over 10 percent were opposed throughout, and a little over 20 percent shifted from opposition to support during the two-year period. As in the case of many foreign affairs issues, slight gender differences did emerge. Men were more likely than women to approve of U.S. involvement in the Gulf. In retrospect, 26 percent of all women thought the United States had done the wrong thing by fighting the Gulf War, while 15 percent of all men held that view.

As in the case of Vietnam, there is some partisan bias in these attitudinal patterns. Republicans were mainly supportive of the effort and of President Bush throughout, and almost no Republicans consistently opposed the deployment of troops. Opposition and switching from opposing to supporting views were found mainly among Democrats and independents.

Issues and Partisanship

A leading assumption is that partisan identification provides guidance for the public on policy matters—that is, most Americans adopt opinions consistent with their partisanship. Of course, it also is likely that policy positions developed independently of one's partisanship but consistent with it will reinforce feelings of party loyalty or that attitudes on issues will lead to a preference for the party most in agreement with them. Furthermore, issue preferences inconsistent with party loyalty can erode or change it. For any particular individual it would be extremely difficult to untangle the effects of partisanship and policy preferences over a long period of time. Common sense suggests that many other elements of personality and circumstances contribute to the development of issue positions, so it is no surprise to find many political views existing quite independently of partisanship.

The relationship between attitudes on public policy and partisanship is not particularly strong in any event. Even though on many issues most partisans of one party will hold a position different from that held by the majority of the other party, large numbers of people with issue positions "inconsistent" with their party identification remain loyal to that party. To account for this, it is variously suggested that: (1) issues are unimportant to many voters; (2) only the issues most important to individuals need be congruent with their partisanship; (3) individuals regularly misperceive the positions of the parties in order to remain comfortable with both their party loyalty and their policy preferences; or (4) the positions of each party are so ambiguous or so dissimilar in different areas of the country that no clear distinction exists between the parties and thus it is not surprising that partisans of different parties appear so similar. Undoubtedly, all these explanations have some degree of truth. A long time has elapsed since there has been a crisis that would realign issues along party lines, so it is understandable that a great many issues are relatively independent of partisan ties. Only on traditional domestic economic issues, which have formed the basic ideological division between the parties since the New Deal, are the differences among the issue positions of partisans at all dramatic.

Political Ideology

A political ideology is a set of interrelated attitudes that fit together into some coherent and consistent view of or orientation toward the political world. Americans have opinions on a wide range of issues, and political analysts and commentators characterize these positions as "liberal" or "conservative." Does this mean, then, that the typical American voter has an ideology that serves as a guide to political thought and action, much the same way partisanship does?

When Americans are asked to identify themselves as liberal or conservative, most are able to do so. The categories have some meaning for most Americans, although the identifications are not of overriding importance. Table 6-4 presents the ideological identification of Americans over the past two decades. A consistently larger proportion of respondents call themselves conservative rather than liberal. At the same time, about a quarter of the population regards itself as middle-of-the-road ideologically. The question wording provides respondents with the opportunity to say they "haven't thought much about this," and fully a quarter to a third typically respond in this way. The series of liberal and conservative responses has been remarkably stable over the years. Ideological identification, in the aggregate, is even more stable than party identification. This should make us cautious of commentary that finds big shifts in liberalism or conservatism in the American electorate.

Table 6-5 shows the relationship between ideological self-identification and partisan self-identification. Democrats are more liberal than conservative, Republicans are disproportionately conservative, and inde-

TABLE 6-4 Distribution of Ideological Identification, 1972-1992

	1972	1974	1976	1978	1980	1982	1984	1986	1988	1990	1992
Liberal	9%	13%	8%	10%	8%	7%	9%	7%	7%	9%	10%
Somewhat liberal	10	8	8	10	9	8	9	11	9	8	10
Middle-of-the-road	27	26	25	27	20	22	23	28	22	25	23
Somewhat conservative	15	12	12	14	14	13	14	15	15	14	15
Conservative	12	14	13	14	15	14	15	15	17	12	15
Haven't thought about it	28	27	33	27	36	36	30	25	30	33	27
Total	101%	100%	99%	102%	102%	100%	100%	101%	100%	101%	100%
(*N*)	(2,155)	(2,478)	(2,839)	(2,284)	(1,565)	(1,400)	(2,229)	(2,170)	(2,035)	(1,987)	(2,481)

SOURCE: Center for Political Studies National Election Studies. Data provided by the Inter-university Consortium for Political and Social Research.

TABLE 6-5 The Relationship Between Ideological Self-Identification and Party Identification, 1992

	Democrats	Independents	Republicans	Total
Liberal	15%	10	2	27%
Middle-of-the-road	11	13	8	32%
Conservative	8	14	19	41%
Total	34%	37%	29%	100%
				N^a = 1,813

SOURCE: Center for Political Studies 1992 National Election Study. Data provided by the Inter-university Consortium for Political and Social Research.

[a] "No opinion" and "don't know" responses have been omitted.

pendents are slightly conservative. But conservatives are twice as likely to be Republicans as Democrats, and liberals are much more likely to be Democrats. The relationship between ideology and partisanship is shown in the low coincidence of Republican and liberal identifications.

Also, the electorate tends to perceive the Democratic party as liberal and the Republican party as conservative. Those who see an ideological difference between the parties believe the Republicans are more conservative than Democrats by a ratio of 5 to 1. Understandably, this has the potential for creating some tension among conservative Democrats and liberal Republicans. Of course, these partisans may perceive their party differently from most people, but substantial numbers of partisans, Democrats mostly, actually appear to see themselves as much closer to the other party ideologically. Perhaps over the years this conflict undermines party loyalty, but in the short run it does not seem to have much impact.

Figure 6-6 presents the relationship between various social characteristics and ideological self-identification. Self-identified liberals are most frequent among blacks and nonsouthern, college-educated whites who claim no religious affiliation. Self-identified conservatives are common outside the South among Catholics and educated, white Protestants, and in the South among Hispanics and other whites. The major impact of education is to reduce the proportion of respondents who opt for the middle category. The college educated are more likely to call themselves either liberal or conservative than the high school educated. This tendency would be even greater if those who offered no self-identification were included.

Approximately half the public identifies itself as liberal or conservative. Do these individuals use this ideological orientation to organize

FIGURE 6-6 Ideological Self-Identification, by Region, Race/Ethnicity, Religion, and Education, 1992

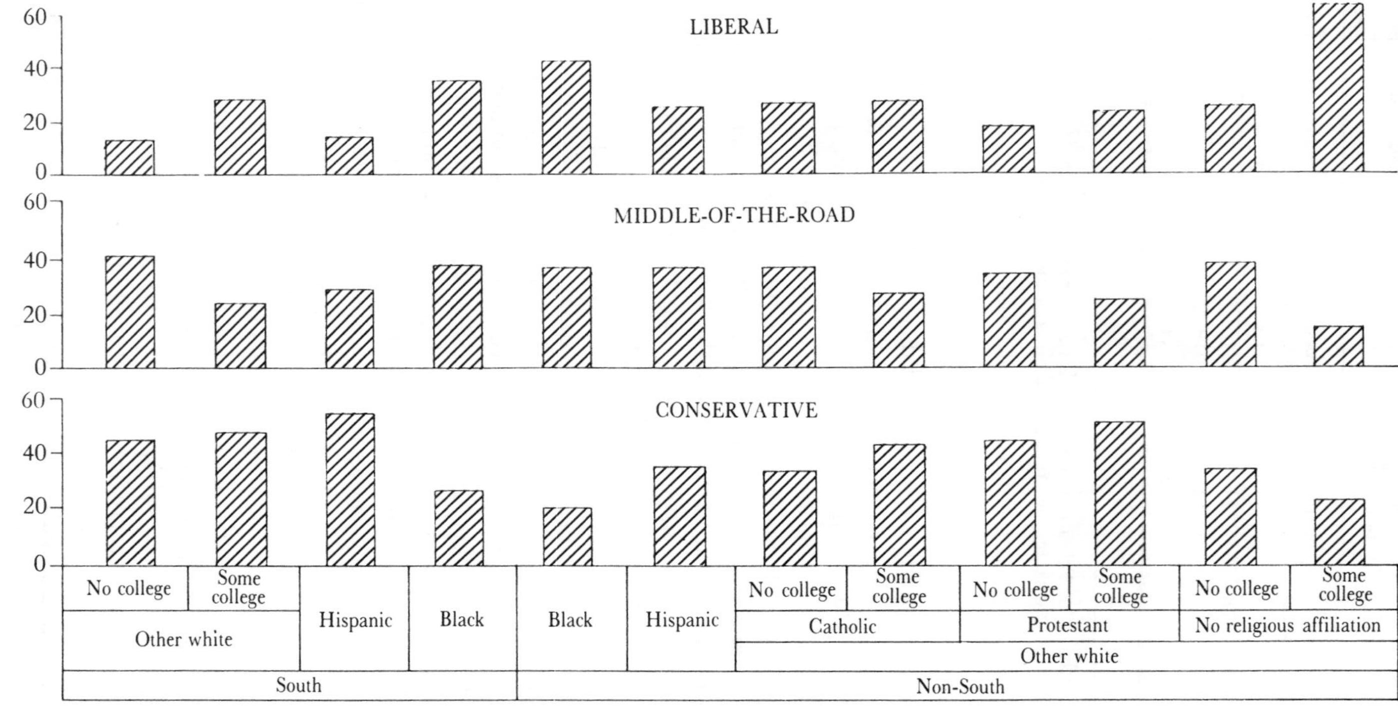

SOURCE: Center for Political Studies 1992 National Election Study. Data provided by the Inter-university Consortium for Political and Social Research.

TABLE 6-6 Distribution of the Levels of Conceptualization, 1956-1988

Levels of conceptualization	1956	1960	1964	1968	1972	1976	1980	1984	1988
Ideologues	12%	19%	27%	26%	22%	21%	21%	19%	18%
Group benefit	42	31	27	24	27	26	31	26	36
Nature of the times	24	26	20	29	34	30	30	35	25
No issue content	22	23	26	21	17	24	19	19	21
Total	100%	99%	100%	100%	100%	101%	101%	99%	100%
(N)	(1,740)	(1,741)	(1,431)	(1,319)	(1,372)	(2,870)	(1,612)	(2,257)	(2,040)

SOURCE: Richard G. Niemi and Herbert F. Weisberg, eds., *Controversies in Voting Behavior,* 3d ed. (Washington, D.C.: CQ Press, 1993), 89.

political information and attitudes? Does political ideology play a role for Americans similar to the role of partisanship as a basic determinant of their specific political views? Analysis has usually centered on two kinds of evidence to assess the extent of ideological thinking in the American electorate: the use of ideological concepts in discussing politics; and the consistency of attitudes on related issues, suggesting an underlying perspective in the individual's approach to politics.

Survey Research Center data reported in Angus Campbell et al.'s *The American Voter* showed that very few members of the electorate discussed their evaluations of the parties and the candidates in ideological language; only 12 percent did so in 1956.[9] The work of John Pierce and others has contributed to similar analysis of subsequent years.[10] As shown in Table 6-6, a change occurred in 1964. In fact, the proportions of "ideologues" doubled in 1964 over 1956 but still constituted only about one-quarter of the electorate. This does not mean that most voters have no notions about what the parties stand for or what they are likely to do when in office. Large proportions of the electorate evaluate the parties with group symbols: "The Democrats help the working man" and "Republicans are good for business." Still, there is a general lack of commitment to some set of abstract principles about the role of government in society on the basis of which the parties are evaluated.

Of course, individuals may simply be unsophisticated in the verbal descriptions of their feelings about politics and political parties. Their ideology may guide their political decisions, but they may be unable to articulate it. In that case, the individuals' attitudes toward public issues might be expected to show a degree of coherence and consistency, since those positions would be arrived at through the application of a common underlying set of political ideals. If individuals are liberal on one issue, one would expect them to be liberal on other related issues; if they are conservative on one, they would be conservative on others. The most sophisticated analysis of ideological perspectives and consistency in issue positions, usually called *issue constraint*, was carried out by Philip Converse using Survey Research Center data from 1956, 1958, and 1960.[11] He found that the strength of relationship among domestic issues and among foreign policy issues was about twice as strong as the relationship between domestic and foreign issues. By normal standards even the strongest relationship among domestic issues did not suggest particularly impressive issue consistency. In 1974 Norman Nie and Kristi Andersen augmented this analysis with the addition of another decade of coverage.[12] As with several other patterns, a change occurred during the campaign of 1964. The degree of issue constraint on various policy matters increased in 1964 and remains relatively high to the present.

As might be expected, the degree of consistency among attitudes on different issues varies with the level of education of the individual; the more educated are substantially more consistent in their views than the less educated. However, increasing levels of education do not appear to account for the increase in issue constraint. The work of Nie and Andersen shows convincingly that interest in politics is more critical. In other words, as the public becomes more concerned with issues and more attentive to political leaders, the public perceives a higher degree of issue coherence. Almost certainly the electorate generally has the capacity for greater issue constraint than it has shown; however, the exercise of the capacity depends much more on political leaders and events than on the characteristics of the electorate. When political leaders use ideological terms to describe themselves and the clusters of issues that they support, the electorate is quite capable of following suit.

The degree of issue constraint will, of course, depend on the range of issues considered. Even in the 1950s, *The American Voter* documents a rather coherent set of attitudes on welfare policies and governmental activity. When the analysis moves to more disparate issues, such as support for welfare policies and civil liberties, the relationship weakens substantially. It can be argued, of course, that little relationship should be expected between positions in these different issue areas because they tap different ideological dimensions with no logical or necessary connections among them. For example, there is nothing logically inconsistent in a person's opposing government regulation of business and believing in racial equality. In the past, internationalist views in foreign policy were considered the liberal position and isolationist attitudes conservative;

however, the Cold War and Vietnam did much to rearrange these notions as liberals argued against American involvement, and conservatives became more aggressive internationalists. In considering the question of issue constraint, two points should be kept in mind: (1) the meaning of the terms *liberal* and *conservative* change with time, as do the connections between these ideologies and specific historical events; and (2) analysts, in studying issue constraint, invariably impose on the analysis their own version of ideological consistency, which, in light of the ambiguities surrounding the terms, is likely to be somewhat artificial.

A less strenuous criterion than issue constraint for assessing the impact of ideology on political attitudes is simply to look at the relationship between individuals' ideological identification and their positions on various issues taken one at a time. Here we find substantial relationships. The relationship between ideological identification and liberal views on various policy matters over the last twenty years is shown in Table 6-7. About one-third of the people sampled did not have an ideological position or did not profess attitudes on these issues and are, therefore, missing in this analysis. Nevertheless, the data in Table 6-7 document strong, consistent relationships between ideological identification and many issue positions. The data do not, however, demonstrate that ideology determines issue positions.

If everyone had a strong ideology, attitudes would be determined by that ideology. To a considerable extent, this appears to happen to the most politically alert and concerned in our society, but this group is only a very small minority of the total adult population. If the major American political parties were ideologically oriented, then by following the parties or political leaders in these parties, Americans would have their opinions determined indirectly by ideology. But the two major political parties are notoriously nonideological. Many of the leaders have personal ideological commitments, but no single ideology dominates either party. Usually specific matters of public policy are of little interest to the electorate; as a consequence, the political parties are unconcerned with dramatizing particular policies.

Public Opinion and Political Leadership

The study of public opinion is of obvious relevance to public officials and political journalists who wish to assess the mood of the people on various topics, but the extent to which decision-makers are

TABLE 6-7 The Relationship Between Ideological Identification and Liberal Positions on Issues of Public Policy, 1972-1992

	Liberal	Somewhat liberal	Middle-of-the-road	Somewhat conservative	Conservative
Increase government services (1992)	59	46	35	24	23
Expand medical care (1992)	74	63	50	43	33
Government guarantee of jobs (1992)	51	35	28	17	18
Pro-choice on abortion (1992)	72	68	49	45	27
Not worth it to fight in the Persian Gulf (1992)	66	45	41	30	24
Cut defense spending (1988)	60	50	36	26	18
Help minorities (1988)	60	35	31	26	14
Get along with Russia (1984)	65	52	34	33	20
Support the Equal Rights Amendment (1980)	91	78	64	48	38
Oppose prayer in schools (1980)	57	41	24	30	14
Legalize marijuana (1976)	60	49	24	24	10
Oppose the Vietnam War (1972)	76	61	39	33	27

SOURCE: Center for Political Studies National Election Studies. Data provided by the Inter-university Consortium for Political and Social Research.

NOTE: The numbers in the table are the percentages taking the liberal position on each issue.

influenced by public opinion on any particular policy is almost impossible to determine. Although policy-makers must have some sense of the public mood, no one supposes that they measure precisely the attitudes of the public or are influenced by public opinion alone.

Political analysts and public officials both have difficulty assessing the likely impact of public opinion as measured by public opinion polls because the intensity of feelings will influence the willingness of the public to act on their views. Public officials who value their careers must be conscious of the issues that raise feelings intense enough to cause people to contribute money, campaign, and cast their ballots solely on the basis of that issue. As a result, public officials may be more responsive to the desires of small, intense groups than to larger, but basically indifferent, segments of the public.

In American society public attitudes toward policies usually can be described in one of two ways: as *permissive* opinion, whereby a wide range of possible government activities are acceptable to the public, or, in contrast, as *directive* opinion, either supportive or negative, whereby specific alternatives are definitely demanded or opposed. Ordinarily, policy alternatives advocated by both political parties are within the range of permissive opinion, a situation that does not create highly salient issues or sharp cleavages in the public even though political leaders may present their various positions dramatically. Only when many people hold directive opinions will the level of issue salience rise or issue clashes appear among the public. For example, undoubtedly there is widespread directive support for public education in this country; most individuals demand a system of public education or would demand it were it threatened. At the same time there is permissive support for a wide range of policies and programs in public education. Governments at several levels may engage in a variety of programs without arousing the public to opposition or support. Within this permissive range the public is indifferent.

On occasion, out-and-out opposition to programs develops, and directive opinion is formed that imposes a limit on how far government can go. For example, the widespread opposition to busing children out of their neighborhoods for purposes of integration has perhaps become a directive, negative opinion. It is no easy matter for political analysts or politicians to discover the boundaries between permissive and directive opinions. Political leaders are likely to argue that there are supportive, directive opinions for their own positions and negative, directive opinions for their opponents' views. One should be skeptical of these claims because it is much more likely that there are permissive opinions and casual indifference toward the alternative views. Indifference is widespread and, of course, does not create political pressure. It frees political leaders of restrictions on issue positions but, on balance, is probably more frustrating than welcome.

Notes

1. Edward G. Carmines and James A. Stimson, *Issue Evolution: Race and the Transformation of American Politics* (Princeton, N.J.: Princeton University Press, 1989).
2. Philip Converse, "The Nature of Belief Systems in Mass Publics," in *Ideology and Discontent*, ed. David Apter (New York: Free Press, 1964), 206-261.
3. Edward G. Carmines and James A. Stimson, "The Two Faces of Issue Voting," *American Political Science Review* 74 (1980): 78-91.
4. These data are available from the Inter-university Consortium for Political and Social Research in a data set with Paul Allen Beck, Jere W. Bruner, and L. Douglas Dobson, *Political Socialization* (Washington, D.C.: American Political Science Association, 1974).
5. Carmines and Stimson, *Issue Evolution*.
6. E. J. Dionne, *Why Americans Hate Politics* (New York: Simon & Schuster, 1991).
7. The most extensive analysis of attitudes toward the Vietnam War is found in John E. Mueller, *War, Presidents and Public Opinion* (New York: John Wiley & Sons, 1973). This work is all the more interesting because of a thorough comparison with public opinion during the Korean War.
8. Ibid., 208-213.
9. Angus Campbell, Philip E. Converse, Warren E. Miller, and Donald E. Stokes, *The American Voter* (New York: John Wiley & Sons, 1960), 249.
10. John C. Pierce, "Ideology, Attitudes and Voting Behavior of the American Electorate: 1956, 1960, 1964" (Ph.D. diss., University of Minnesota, 1969), Table 3.1, 63; and Paul R. Hagner and John C. Pierce, "Conceptualization and Consistency in Political Beliefs: 1956-1976" (Paper presented at the annual meeting of the Midwest Political Science Association, Chicago, 1981). See also Norman H. Nie, Sidney Verba, and John R. Petrocik, *The Changing American Voter* (Cambridge, Mass.: Harvard University Press, 1976), chap. 7.
11. Converse, "The Nature of Belief Systems in Mass Publics," 206-261.
12. Norman H. Nie and Kristi Andersen, "Mass Belief Systems Revisited: Political Change and Attitude Structure," *Journal of Politics* 36 (September 1974): 541-591.

Suggested Readings

Carmines, Edward G., and James A. Stimson. *Issue Evolution: Race and the Transformation of American Politics*. Princeton, N.J.: Princeton University Press, 1989. A fascinating account of the role of racial issues and policies in American politics in recent decades.

Converse, Philip E. "The Nature of Belief Systems in Mass Publics." In *Ideology and Discontent*, ed. David Apter. New York: Free Press, 1964. A classic analysis of the levels of sophistication in the American public.

Hochschild, Jennifer L. *What's Fair*. Cambridge, Mass.: Harvard University Press, 1981. An intensive, in-depth study of the beliefs and attitudes of a few people that deals with traditional topics from a different perspective.

Mayer, William G. *The Changing American Mind.* Ann Arbor: University of Michigan Press, 1992. Analysis of changes in issue positions between 1960 and 1988.

Page, Benjamin J., and Robert Y. Shapiro. *The Rational Public.* Chicago: University of Chicago Press, 1992. Analysis of the American public's views on policy issues over the past fifty years.

Sniderman, Paul M., Richard A. Brody, and Philip E. Tetlock. *Reasoning and Choice.* Cambridge: Cambridge University Press, 1991. A political psychological approach to the study of issues and ideology.

chapter seven

Political Communication and the Mass Media

MUCH ATTENTION has been focused on the process of change in political opinions, both in terms of the conditions for such change and the possibilities of instigating widespread changes in political beliefs through the mass media. At the extremes, the process of influencing political opinions is labeled brainwashing or propaganda; in reality, only a matter of degree separates these forms of influence from political persuasion, campaigning, or even education. All the efforts covered by these terms are directed toward changing individuals' political ideas, values, and opinions or toward fostering some political action. Enormous amounts of time and money are expended in American society to change political views. The very diversity of these efforts to influence the public mind, along with the diversity and complexity of the society itself, make highly unlikely a quick or uniform public response to any one of these attempts. Only dramatic events or crises can quickly change the public's views. Although news of these events comes through the media, the impact results from the events themselves, not the media imagery.

Political persuasion probably is most effective in casual personal relationships. The impact of the mass media is probably important in shaping the contours of political discourse but only gradually and over fairly long periods of time. At the same time, the role that the media have in making information widely available is extremely important in creating the conditions under which attitude change occurs. In this chapter we will consider the basic processes of opinion change and the impact of the mass media and election campaigns on individual political behavior.

Functions of Opinions for Individuals

Social psychology suggests that an individual's opinions can serve various purposes: cognitive, social, and psychological. Cognitive functions of opinions cover the efforts to give meaning to our social environment and to relate elements of belief and knowledge to one another. Opinions generally relate directly or indirectly to an individual's most significant goals or values. Somehow the policy supported by a political opinion is expected to be consistent with one's most important political values.

Opinions serve a social function if they aid the individual in adjusting to others or in becoming part of a group. In some cases individuals may use opinions to set themselves apart from others. Political and social issues may be too unimportant generally to serve social purposes for most people, and there is little evidence to indicate that strong social conformity pressures affect their views on most political issues. Nevertheless, for highly salient issues an individual is apt to find that holding a socially unacceptable view is both uncomfortable and costly.

An opinion also may serve purposes for an individual that are not dependent upon its social, economic, or political meaning but, rather, upon its special psychological significance for the individual. For example, an individual might hold strongly prejudicial opinions against some group because it enhances self-esteem to feel superior to others, or an individual might project undesirable qualities onto a certain group and thereby disassociate himself or herself from those qualities. The danger or disadvantage of psychological attachments of this kind is that the opinions so based are not responsive to ordinary influence because of their psychological importance to the individual. Most Americans do not appear to attach strong psychological meaning to their political opinions. Furthermore, in a modern pluralistic society with its open political processes, opinions on significant political subjects are unlikely to remain privatized and solely of psychological relevance to the individual; opinions also take on social and cognitive functions.

Most discussions of political opinions imply a more or less reasoned handling of opinions by individuals. They imply that individuals intelligently relate their opinions to one another and that a logical relation exists between a goal and a preference for policies leading to that goal. The implication of this perspective, as we shall see in the next section, is that opinions can be changed if the cognitive content of the attitude is changed, that is, if new information is brought to the attention of the individual. However, if individuals hold their opinions for the social or psychological purposes they serve, rather than for the cognitive, providing these individuals with more information or altering the policy implications of the opinion will not necessarily lead to opinion change.

Opinion Consistency and Dissonance

The analysis of inconsistency in opinions has much in common with the cross-pressure hypothesis considered in Chapter 5. In psychology this analysis of opinions has taken the form of identifying elements of several opinions as consistent with one another or as being in conflict (dissonant). Because dissonance is assumed to be disturbing, an individual presumably will try to avoid or reduce dissonance. An example of dissonance should clarify these concepts.[1]

Suppose a Republican believes that all Democratic administrations are corrupt and that Republicans stand for honest government, and the individual's party loyalty is justified on this basis. If the individual hears that a Republican governor is taking bribes, this information conflicts with the person's earlier views and may create dissonance among them. The dissonance could be reduced by justifying his or her loyalty on a new basis or by denying or discrediting the new information. A denial might take the form of deciding that the governor is being framed by opponents.

Individuals have many psychological defenses against the potential dissonance represented by new information that conflicts with their existing attitudes: *selective exposure,* or not paying attention to conflicting information; *selective perception,* the misinterpretation of such information, or rejecting the sources of the information as lacking credibility; *compartmentalization,* not making the connections between dissonant attitudes; and *rationalization,* the development of an unwarranted interpretation of a situation to avoid confronting the real one. Should the meaning of the information be unavoidable, attitude change to restore harmony may result. Typically, individuals will change dissonant patterns in the easiest way; the opinions or beliefs that are least important to the individual will be changed rather than important ideas or values.

Political opinions are probably most often changed simply by providing individuals with more information. This additional information may be no more than some new facts about the environment or indications that many political leaders whom an individual respects hold a particular view. The low salience of most political issues, plus the widespread emphasis on debate and discussion, leads to circumstances that improve the opportunities for changing opinions with information.

Political Communication and Attitude Change

Individuals in the public receive ideas and information intended to alter their political opinions from a variety of sources. Some sources are political leaders and commentators whose views arrive impersonally through the mass media; others are friends, co-workers, and family members who influence opinions through personal contact. Much remains to be learned about political persuasion and communication, but at least occasionally many Americans engage in attempts to influence others, and almost everyone is regularly the recipient of large quantities of political communication.

A somewhat oversimplified view of the transmission of political information would have the media beaming a uniform message to a mass audience made up of isolated individuals. The audience would receive all or most of its information from the media; thus, public opinion would be a direct product of the information and perspective provided through the media. A more complex view suggests that information is transmitted in what is called a "two-step flow of communication." [2] Information is transmitted from "opinion elites" (leaders in the society, such as politicians, organizational leaders, news commentators) to a minority of the public—the "opinion leaders"—and from them to the remainder of the public:

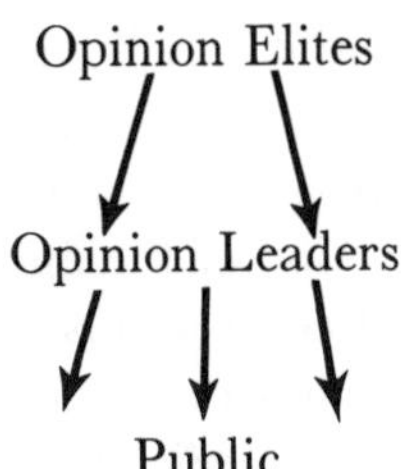

The information from opinion elites usually is sent through the mass media, but this view implies that only a portion of the audience, the opinion leaders, is attentive to any particular type of information such as political news. These opinion leaders, as intermediaries, then interpret, modify, and explain facts and events to those friends and neighbors who are less interested in or concerned with these happenings. In the process, the original message conveyed through the media becomes many somewhat different messages as it reaches the public.

The two-step flow model may not be literally true in most cases, and public opinion research has generally failed to turn up many people who recognize themselves as opinion leaders. Even so, most members of the public probably do receive information from the mass media in the context of their social groups. Thus, they filter the information and interpretations of the media through not only their own perceptions, experiences, and existing attitudes but also those of people around them. Only when the media have the attention of most members of the audience and a virtual monopoly over the kinds of information received by a public that has few existing attitudes about the subject can the media produce anything like a uniform change in public attitudes.

A somewhat different argument, also based on the role of social influences on the development of public opinion, has been made by Elisabeth Noelle-Neumann in *The Spiral of Silence.*[3] She argues that members of society sense that some views are increasing in popularity, even if these ascending viewpoints are held only by a minority. Under such circumstances people become reluctant to express opinions contrary to the presumed ascending view, while individuals holding that view are emboldened and express themselves more freely. This furthers the illusion that one viewpoint is widely shared. People then adopt the viewpoint because of this largely imaginary public pressure. Although intriguing, the attractiveness of this argument is diminished somewhat by the almost total lack of evidence in support of it.

In the remainder of this chapter we will consider the impact of the mass media on political attitudes in the context of election campaigns. Since the media can be influential only if people are paying attention, we will look at the question of the overall attentiveness of the public to political news. Since the impact of the media varies depending on the existing attitudes and information of the audience, we will examine the impact of the media on different kinds of people and in different campaign contexts. To begin, however, we need to draw some distinctions among the various types of media. First, the impact of information may be different depending on the type of media through which it is received. Precisely the same information received through television, radio, or a newspaper may impress the recipient quite differently. For example, viewing a television picture of a speech may be more dramatic than hearing it on radio or reading the text in a newspaper. Something like this occurred in 1960 when television viewers of the first of three presidential debates between John Kennedy and Richard Nixon had a less favorable impression of Nixon than did radio listeners. A difficult topic, however, may be more easily absorbed by reading and rereading a newspaper article rather than having a story flash by once on television.

Second, the media differ in what they offer. Simple elements of information are more quickly and dramatically presented to a large audience on television than through the print media. Television, however, may systematically underinform its audience by rarely offering more than a "headline service" of a minute or two on any one story. The more the public wants information and is motivated to seek it, the more important newspapers and magazines become. It is easy to search for items of information in newspapers, quite difficult with radio and television. The characteristics of the media give them different roles in the formation of public opinion. Generally, television alerts the public to a variety of topics; newspapers inform a smaller segment of the public in greater depth.

Third, there exists an increasing diversity of news sources available through television, especially over the past ten years. The Cable News Network (CNN) is a genuine alternative to the broadcast networks, especially when it comes to fast-breaking international news. The C-SPAN channels provide extensive coverage of both the U.S. House of Representatives and the Senate, as well as other political events, without the intermediary of network editing and commentary. Call-in television and radio provide lengthy discussions of public issues and, in 1992, offered a mechanism whereby candidates could bypass the normal news channels and receive unmediated coverage.

Fourth, the impact of political advertising in the media should be treated differently from other elements. The growth of television advertising has changed campaign financing drastically, though it has been difficult to establish an impact on vote choice that justifies the investment in television advertising. The major impact of television advertising as well as other campaign activities appears to be increasing voters' awareness of the issue stands of the candidates—mainly after the voters have made up their minds on a preferred candidate. A study by Thomas Patterson and Robert McClure in the Syracuse, New York, area in 1972 attempted to assess the relative impact of television news versus television political advertising on voters' perceptions of the candidates.[4] They concluded that television advertising contained more explicit information about the candidates' stands on issues than did news stories and had a correspondingly greater impact on voters' awareness of the issue positions of candidates. Television news stories were too brief and focused too much on campaign action to convey much issue information to the viewer. The impact of political advertising on TV was greatest among voters with limited exposure to other news sources. For those more attentive to the mass media in general, newspapers were the greater source of political information.

Finally, the impact of editorial endorsements by newspapers (television and radio stations rarely make endorsements) should be assessed independently of news coverage, although editorial preferences may bias news stories. Newspaper endorsements seemingly have a minimal impact in presidential elections where many other sources of influence exist.[5] In less visible, local races, a newspaper editorial may influence many voters.[6] Some concern exists that major newspaper chains could wield significant power nationally by lining up their papers behind one candidate. In recent years the large chains have left their papers free to make decisions locally, and while this might change at any time, the impact on a national election might not even be discernible.

Attention to the Media

Obviously, for the media to have an impact on an individual's political attitudes and behavior, the individual must give some degree of attention to the media when political information is being conveyed. Almost all Americans have access to television and watch political news at least some of the time. A majority of Americans read a daily newspaper for political news.

There is much discussion in the scholarly literature on mass media of the capacity to bring matters to the attention of the public or to conceal them.[7] This is usually referred to as *agenda setting*. The literature suggests that the media have great influence over what the public is aware of and concerned with. Television news and front-page stories in newspapers focus the public's attention on a few major stories each day. This function, sometimes called "headline service," tells the public: Here are important developments you should be aware of. Major crises like the invasion of Kuwait by Iraq and the deployment of U.S. troops in Saudi Arabia push other stories off the agenda. For example, in the summer of 1990 the savings and loan scandals were all but removed from nightly news coverage and replaced on the front pages by news from the Persian Gulf. The media made it almost impossible for an ordinary American to be unaware of the Persian Gulf crisis—that is agenda setting.

Television often plays a critical role in bringing events and issues, such as the Persian Gulf War and the Clarence Thomas-Anita Hill hearings, to the attention of the American public. Without television, the basic information about the Persian Gulf and the Thomas-Hill hearings would have reached the public, but television appears to have presented certain types of information in an exceptionally dramatic or impressive way.

The news media, particularly television, can rivet public attention on certain issues and, in doing so, limit the policy-making options of political leaders. The range of subjects on which this can be done is rather narrow, however. Death, destruction, intrigue, or pathos is generally an essential ingredient. More abstract or mundane political issues are easily ignored by most of the public.

The Persian Gulf War was televised to an unprecedented extent. The American public watched a real-life video arcade of modern warfare. Sixty-seven percent of a national sample reported following the war "very closely." [8] In the short run, this coverage created the impression of an overwhelming military victory and great satisfaction with television news coverage. In just ten days, from January 7 to January 17, approval of President George Bush's handling of the crisis jumped from 57 percent to 85 percent, and those supporting military action increased from 47 percent to 78 percent.[9] With the passage of time, evaluations became more mixed.

It is also true, however, that many potential news items are never reported, either in the print media or on television. This is the result of a process often referred to as *gate keeping.*[10] The media are more selective than a phrase such as "all the news that's fit to print" suggests. Bias in gate keeping and agenda setting can occur when items are kept from the public that would have been of considerable interest or when items the public otherwise would have ignored are made to seem important. Neither of these effects is easily demonstrated with political information and opinions. It is fairly easy to show that a particular newspaper or a given television station may ignore certain topics or exaggerate others, but it is extremely difficult to find evidence of any impact of selective coverage on the public.

While the media may focus on certain news items, the public has an enormous capacity for ignoring the coverage and being highly selective in what to take an interest in. The *Los Angeles Times Mirror* has engaged in an extensive project to explore the public's awareness of and interest in news stories.[11] Its analysis shows that some news stories, like the explosion of the space shuttle *Challenger* or the 1989 San Francisco earthquake, are

TABLE 7-1 Closely Followed Major News Stories and Other Selected News Items, 1986-1991

News stories	Percentage following very closely
Closely followed news stories	
Explosion of space shuttle *Challenger* (January 1986)	80
Clarence Thomas hearings (October 1991)	75
San Francisco earthquake (November 1989)	73
Rescue of little girl in Texas who fell into a well (October 1987)	69
Persian Gulf War (January 1991)	67
Iraq's invasion of Kuwait (August 1990)	66
Deployment of U.S. forces in the Persian Gulf (September/October/November 1990)	63
Invasion of Panama (January 1990)	60
Hurricane Hugo (October 1989)	60
U.S. air strikes against Libya (April 1986)	58
Crash of United Airlines DC-10 in Sioux City, Iowa (August 1989)	53
Alaska oil spill (March 1989)	52
Other news stories	
Breakup of the Soviet Union (October 1991)	47
Video of Rodney King beating (March 1991)	46
Sentencing of Oliver North (July 1989)	37
Democratic convention (July 1988)	30
Republican convention (August 1988)	27
Nelson Mandela's visit to the United States (July 1990)	24
Nomination of Robert Bork to the U.S. Supreme Court (September 1987)	17
Investigation of the "Keating Five" (March 1991)	12

SOURCE: Times Mirror Center for The People and The Press, *Times Mirror News Interest Index,* October 15, 1991, 16-21.

followed with great interest by most of the public. As shown in Table 7-1, almost all the news stories from January 1986 to October 1991 that were followed "very closely" by the largest percentages of the public were military operations or disasters of one sort or another. Still, by most standards, half of the stories were political. On the other hand, less than 20 percent of the public paid close attention to news stories about Robert Bork's nomination to the Supreme Court or the ethics hearings on the five senators (the Keating Five) who had done favors for Charles Keating, a bank executive convicted in the savings and loan scandal.[12]

The combination of television, newspapers, radio, and magazines represents an extraordinary capacity to inform the public rapidly and in considerable depth about major political news items. Add to this the informal communication about the news of the day that most people engage in, and it is easy to see that the American public is in a position to be well informed. That as many people persist in not informing themselves about most political news is not a failure of the mass media to make the news available in a variety of forms. Only a minority of the public, albeit a sizable minority, are motivated to follow political news closely and inform themselves broadly about public affairs.

In 1976 Thomas Patterson found a strong relationship between political interest and media attention.[13] He collected extensive data on samples of adults in Erie, Pennsylvania, and Los Angeles during the primary and general election campaigns. This is an unusual collection of data among public opinion studies because it focuses explicitly on media behavior. Patterson's analysis, reported mainly in *The Mass Media Election,* permits a distinction between reported media attention and the ability to recall political information from the media. Both attention to and recall of political news either on television or in a newspaper are greatest among the highly interested. In this most interested group there is some overlap between careful attention to television and newspapers, but in the rest of the public very few people are making great use of both media.

For as long as scholars have studied the media behavior of the public, they have found a strong relationship between interest in politics and attention to political news. This, of course, is not surprising, but it has several consequences for political communication. The most interested are also the most partisan, so there is a relationship between news attention and partisanship. Furthermore, high interest and the attention to news lead to the acquisition of more political information. These individuals are better equipped than the uninterested and inattentive to retain and use new elements of information that come their way.

The fact that strong partisans and politically interested people are most attentive to the media accounts for the somewhat paradoxical finding that those with the most exposure to the media are among the least affected by it. The impact of mass media exposure on voting behavior in elections in the 1950s was studied by Philip Converse of the Center for Political Studies, who drew several conclusions based on findings similar to those represented in Figure 7-1.[14] The voters most stable in their preferences (whether stability is measured during a campaign or between elections) would be those who are highly attentive to mass media but firmly committed, and those who pay no attention to

FIGURE 7-1 Hypothetical Relationship Between Mass Media Attention and Stability of Voting Behavior

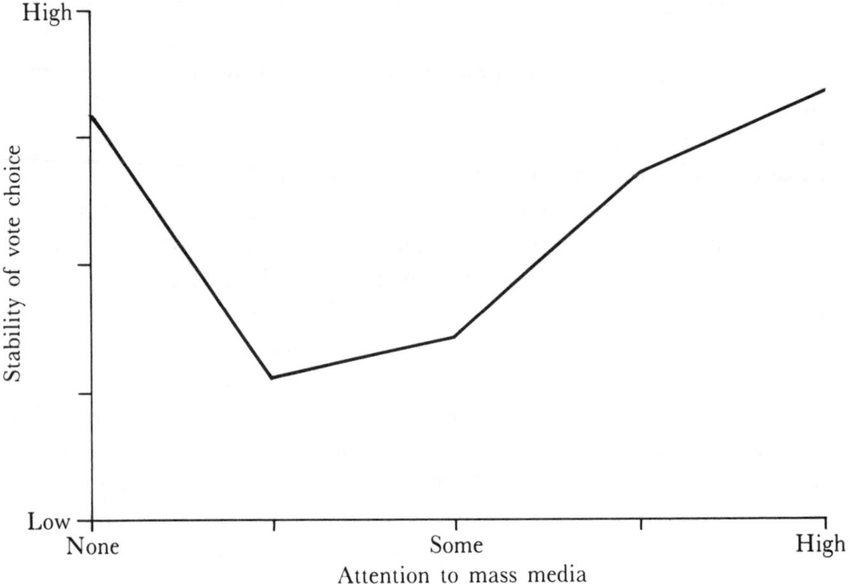

media communication and remain stable in their vote choice because no new information is introduced to change their vote. The shifting, unstable voters are more likely to be those with moderate exposure to mass media. Unfortunately, efforts at replicating Converse's findings for other election years have failed to uncover similar patterns. One difficulty may be the virtual disappearance of voters with no exposure to the mass media in recent years. Nevertheless, the reasoning behind this expected relationship is quite compelling: The impact of the media is likely to be greatest when the recipients of the message have little information and few existing attitudes.

The Media and Presidential Approval Ratings

Presidential approval ratings, regularly measured by public opinion polling organizations, reflect both the effect media coverage can have on political attitudes and its limitations. Media polls regularly ask about and report on the public's views on how the president is handling his job.

The various polling organizations ask the question in different ways, but basically what they report, and what we report here, is the percentage of the public that approves of the way the president is doing his job—not the degree of enthusiasm people feel. The approval measure sometimes behaves oddly. For example, President Ronald Reagan's approval rating jumped 10 percent after he was shot, presumably a sympathy vote and not an assessment of the job he was doing.

In one sense, the ratings are a function of media content, since media coverage is the only source of information about the president for most people. The most precipitous changes in approval ratings, though, result from dramatic and important events. Although the media coverage colors the recipient's perception of these events, the media are usually not free to ignore them; it is the events themselves, not just the coverage, that makes them compelling.

Most presidents begin a term with high ratings, a phenomenon referred to as a "honeymoon effect." President Bill Clinton began his first term with lower ratings than most recent presidents, as is evident in Figure 7-2. Presidents usually suffer a decline in approval ratings the longer they are in office.

We not only expect the ratings to decline over time, but as the public becomes more knowledgeable about a president, the approval ratings should become more stable and more retrospective. In other words, the more people know about the president, the less impact some new element of information has and the more their approval or disapproval represents a summary judgment. As this happens, the day-to-day events covered by the media, and the coverage itself, have less impact in shaping the attitudes of the public.

At first glance, the approval ratings of Bush seem to defy these tendencies. Far into his term as president, Bush's approval ratings improved dramatically during the 1991 Persian Gulf War. Poll results varied, but generally he was getting approval ratings as high as any president had ever received. A year later, by the fall of 1992, his ratings had dropped to half their previous height, and he was receiving ratings about as low as any past president.

What happened to Bush's ratings illustrates the public's shifting focus on what matters in the assessment of the president. Before and after the Persian Gulf conflict, the public's attention was on the economy. Throughout 1990, 1991, and 1992, President Bush received low ratings for his handling of the economy, so when the economy mattered most to people, his overall approval ratings were low. During the Persian Gulf War, attention shifted to foreign affairs, an area in which Bush had always enjoyed high ratings, and this translated, for a while, into high overall approval ratings.

FIGURE 7-2 Range of Positive Approval Ratings of Last Five Presidents Compared with Those of President Clinton

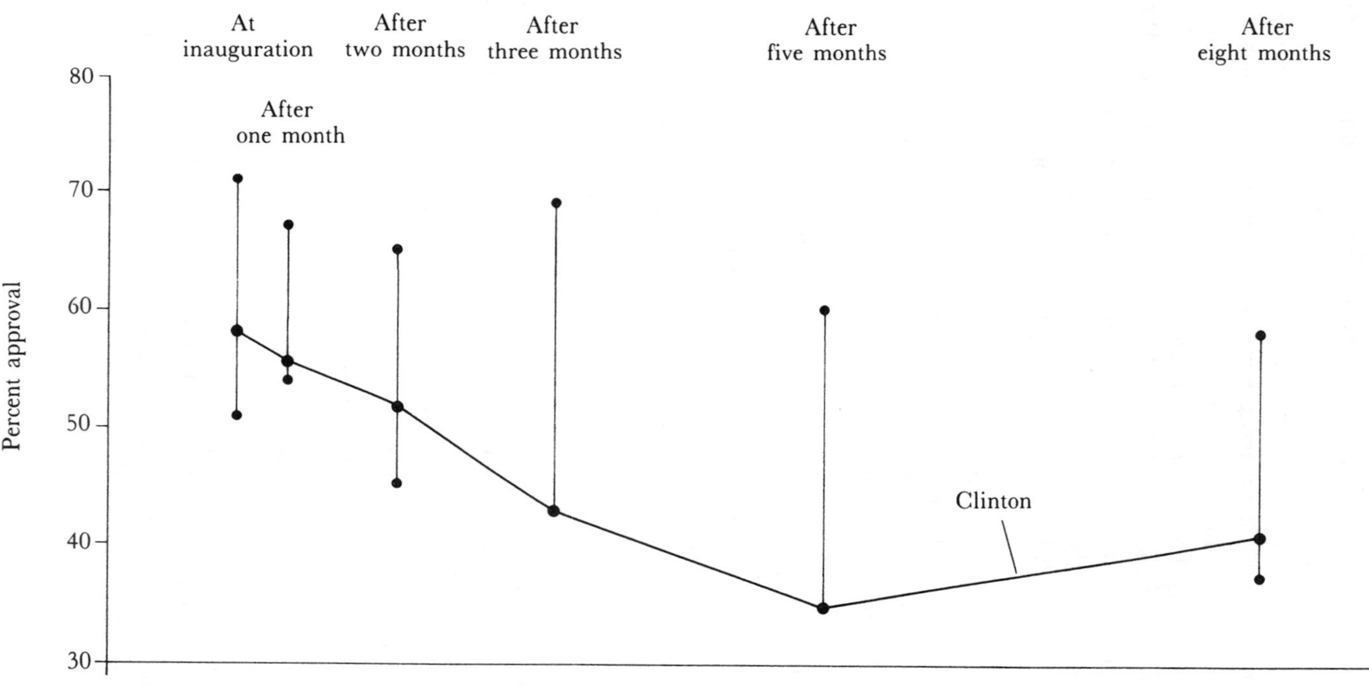

SOURCE: Surveys by Louis Harris and Associates, reported in *The Public Perspective* 4:6 (September/October 1993): 19; and surveys by the Gallup organization reported in *The American Enterprise* 4:2 (March/April 1993): 94.

TABLE 7-2 Approval Ratings of Bush Before and After the Persian Gulf War, by Party Identification

Date	Strong Democrat	Weak Democrat	Independent	Weak Republican	Strong Republican	Total
November 1990	38	61	67	85	90	65
June 1991	56	77	79	96	98	80
September-October 1992	12	28	38	69	89	42

SOURCE: Center for Political Studies National Election Studies. Data provided by the Inter-university Consortium for Political and Social Research.

NOTE: Figures are percentage of respondents approving Bush's handling of his job.

With approval ratings, as with so many attitudes, partisanship filters and colors the content of the mass media. Table 7-2 shows the approval ratings of Bush according to partisan categories in 1990 before the Gulf War, shortly after the Gulf War in 1991, and in the fall of 1992. All partisan categories showed an increase in approval in 1991 and then a decrease in 1992. Strong Republicans, however, were always extremely positive; strong Democrats, conversely, never were. Partisanship as well as information anchor many individuals in their opinions, a point we will return to below.

Impact of the Media During Election Campaigns

Since the impact of the media depends, in part, on the amount of prior information the audience has about a subject, we would expect there to be considerable variation in its impact depending on the stage of the election campaign and the level of public knowledge about the candidates.

Although research has shown little individual change in vote choice or issue positions during campaigns, to some degree this is because studies have devoted most attention to highly visible general elections—the types of elections in which voters are most likely to have made up their minds early and firmly. On the other hand, prior to the general election campaign, the public's choices appear volatile even between well-known candidates. In the summer of 1979 Democrats preferred Sen. Edward Kennedy over President Jimmy Carter by a margin of 3 to 1 as their party's nominee for president.[15] By the end of the year the two candidates were even, and by March 1980 Carter was ahead of Kennedy by 2 to 1 among Democrats.[16] Nothing comparable to this magnitude of change was observed between the nominating conventions and the election in November.

The media can have considerable impact when attitudes are not well formed or strongly held. For example, Patterson reports data showing that in 1976 the initial public reaction to the second televised debate between Gerald Ford and Carter was favorable to Ford. As news commentary, especially on television, emphasized a mistaken statement by President Ford about the absence of communist domination in Eastern Europe, public opinion shifted toward Carter as the perceived winner. In the course of two days, public evaluation flipped from 53 percent to 35 percent in favor of Ford to 58 percent to 29 percent in favor of Carter.[17] Without arguing that the public's opinion on who won the debate had any special consequences, it must be conceded that this represents an impressive instance of media influence over public opinion.

The impact of the media is probably greatest in its ability to make some potential nominees well known to the public or to consign them to obscurity. Patterson's study of the role of the media in 1976 shows that during the primaries, Carter benefited from the tendency of the press to cover only the winner of a primary, regardless of the narrowness of the victory or the number of convention delegates won.[18] Even the accident of winning primaries in the eastern time zone gave Carter disproportionately large, prime-time coverage on evenings when other candidates enjoyed bigger victories farther West.[19] It is important to realize that while the media doubtless contributed to the Carter bandwagon in 1976, this was possible because few voters were well informed about or committed to any of the many Democratic candidates. During the same period the media exaggerated the significance of Ford's early primary victories without noticeably influencing the public's feelings about him or Reagan.[20] It is much more difficult to influence voters who have well-informed preferences.

The "winner-take-all" commentary on the presidential primaries has been replaced in recent years by commentary on "unexpected" winners and losers. Attention focuses on who does much better or much worse than expected, regardless of the number of votes they receive. The most favorable coverage may be given to a second- or third-place finisher, while the real winner in terms of numbers of votes is treated as a loser. The irony of this type of commentary is that it essentially converts the errors in the media's pre-election coverage into newsworthy political change.

Prior to 1988, southern Democratic leaders decided that concentrating many primaries early in the election year would focus candidates' attention on southern states and the large number of convention delegates to be won there. Furthermore, media attention and campaigning would be drawn to the South, and this would cast a more conservative tone over the campaign that would give an advantage to candidates who appealed to southern voters. So far this strategy has not worked. As a media event, Super Tuesday (the day of many southern primaries) lacks focus because there are too many states to cover and too many dissimilar results. Moreover, candidates have neither the time nor the resources to campaign in all of the states, so there is little attempt to appeal to a general southern electorate.

Political Learning During a Campaign

Over the course of a presidential campaign, particularly during the primaries, a great deal of political learning goes on. Voters become aware of candidates they had never heard of and gain an impression of these candidates' stands on issues. Even well-known candidates such as an incumbent president may not have a clearly defined set of issue positions in the public's view before the campaign.

In studying the 1976 election, Patterson found that the association between voters' issue positions and their candidate choices increased over the course of the campaign.[21] Voters in his sample did not appear to be persuaded to change their attitudes on issues by candidate appeals or to switch their vote choices; rather, as they learned which positions the candidates took, voters discovered (in many instances) that they were closer to their preferred candidate. This finding might be used to argue that the campaign is a process of clarification, an articulation of issue linkages that were potential all along. Voters are also more likely to perceive the candidates' positions on issues as more extreme, more distinct from each other, by the end of the campaign. Since the voters themselves do not seem to become more polarized or extreme on issues over the course of the campaign, this evidence suggests that the public is learning about the candidates rather than being persuaded by them.

The opportunities for political learning in a campaign are obviously lessened to the extent that selective exposure occurs. Selective exposure refers to a tendency to select information that conforms to one's ideas and values. Individuals allegedly avoid media content that would conflict with their present point of view and seek out information that reinforces their views. Presumably, committed Bush and Clinton supporters were not as interested in independent candidate Ross Perot's half-hour infomercials as were his supporters or those undecided between Perot and another candidate. Using the terms introduced above, an individual selects mass-media content to avoid or reduce dissonance. It is persuasive to argue that Democrats are more likely than Republicans to read news stories about Democratic candidates or to watch a Democratic television commercial. Common sense—if not empirical evidence—suggests that something like this does occur. However, there is no factual basis for believing that most voters successfully avoid all political information that is in conflict with their present views. Most Americans are unavoidably exposed to political ideas and values with which they do not agree.

A clear example of a situation in which selective exposure almost certainly does not operate is a televised debate between presidential candidates. Here it would be practically impossible to ignore one candidate and pay attention to the other. The debates illustrate the substantial impact of the mass media under the right circumstances. Nearly everyone in the American electorate watches one or more televised presidential debates during a campaign. According to several different public opinion polls in 1960, about half of the voters reported that they were influenced by the debates in their evaluation of Kennedy and Nixon. Among voters reporting that the debates determined their vote choice, Kennedy held an advantage of 3 to 1 over Nixon.[22]

In the most recent presidential elections, television debates between presidential candidates have been a major focus of public attention. For all the worry of campaign staffs that their candidate will self-destruct before a huge national audience, the candidates have generally performed adequately. Each of the three presidential debates in 1992 turned out differently, perhaps because they each had a different format. Perot benefited the most from the first debate (47 percent thought he did the best job), and Clinton was most impressive in the second (58 percent said he won). The third debate was a draw with no clear "winner."[23] It continues to be the case that substantial numbers of voters believe they acquire valuable information about the candidates from the debates.

The vice-presidential debates probably have more impact on attitudes, simply because the vice-presidential candidates are generally less well known. The public impression of James Stockdale, Perot's running mate, was essentially determined by his disastrous performance in the 1992 vice-presidential debate, which was virtually his only campaign appearance.

In recent campaigns no other opportunity for winning over so many uncommitted voters or converting opponents has compared with the television debates. However, another significant political opportunity regularly offered to candidates is the party nominating convention. A large television audience is available to each party during the convention, although holding the attention of the audience for extended periods of time appears to be difficult, particularly if there is no contest for the presidential nomination. Furthermore, strong partisans follow their party's convention more intently than do other members of the electorate. The battle-marred Democratic convention in 1968 and George McGovern's acceptance speech long after midnight in 1972 represent dramatic failures to use this opportunity to benefit the party's nominee. Usually, however, candidates receive a convention "bounce," a noticeable jump in their trial heat results immediately after their party's convention.[24]

Much political commentary has deemed the 1992 Democratic convention a triumph for Clinton and the Republican convention a disaster for Bush. This interpretation exaggerates the impact of the conventions, particularly the damage done by the Republican convention. For all the negative reaction to the moral majoritarian tone of the convention, Bush received the same bounce that he did after the 1988 convention, which had been considered quite a success, despite the selection of Dan Quayle as his vice-presidential running mate. The crucial difference between 1988 and 1992 was not the bounce but rather the fact that Bush came out of the 1988 convention leading the race and out of the 1992 convention trailing badly. A far more important factor in the changing fortunes of Bush and Clinton during July and August of 1992 was the temporary withdrawal of Perot. Perot's departure gave Clinton a large bloc of new supporters going into the Democratic convention. Prior to the Republican convention, Bush gained few former Perot followers even though many had indicated Bush was their second choice. Perot's withdrawal immediately prior to the Democratic convention probably focused increased attention on the convention and on Clinton as the only available alternative to Bush. It gave Clinton a rather unique opportunity to create an impression with undecided voters.

Campaign organizations work tirelessly to affect the learning that takes place during a political campaign by supplying the news media with information favorable to their candidates. An especially attractive way to do this is to stage media events that provide the media, particularly television, with an attention-grabbing headline, sound bite, or photo opportunity. The campaigns of Nixon in 1968 and Bush in 1988 were particularly successful in manipulating news coverage favorable to their candidates by staging media events and otherwise limiting access to the candidates. Television news directors and newspaper editors have become increasingly resistant to carrying stories rigged by campaign organizations. A more certain way to control the content of the media is through advertising. After all, the campaign organization is free to package and "sell" the candidate anyway it can through advertising.

Selling a Candidate

To successfully sell a candidate with advertising techniques, image makers must be able to control the information available about their candidate, thereby controlling the perceptions the voters hold about him or her. For a relatively unknown challenger, such as McGovern in 1972 or Carter in 1976, this type of strategy would appear self-defeating because few candidates (Perot in 1992 would be an exception) have had the resources to become well known nationwide through advertising and staged appearances alone. Instead, unknowns must scramble for exposure in any forum they can find, and this prevents the careful manipulation of an image. Conversely, well-known candidates or incumbents, who can afford to sit back and let the public relations people campaign for them, probably already have images that are impossible to modify in any significant way over the relatively short period of time available in an election campaign. The most famous alleged attempt to "repackage" a candidate was the effort of the Nixon campaign staff in the 1968 presidential election.[25] The evidence here suggests that more voters decided to vote for other candidates during the course of the campaign than decided to vote for Nixon. After about twenty years of nationwide public exposure, a "new Nixon" reinforced existing images, both negative and positive; he simply could not create a new, more favorable image.

In the rare case in which a virtual unknown gains rapid political prominence without the usual exposure, the lack of information about him or her allows public attitudes to fluctuate. In 1974, when Ford became president, he was not well known to the American public. The highly favorable but rather vague impression of him that accompanied his taking office changed dramatically within a month when he pardoned Nixon. Early in 1976 Carter was little known, and public perceptions of him varied widely. After his nomination, however, he became clearly recognizable to the public, though his supporters and detractors alike confessed to uncertainty over his issue positions. The relatively small amount of information available to the public about Carter prior to the start of the campaign made his early support subject to erosion. Since attitudes about him were not well formed, the information gained through the course of the campaign had a potentially greater impact on his popularity than it would have had on a better-known candidate.

Attitudes toward Geraldine Ferraro displayed a similar volatility. When, as a virtual unknown, she was picked by Walter Mondale to be his running mate in 1984, the response was overwhelmingly favorable; as questions began to arise about her husband's business dealings, her approval ratings quickly turned downward, and she went from being an asset to the ticket to a liability. In contrast to Ferraro, Mondale, as a former vice president, was very well known long before the primary campaign began in 1984. Continuous monitoring of Mondale's image through surveys conducted from January to November of 1984 by the Center for Political Studies reveals a very high degree of stability.

Reagan was more successfully handled as a candidate than were most of his predecessors. Perhaps his professional training as an actor made him more susceptible to management by his advisers. But, to a considerable degree, image building for political figures depends on protecting them from the press and public exposure rather than manipulating publicity by selling particular content. This approach was especially effective in the campaign of 1980 when the focus of attention and public dissatisfaction rested on President Carter rather than Reagan. As president, Reagan was quite inaccessible, making few uncontrolled public appearances.

While it may be difficult to sell a candidate by manipulating an image in a positive way, there appears to be a far greater opportunity to hurt an opponent's image through negative campaigning and advertising. In recent years candidates' campaigns and independent organizations have attacked the images of candidates in personal and political terms. Although the Bush campaign had used negative campaigning with considerable success against Michael Dukakis in 1988, it was much less successful in attacking Clinton in 1992. Two generalizations about negative campaigning can be made: (1) the public disapproves of negative campaigning; and (2) even so, it sometimes works.

If negative campaigning illustrates the capacity of the media to accomplish political purposes, the difficulty candidates have in using the media to respond to these attacks reveals the limitations of the media. Victims of negative campaigning have tried to ignore the attacks, attempted to answer the charges, or counterattacked with their own negative campaign. None of these responses appears to be notably successful—a fact that encourages the continued use of negative campaigning. Attacks in the form of ridicule or humor may be particularly difficult to answer. Some strategists have urged the victims of negative campaigning to respond immediately and defend themselves aggressively. This may be good advice, but it requires a lot of the victim. To respond promptly with advertising requires a great deal of money (perhaps near the end of a campaign when resources are limited) and a skilled staff. Moreover, victims of negative campaigning need to have a strong, effective answer to such attacks.

There are other circumstances in which public relations and mass advertising techniques could conceivably be successful in foisting a candidate on an unwitting public. In a single state a previously unknown candidate could saturate the mass media with prepackaged information. If the opponent were likewise unknown and without the financial resources to wage a countercampaign, such a strategy might well succeed. This is particularly true in party primaries or in nonpartisan elections in which the partisanship of candidates does not become involved in the evaluation of their attributes.

Do Election Campaigns Change Votes?

Although most professional politicians take for granted the efficacy of political campaigns, scholarly analysis has often questioned their impact. In most elections the majority of voters decide how they will vote before the campaign begins. Beyond this, the general low level of political information in the American electorate throws doubt on the ability of undecided voters to absorb ideas during a campaign. Andrew Gelman and Gary King have offered an especially interesting form of this argument.[26] They contend that a voter's eventual choice can be predicted quite satisfactorily at the start of a campaign, well before the candidates are even known. Furthermore, since a voter may vacillate away from this ultimate choice during the course of a campaign, intermediate predictions, so popular in media coverage and campaign organizations, are misleading.

That an individual voter's choice is determined at the start of a campaign may be difficult to believe. Yet evidence indicates that in most years the vote choices of most voters are not affected by political campaigns. However, the possibility exists that campaigning influences a small but crucial proportion of the electorate, and many elections are close enough that the winning margin could be a result of campaigning. Clearly, professional politicians drive themselves and their organizations toward influencing every undecided voter in the expectation that they are the key to providing, or maintaining, the winning margin. The Gelman and King analysis predated 1992 when Perot's candidacy made vote choice less predictable, both before and during the campaign. Also, Perot's presence left a greater number of voters than usual undecided well into the fall, making them prime targets of intense campaigning.

One way of approaching the question of campaign impact is to see how many voters make up their minds before the campaign starts. As shown in Table 7-3, in presidential elections from 1948 to 1992 voters made their vote choice at about the same time: In most years about one-third of the electorate decided before the conventions, another one-third decided during the conventions, and a final one-third decided during the campaign.

The 1992 presidential election was unusual in that so many voters left their vote choices open until the campaign. Almost 1 in 5 voters report they did not decide for whom to vote until the last few days before the election. Perot voters were especially likely to make their decision at the last minute, as were those who were considering Perot but ultimately voted for another candidate. The presence of Perot in the 1992 race definitely delayed the decisions of many voters.

The decision times of partisans and independents vary because the loyal party votes line up early behind the party's candidate. In all recent elections, the independents and weak partisans were more likely to make up their minds during the campaign, while strong partisans characteristically made their decisions by the end of the conventions. To put it differently, the less committed are still undecided at the start of the campaign. In fairly close elections, this relatively uncommitted group can swing the election either way with 10 to 15 percent of the voters making a decision in the last days of the election campaign.

It is widely reported that the most interested voters make their vote decisions early and that the least interested voters remain undecided during the campaign. A great deal has been made of this generalization and its implications for campaign strategy. Essentially, the consideration has taken this form: The least interested (and least concerned and least informed) are the only voters still available during the campaign. And, to influence them, very simple campaign appeals are necessary. The interested voters (mainly partisan and already committed) are held in line with appeals to party loyalty.

TABLE 7-3 Distribution of Time of Decision on Vote Choice for President, 1948-1992

Time of Decision	1948	1952	1956	1960	1964	1968	1972	1976	1980	1984	1988	1992
Before conventions	37%	34%	57%	30%	40%	33%	43%	33%	42%	49%	32%	39%
During conventions	28	31	18	30	25	22	17	20	17	16	28	14
During campaign	25	31	21	36	33	38	35	45	40	29	37	45
Don't remember, not ascertained	10	4	4	4	3	7	4	2	1	5	3	2
Total	100%	100%	100%	100%	101%	100%	99%	100%	100%	99%	100%	100%
(*N*)	(424)	(1,251)	(1,285)	(1,445)	(1,126)	(1,039)	(1,119)	(1,667)	(958)	(1,376)	(1,209)	(1,684)

SOURCE: Survey Research Center; Center for Political Studies National Election Studies. Data provided by the Inter-university Consortium for Political and Social Research.

This description is appropriate for some recent campaigns, but it is not a permanent characteristic of the American electorate. It fits the Eisenhower elections, perhaps the later Roosevelt elections, as well as the elections beginning in 1976. Interest was unusually high in the 1992 campaign, and the most interested voters made their decisions before the general election campaign began. Those voters who remained undecided into the last two months before election day revealed less interest in the campaign. In contrast, in 1960 the least interested voters showed a slight tendency to decide early rather than late; in 1964, 1968, and 1972 the time of decision of the most interested and least interested was no different. In other words, under many circumstances interested voters are as likely as uninterested voters to enter the campaign still undecided on their vote choice. This is not to say that these interested voters are completely without preferences or that they are extremely well informed. They are neither. But it is not true that in all political campaigns the only voters still undecided at the start of the campaign are uninterested in politics.

Campaign Strategy

Those attempting to communicate with the American public on political matters face an awkward dilemma. The attentive members of the public, the individuals most likely to receive political messages, are least likely to be influenced by one or a few items of information. On the other hand, the individuals who are open to persuasion are uninterested in politics and not likely to pay attention to politics in the media.

In conclusion, we can use material from this chapter as a basis for generalizing about political communication and campaign effects from the perspective of a candidate. In political campaigns, candidates stand little chance of altering the electorate's issue preferences on policies that are sufficiently prominent to affect their vote choices. In the short run, to change individuals' preferences on issues that they care about is difficult by any means, and it is particularly difficult through the impersonal content of mass media. To change an individual's preferences or pattern of behavior, personal contact is more effective than the media; therefore, vote choice or turnout is likely to be influenced, if at all, by an acquaintance of the individual.

To a limited degree, candidates can alter the prominence of a few issues for some segments of the public, but their capacity to increase or decrease the importance of issues is slight in comparison with what will happen in the ordinary course of events. For example, a candidate cannot make corruption in government a salient issue solely through his or her campaign, but a major scandal can make it an issue whether the candidates want it or not. Nevertheless, it is worth some effort to increase the visibility of issues that are expected to benefit the candidate, even though that effort will probably fail. Correspondingly, it is also worth some effort to attempt to reduce the salience of issues that hurt a candidate, though, again, this strategy is not likely to succeed.

The public's perceptions of candidates' positions on issues are much more susceptible to change. News and advertising through the mass media can convey a lot of information on issue stands and dramatize the differences between candidates. The more factual this information and the more the candidates agree on the respective characterizations, the more fully this information is absorbed by the public. This is the area of attitude change and public awareness in which candidates can accomplish the most.

In the final analysis, candidates are most interested in winning votes, regardless of how strong a preference each vote represents. But there are grounds for wanting large numbers of supporters with very strong preferences. Individuals with an overwhelming preference, holding no significant conflicting views, form the base of support for a candidate that yields campaign contributions and workers. These are the individuals all through society who casually influence the people around them to hold views favorable to a candidate. These are the opinion leaders who interpret and misinterpret the news on behalf of their candidate.

The more obviously partisan or one-sided the content of either media message or personal contact, the less likely it is to influence the uncommitted, not to mention the hostile. This poses a problem for the campaigner. Even though extreme messages are most likely to attract the attention of the relatively apathetic uncommitted voter, those same messages are least likely to get results. For this reason, in part, events dramatizing an issue can be so valuable or damaging to a candidate. Events that affect a candidate's personal image are especially important because these perceptions are the most difficult to change through direct appeals in campaign advertising.

The overall implications of this discussion are several. It takes a long time and probably noncampaign periods of low intensity to switch individual issue stands or party loyalties. The media presentation and personal discussion of political and social conditions or events have a greater impact on attitudes than advertising or party contacts.

To a considerable degree, these generalizations about political influence and communication imply that by the time a candidate wins nomination, he or she faces a constituency whose basic values and preferences can be changed only by events over which the candidate probably has little or no control. The only impact the candidate can have through campaigning is to make issue positions known as dramatically as possible and to contrast those positions with the opponents'. No candidate will know in advance what the net effect of these efforts will be, and most will never know. But most elections are contested under conditions that give one candidate a great initial advantage in the partisan loyalty and issue preferences of the constituency. The best chance for candidates is to exploit what they believe are their advantages, but in most cases the stable party loyalties and unchanging issue preferences of a constituency impose significant constraints on how much difference campaign strategies can make.

Speculation on the nature of political communication has ranged from alarm over the vulnerability of the mass public to manipulation through the media, to annoyance at the difficulty of reaching the public. The American people make use of the mass media to inform themselves on matters of interest, but this does not mean that the public pays attention to everything in the media. Individuals have a remarkable ability to ignore information—a capacity as fully developed as the ability to absorb information. Influencing individuals on a subject about which they feel strongly is extremely difficult because they reject the media content, and influencing individuals on a subject about which they are indifferent offers problems because they ignore the media content.

Also, the media are difficult to use for manipulation because so many different points of view are found there. An extremely wide range of political perspectives is available to some degree in the mass media, although some perspectives are much more frequently available and more persuasively presented than others. The media in American society allow all views to enjoy some expression, although media coverage of many topics may be expressed in a manner extremely favorable to some viewpoints and unfavorable to others. It would be very difficult to disentangle the bias associated with the news and commentary in the media from the distortion found in the individual's reception of political information. The public has a considerable capacity for ignoring media content or misinterpreting that content. Either of these conditions would be adequate to account for considerable discrepancy between political reality and the public image of that reality. No analyst of public opinion would contend that the American people are extremely well informed politically or hold views that are free of systematic bias. There is, however, quite a difference between this recognition and the contention that the mass media cause particular misperceptions. On the other hand, the long-term impact of the biases and style of the mass communication channels on public attitudes has not received adequate attention. Universal exposure to the prevailing political culture as offered through the mass media in news reporting, popular commentary, and the arts will certainly make subcultural variations more difficult to establish and maintain.

Notes

1. The classic statement on cognitive dissonance is Leon Festinger, *A Theory of Cognitive Dissonance* (Evanston, Ill.: Row, Peterson, 1957). For some of the most interesting experimental work in this field, see Milton J. Rosenberg, Carl I. Hovland, William J. McQuire, Robert P. Abelson, and Jack W. Brehm, *Attitude Organization and Change* (New Haven, Conn.: Yale University Press, 1960).
2. Elihu Katz and Paul F. Lazarsfeld, *Personal Influence: The Part Played by People in the Flow of Mass Communications* (New York: Free Press, 1964).
3. Elisabeth Noelle-Neumann, *The Spiral of Silence* (Chicago: University of Chicago Press, 1984).
4. Thomas E. Patterson and Robert D. McClure, "Television News and Televised Political Advertising: Their Impact on the Voter" (Paper presented at the National Conference on Money and Politics, Washington, D.C., 1974); and Thomas E. Patterson and Robert D. McClure, *Political Advertising: Voter Reaction to Televised Political Commercials* (Princeton, N.J.: Citizens' Research Foundation, 1973).
5. Everette E. Dennis, *The Media Society* (Dubuque, Iowa: Wm. C. Brown, 1978), 37-41.
6. Michael B. MacKuen and Steven L. Coombs, *More than News* (Beverly Hills, Calif.: Sage Publications, 1981).
7. For an early statement of this point, see Bernard C. Cohen, *The Press and Foreign Policy* (Princeton, N.J.: Princeton University Press, 1963).
8. Times Mirror Center for The People and The Press, *Times Mirror News Interest Index,* October 15, 1991, 16-21.
9. CBS News/*New York Times* Poll press release, January 17, 1991.
10. See Dennis, *The Media Society,* chaps. 5, 7.
11. A variety of publications, including monthly reports, are available from the Times Mirror Center for The People and The Press in Washingon, D.C.
12. News release by the Times Mirror Center for The People and The Press, *Times Mirror News Interest Index,* October 15, 1991, 16-21.
13. Thomas E. Patterson, *The Mass Media Election* (New York: Praeger, 1980), 14-15.
14. Philip Converse, "Information Flow and the Stability of Partisan Attitudes," *Public Opinion Quarterly* 26 (Winter 1962): 578-599.
15. *Gallup Opinion Index,* No. 183, December 1980, 51.
16. "Opinion Roundup," *Public Opinion* 3 (April/May 1980): 38.

17. Patterson, *The Mass Media Election,* 123, 125.
18. Thomas E. Patterson, "Press Coverage and Candidate Success in Presidential Primaries: The 1976 Democratic Race" (Paper presented at the annual meeting of the American Political Science Association, Washington, D.C., 1977).
19. James D. Barber, ed., *Race for the Presidency* (Englewood Cliffs, N.J.: Prentice-Hall, 1978), chap. 2.
20. Patterson, *The Mass Media Election,* 130-132.
21. Thomas E. Patterson, "Vote Choice in the 1976 Presidential Primary Elections" (Paper presented at the annual meeting of the Southern Political Science Association, New Orleans, 1977).
22. Recomputed from Elihu Katz and Jacob J. Feldman, "The Debates in the Light of Research: A Survey of Surveys," in *The Great Debates: Background, Perspective, Effects,* ed. Sidney Kraus (Bloomington: Indiana University Press, 1962), 212.
23. *The Gallup Poll Monthly,* No. 325, October 1992, 19.
24. James E. Campbell, Lynna L. Cherry, and Kenneth A. Wink, "The Convention Bump," *American Politics Quarterly* 20 (July 1992): 287-307.
25. Joe McGinniss, *The Selling of the President* (New York: Trident Press, 1969).
26. Andrew Gelman and Gary King, *Why Do Presidential Election Campaign Polls Vary So Much When the Vote Is So Predictable?* (Cambridge, Mass.: Littauer Center, 1992).

Suggested Readings

Ansolabehere, Stephen, Roy Behr, and Shanto Iyengar. *The Media Game: American Politics in the Television Age.* New York: Macmillan, 1993. A readable discussion of the way politicians use the media and the impact on public attitudes.

Graber, Doris. *Processing the News.* New York: Longman, 1988. An in-depth study of a few respondents on the handling of political information from the media.

Jamieson, Kathleen H., and Karlyn K. Campbell. *The Interplay of Influence.* Belmont, Calif.: Wadsworth, 1988. A survey of news processes and advertising and their impact on the public.

Neuman, W. Russell, Marion R. Just, and Ann N. Crigler. *Common Knowledge.* Chicago: University of Chicago Press, 1992. An interesting analysis of mass media and political attitudes.

Patterson, Thomas E. *The Mass Media Election.* New York: Praeger, 1980. A major study of the impact of mass media on public opinion and voting behavior.

Popkin, Samuel L. *The Reasoning Voter.* Chicago: University of Chicago Press, 1991. A wide-ranging discussion of campaigning and presidential vote choice.

chapter eight

Vote Choice and Electoral Decisions

THE CENTRAL focus of research on American political behavior is vote choice, especially presidential vote choice. No other single form of mass political activity has the popular interest or analytic significance that surrounds the selection of a president every four years. Most Americans follow presidential campaigns with greater attention than they give other elections, and eventually about 50 percent of the electorate expresses a preference by voting. The results of presidential balloting are reported and analyzed far more extensively than any others. This chapter will explore the main determinants of vote choice and the interpretation of election outcomes in light of these determinants. We will attempt to generalize the discussion beyond presidential choice, but inevitably most of the illustrations are drawn from recent presidential election studies.

Election analysts found 1992 a fascinating year—and an exasperating one. Ross Perot's in-out-in-again candidacy caused most of the problems. Because of his late re-entry into the campaign, the pre-election survey by the National Election Study (on which most of our analysis in this book is based) largely ignored Perot. Furthermore, the techniques that election analysts have used for decades are not readily adaptable to three-candidate races. Nevertheless, precisely because of its unusual features, there is much to learn from the 1992 election.

Earlier chapters have emphasized party loyalty as a basic characteristic that influences many aspects of an individual's political behavior. In regard to vote choice, an individual's partisanship can be construed as a long-term predisposition to vote for one party or another, other things being equal. In other words, in the absence of any information about candidates and issues or other short-term forces in an election, individuals can be expected to vote according to their partisanship. On the other hand, to the extent that such short-term forces have an impact on them, they may be deflected away from their usual party loyalty toward some other action. Clearly, the more short-term forces there are in an election—or the more a voter is aware of them—the less will be the impact of partisanship. This idea is crucial for understanding the relative impact of partisanship in different types of elections. In highly visible presidential elections, when information about candidates and at least some issues is widely available, partisanship will typically be less important to the voter's decision than in less visible races down the ticket. Clearly, too, more potent short-term forces would be required to cause a very strong partisan to vote for another party than would be necessary to prompt a weak partisan to defect. An individual's vote in an election can be viewed as the product of the strength of partisanship and the impact of the short-term forces on the individual.

In most elections, both candidates and political commentators give their attention to short-term forces, such as the personalities of the candidates, issues, and the parties' records, since these are the variable elements that the actions of candidates and campaign strategies seek to modify. Although in many respects partisanship is the most important element, it is taken as a constant since, in the short run, it is not likely to change. This chapter will consider the impact of the short-term forces of candidate image, current party images, and issues within a setting of stable party loyalties.

Candidate Image

The appeal of candidates has been given more attention in recent elections than any other short-term influence. During the past forty years national samples have been extensively questioned about likes and dislikes concerning the presidential candidates. During this period there have been several very popular candidates with extremely favorable images, as well as several who were rejected by the electorate largely on the basis of their personal attributes.

The specific content of candidates' images has varied greatly, and, as can be seen in Figure 8-1, no single pattern appears associated with either party. Perhaps the most prominent feature of this series is its downward trend. Presidential candidates of both parties are viewed far less favorably now than in the past. The disenchantment with govern-

FIGURE 8-1 Images of the Democratic and Republican Presidential Candidates, 1952-1992

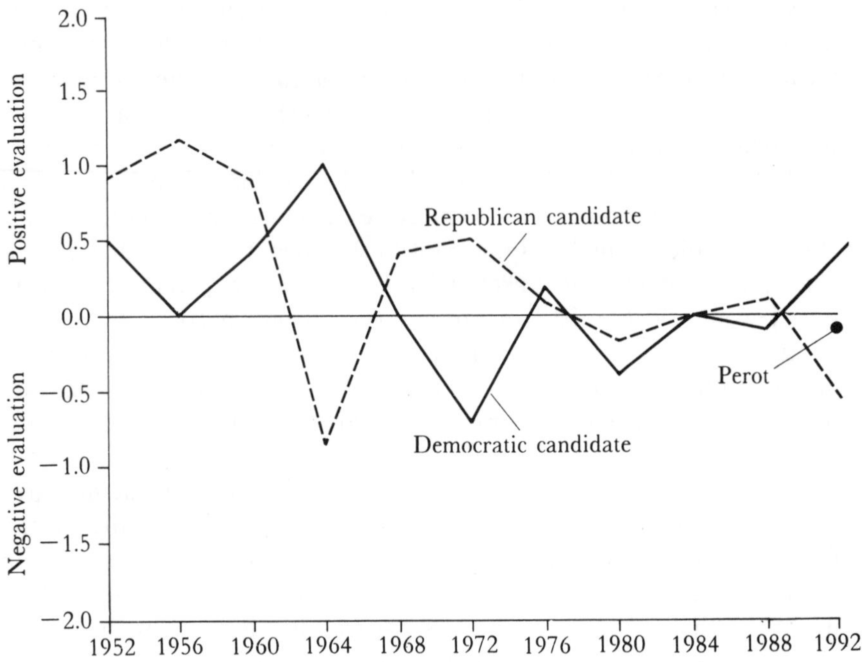

SOURCE: Warren E. Miller and Santa Traugott, *American National Election Studies Data Sourcebook, 1952-1986* (Cambridge, Mass.: Harvard University Press, 1989), 113, 115; Center for Political Studies National Election Studies.

ment and politics, catalogued in Chapter 1, clearly extends to the personal images of the presidential candidates.

Dwight D. Eisenhower in 1952 and 1956 and Lyndon Johnson in 1964 had very positive images. Richard Nixon enjoyed a more favorable image than his various opponents in several elections. Although most American voters would ultimately revise their evaluations, in 1960 Nixon was more favorably perceived in personal terms than John Kennedy; his personal image rivaled Eisenhower's. Kennedy's image improved during his presidency, but his extraordinary popularity came after his assassination.

Sometimes a candidate enjoys an advantage because the opponent is extremely unpopular. Johnson had such an advantage over Barry Goldwater, as did Nixon over George McGovern. In 1972 McGovern was held in very low esteem; only about one-third of the public thought he could be trusted as president. Almost 60 percent thought Nixon could be trusted; George Wallace, although no longer a candidate, was viewed as more trustworthy than McGovern.

In both 1980 and 1984 the public's view of Ronald Reagan was more negative than positive. In both years a very large share of the negative comments referred to his age; while many people mentioned this point, it does not seem to have been an intensely unfavorable evaluation. One might say that Reagan did not need to be seen favorably because he had the good fortune to face opponents who were even more negatively evaluated by the public. Both Jimmy Carter and Walter Mondale were viewed as weak. Many people thought Mondale was dishonest or unprincipled. In the elections of 1980 and 1984 all the candidates were viewed more negatively than positively, which represented a new low in candidate appeal.

In 1988 the images of George Bush and Michael Dukakis were quite evenly balanced, with Bush's image slightly more positive than negative and Dukakis's image slightly more negative than positive. Bush was seen as vastly more experienced than Dukakis, an advantage that more than offset the negative evaluations associated with Bush's involvement with the Iran-contra scandal during the Reagan administration. For the first time in many years the public viewed a candidate's Republicanism more favorably than his opponent's affiliation with the Democratic party.

By 1992 Bush's image had deteriorated to one of the worst in forty years; only Goldwater and McGovern had been viewed more unfavorably. Bush's reneging on his promise about "no new taxes" and his perceived responsibility for the bad state of the economy were the most damaging contributors to his image problem. By contrast, Bill Clinton had, on balance, a quite positive image. He was not viewed so favorably in personality terms (for example, on traits such as honesty and experience, or for his avoidance of military service during Vietnam), but this perception was more than offset by positive comments about his views on a wide range of issues. Respondents mentioned Clinton's positions on health care or the deficit as things they liked about him. By any standards, Clinton's image was unusually issue-based.

Perot strongly influenced the tone and content of the 1992 presidential election, but his success was not based on a positive image with the general public. Actually Perot's image was slightly negative, in significant part because of concerns about his lack of experience and his temporary withdrawal from the race in mid-summer. Ironically, the most positive aspect of Perot's image was, likewise, his lack of experience. His background as a businessman and not as a politician appealed to many. For all his prominence as a third candidate in the race, Perot remained less well known than Bush and Clinton throughout the campaign.

This form of analysis, which simply counts the number of positive and negative comments about the candidates, should be viewed cautiously since the relative seriousness of the complaints—for example, being old versus being unprincipled—is not taken into account. In addition, the comments about the candidates are in response to a question about what the respondent likes and dislikes about the candidate. They range from comments on very personal traits ("He's dishonest.") to those quite removed from the personality of the candidate ("I like what he's saying about health care."). Although both are counted as reflecting feelings about the candidate's image, they are quite different in tone. Given the unusually high number of issue-related comments about Clinton in 1992, we need to be careful not to interpret his candidate image as reflecting only personality traits.

A good deal of nonsense has been written in recent years about winning elections by manipulating the images of the candidates, mainly through the mass media. The implication has been that the images of candidates are easily created and altered, but actually to do either appears difficult and expensive. Some elements in candidate images may be susceptible to manipulation through skillful public relations work, but many elements are not.[1] In 1960 Kennedy's Catholicism prompted both positive and negative reactions, but such impressions cannot be controlled or altered much by candidates or their agents. The Kennedy organization did have some choices about making an issue of religion, but once the decision was made there was less leeway in controlling the impact of the issue.

In most other cases, candidates have little control in deciding whether to raise certain topics, for often the opponent will do so anyway. In 1972 McGovern could do little about the impression he created by dropping his vice-presidential candidate, Thomas Eagleton, from the ticket, nor could Gerald Ford erase the effects of his pardon of Nixon. Carter would not have been able to create the impression that the hostages had been freed while they were still held in Teheran.

An incumbent candidate or a former vice president benefits from a perception of being experienced, which is not purely a result of campaign advertising. Neither can negative reactions aroused by being involved in an unpopular administration be avoided. As an example,

Bush, like most incumbents, was seen as experienced, but in 1992 this positive trait was overwhelmed by the view that he had mishandled the economy.

The public's impressions of candidates for major office seem to be realistic, gained primarily through ordinary news coverage. This is not to say that these images are completely accurate or fair or sophisticated, but neither are they fictitious pictures created by public relations personnel.

Unlike incumbents and established candidates, presidential candidates who are less well known have a greater opportunity to create a favorable image during the relatively brief period of the campaign. Conversely, such candidates are also more vulnerable to an attempt by an opponent to pin an unattractive image on them. The relatively unknown Clinton was vulnerable to this phenomenon throughout 1992. It is quite remarkable that he survived the series of unfavorable additions to his personal image. To some extent he compensated for his personal image problems by making a favorable impression on so many voters with his spirited discussion of issues.

The 1992 election year was typical of the volatility of support for less well-known candidates such as Clinton and Perot. Trial heat data from the Gallup Poll when all three candidates were in the race showed Perot's support varying from a high of 39 percent to a low of 7 percent between June and November. We might suppose that this marked variation was a function of Perot's temporary departure from the race, but Clinton's support fluctuated almost as much during the same period, from a low of 24 percent to a high of 52 percent. In contrast, during the same months Bush's support varied only between 31 and 37 percent.

Very few candidates for other offices are as well known or as well publicized as candidates for the presidency. Most candidates in most elections are unknown quantities for the average voter. Typically, voters will be aware of the candidate's party affiliation and whether he or she is an incumbent, but not much more. In fact, these pieces of information may come to the attention of the voter only if they are indicated on the ballot.

Normally, the impact of candidate image on vote choice declines as one goes farther down the ticket to less visible and less well-known offices. This does not mean that the candidate's personal qualities are unimportant in winning election to these offices. They may be of paramount importance in obtaining the nomination or endorsement of the party organization, in raising financial support, in putting together a campaign staff, and in gaining backing from the leadership of influential organizations. But these personal attributes are unlikely to influence the decisions of the average voter simply because the voter is unlikely to be aware of them.

Party Image

The images of the parties are another factor that can influence the voting decisions of the electorate. Even though party images are strongly colored by longstanding party loyalties, the focus of this analysis is a set of potentially variable attitudes toward the parties that can be viewed as short-run forces at work in an election. Party images also affect and are affected by the images of the candidates running under the party label and by the attitudes toward issues espoused by the candidates or the party platforms. These factors can be kept distinct conceptually, though it may be impossible to disentangle the various effects in any actual situation.

The changing perceptions of the parties' abilities to keep the country out of war are shown in Figure 8-2. Traditionally, the Republican party has been favored in this area during presidential contests, with the advantage being reversed several times in the past forty years. Until recently the Democratic party has been viewed fairly consistently as the party of prosperity. There are brief lapses in this pattern, displayed in Figure 8-3, but overall the Democrats have enjoyed a clear advantage over the Republicans. With the start of the Reagan administration, the Republicans became the party of prosperity in the public's view. This image lasted through 1981 and then reverted for two years as the economy slid into recession. In 1984 and 1985, the Republican party's image as the party of prosperity was restored by margins greater than either party had enjoyed since before 1980. By late 1992 the Democratic party had regained the advantage on both dimensions over the Republicans.

The role of party images in vote choice has been labeled "retrospective voting" by Morris Fiorina, who argued that voters continuously evaluate the performance of the political parties, especially the president's party.[2] Voters use this evaluation of past performance as an indicator of future performance, and they take this retrospective assessment into account in making their vote choices. Since these assessments are likely to involve the performance of the current administration, questions about the incumbent president's handling of various policy areas have been used as indicators of the extent of retrospective voting. In a sophisticated analysis of presidential voting in 1988, Warren Miller

FIGURE 8-2 Attitudes on Which Party Is More Likely to Keep the Country Out of War, 1939-1992

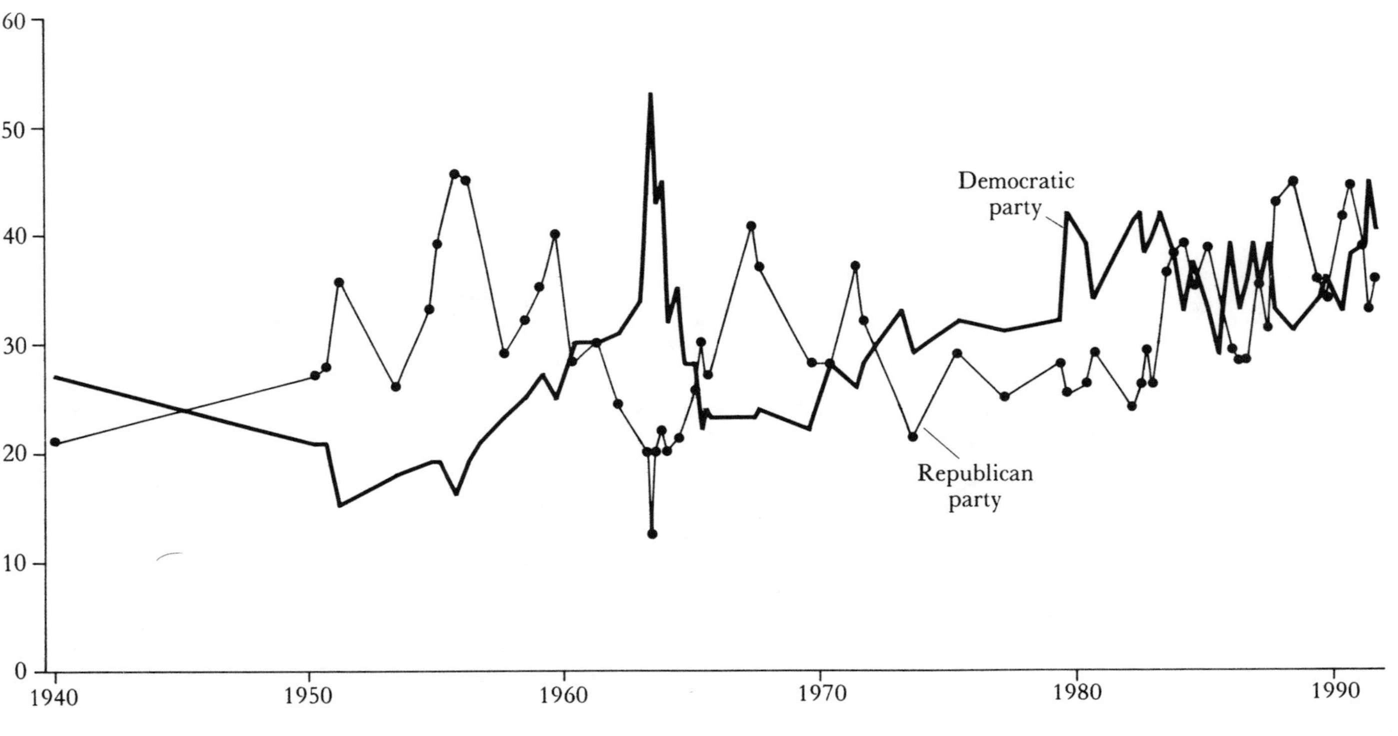

SOURCE: *The Gallup Report*, No. 277 (October 1988): 5; No. 286 (July 1989): 4; No. 322 (July 1992): 47; No. 325 (October 1992): 27.

FIGURE 8-3 Attitudes on Which Party Will Do a Better Job of Keeping the Country Prosperous, 1951-1992

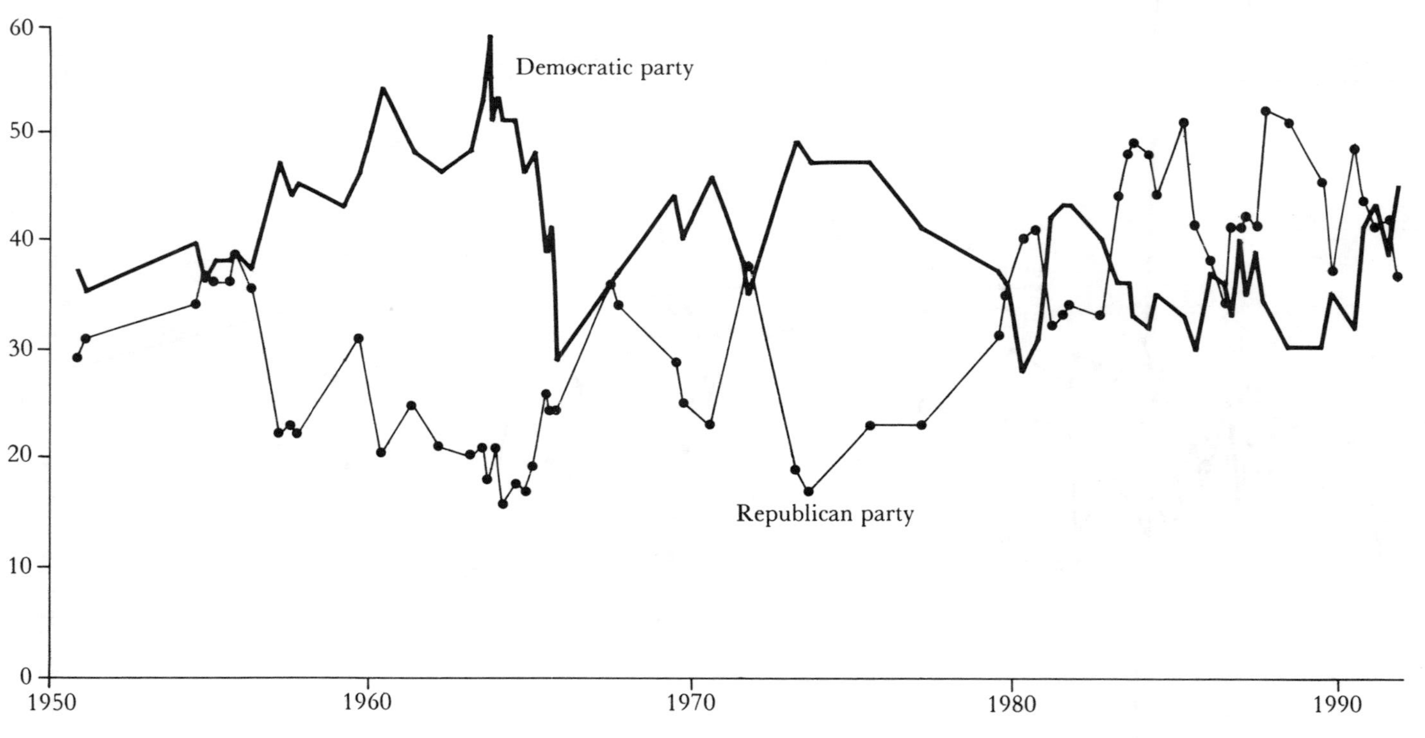

SOURCE: *The Gallup Report*, No. 277 (October 1988): 5; No. 286 (July 1989): 4; No. 322 (July 1992): 46; No. 325 (October 1992): 27.

and Merrill Shanks demonstrated that voters' approval or disapproval of Reagan's performance as president had a noticeable impact on the choice between Bush and Dukakis.[3] We will use President Bush's approval ratings as an indicator of retrospective evaluations in a later section on the determinants of vote choice.

Party images and presidential evaluations are strongly related to partisanship, with partisans more likely to embrace positive images of their party and to reject negative ones than independents or partisans of the opposition. Partisanship and party image, however, are not synonymous, for individuals often share unfavorable perceptions of their party without changing party identification. Yet, at some point, negative images of one's own party or positive perceptions of the other party undoubtedly lead to partisan change.

The images of local or state parties may be considerably different from and independent of those of their national counterpart. A state or local party organization may be perceived in different terms from the national party, and many a local or state party has gained a reputation for ineptitude or corruption that did not influence voting decisions for national offices. At the same time, these local images may become increasingly important in voting for offices at lower levels since party labels become a more important identifying characteristic in those races.

Issue Impact

Obviously, candidate images and party images may be closely related to issues, and under some circumstances are indistinguishable. The perception of the stands of candidates and parties on issues is a basis for making vote choices, a basis usually distinct from either personality characteristics or longstanding symbolism. Most significantly, candidates can establish issue positions or alter their appeals through their presentation of issues in ways that are not applicable to personal images or party characteristics. Candidates cannot change their experience or religion or party, but they can take new stands on issues or attempt to change the salience of issues. It is feasible, then, for candidates to attempt to appeal for votes on the basis of issues.

Over the years, considerable commentary has focused on the rise of single-issue voting. Collections of voters, caring intensely about a particular issue, vote for whichever candidate is closest to their views on that issue, regardless of the candidate's party, personal characteristics, or positions on other issues. There is nothing new about this phenomenon.

The classic example of single-issue voting in American politics was abolition, an issue of such intensity that it destroyed the Whig party, launched several new parties including the Republican party, and was a major contributing factor to the Civil War. Abortion is currently an issue that determines the way many people will vote.

Although organizational sophistication and increased opportunities for dissemination of information make single-issue groups a potent force in American politics today, politically ambitious candidates have always searched for issues of this type to help them gain a following. At the same time, incumbent candidates and the broadly based political parties have seen advantages in avoiding or glossing over such issues. Intense concentration on a single issue is potentially divisive and damaging to parties that must appeal to a broad range of voters or to those in office who must cast votes on a wide range of issues. Nevertheless, the political opportunity for the candidate who can capture a group of voters willing to vote on the basis of a single issue or cluster of issues is so great that it is unlikely that any intense concern in the electorate will be long ignored.

Several characteristics of electoral behavior conflict with this description of the role of issues in influencing vote choice. For one thing, in most elections many voters are unaware of the stands taken by candidates on issues. Voters commonly believe that the candidates they support agree with them on issues. This suggests that voters may project their issue positions onto their favorite candidate more often than they decide to vote for candidates on the basis of their position on issues. Furthermore, when voters agree on issues with the candidate they support, they may have adopted this position merely to agree with their candidate. Actually, candidates and other political leaders frequently perform this function for members of the electorate; they provide issue leadership for their following.

Within the enormous range of possible issues at any given time, complete indifference to many is quite common. Most issues important to political leaders remain in this category for the general public. In general, American voters are assumed to care about domestic economic issues, if they care about any issue, and to be indifferent to foreign policy issues. A related but different emphasis casts this relationship in a broader pattern: Voters care intensely about an issue when they are suffering or perceive a threat. Usually the easiest threat to understand is economic, whereas the most difficult threats to comprehend are in the area of foreign policy. The famous reminder in the 1992 Clinton campaign headquarters, "It's the economy, stupid," recognized the truth behind this generalization.

The extent to which voters are concerned with issues in making vote choices is a subject of considerable debate. Several prominent scholarly efforts were designed to rescue the voter from an undeserved reputation for not being issue oriented.[4] *The Changing American Voter,* by Norman Nie, Sidney Verba, and John Petrocik, documents a rise in issue voting associated with the election of 1964.[5] According to their data, the correlation between attitudes on issues and vote choice peaked in the ideological Johnson-Goldwater campaign but remained through 1972 at a considerably higher level than in the "issueless" 1950s. More recently, in a thorough assessment of the impact of issues in the elections of 1980, 1984, 1988, and 1992, Merrill Shanks and Warren Miller found relatively low levels of issue impact.[6]

Apart from the depressed condition of the economy, there were no particularly influential issues in the 1992 election, but people with different positions on issues varied in their vote preferences in many instances. We find this pattern in the choice between Bush and Clinton, at any rate, although there is relatively little connection between issue positions and voting for Perot.

Tables 8-1 through 8-4 show the relationship between voters' positions on a series of issues and their votes for Bush, Clinton, or Perot. In many respects, these tables are what we would expect. Voters taking the more liberal position are more likely to vote for Clinton than those taking the more conservative position. Conversely, as voters take the more conservative position, the vote for Bush increases. This pattern is strongest on the issues analyzed in the first two tables.

Table 8-1 shows the rather traditional domestic economic issue of decreasing government services to reduce spending versus increasing services and spending. Those voters who favor cutting services and spending supported Bush strongly and by a large margin over Clinton or Perot. Clinton's vote increases and Bush's declines as one moves across the table to voters who favor increased services. Table 8-2 shows that voters who favor government programs to help blacks overwhelmingly supported Clinton. Support for him diminished considerably while it increased for Bush among those voters who thought blacks should help themselves. On these, as with most other issues, there is very little relationship with the Perot vote; his support is quite similar across the whole range of opinion.

Since both these issues deal with themes that long have divided the parties, it is not surprising that we find substantial relationships between holding a certain view and supporting a particular candidate. As we

TABLE 8-1 Presidential Vote and Attitude toward Increasing or Decreasing Government Services, 1992

	Decrease government services	←		Neutral		→	Increase government services
Bush	59%	61%	49%	28%	22%	15%	19%
Clinton	23	17	27	53	65	63	68
Perot	18	22	24	20	13	22	13
Total	100%	100%	100%	101%	100%	100%	100%
(*N*)	(86)	(155)	(240)	(468)	(263)	(125)	(110)

SOURCE: Center for Political Studies 1992 National Election Study. Data provided by the Inter-university Consortium for Political and Social Research.

TABLE 8-2 Presidential Vote and Attitude toward Government Help for Blacks, 1992

	Government help for blacks	←		Neutral		→	Let blacks help themselves
Bush	10%	11%	22%	30%	46%	46%	42%
Clinton	83	72	61	51	38	30	38
Perot	7	17	17	19	16	24	20
Total	100%	100%	100%	100%	100%	100%	100%
(*N*)	(83)	(82)	(180)	(426)	(229)	(224)	(299)

SOURCE: Center for Political Studies 1992 National Election Study. Data provided by the Inter-university Consortium for Political and Social Research.

TABLE 8-3 Presidential Vote and Attitude toward Defense Spending, 1992

	Cut defense spending	←		Neutral		→	Increase defense spending
Bush	10%	13%	33%	45%	44%	41%	36%
Clinton	75	62	49	36	39	36	51
Perot	16	25	18	19	17	23	13
Total	101%	100%	100%	100%	100%	100%	100%
(*N*)	(126)	(236)	(364)	(507)	(172)	(55)	(39)

SOURCE: Center for Political Studies 1992 National Election Study. Data provided by the Inter-university Consortium for Political and Social Research.

TABLE 8-4 Presidential Vote and Attitude toward Abortion, 1992

	Pro-life ←			→ Pro-choice
Bush	47%	46%	42%	22%
Clinton	40	38	39	58
Perot	12	16	19	20
Total	99%	100%	100%	100%
(*N*)	(139)	(435)	(236)	(801)

SOURCE: Center for Political Studies 1992 National Election Study. Data provided by the Inter-university Consortium for Political and Social Research.

move to issues not traditionally associated with either party, the relationships are less strong, though still clear.

The relationship between defense spending and vote choice in Table 8-3 shows Clinton's support highest among those voters who want to cut defense spending, whereas Bush had little support among such voters. Table 8-4 shows that a voter's position on abortion also is related to his or her vote for a particular presidental candidate. Pro-life voters favored Bush, while pro-choice voters favored Clinton. This is the only issue that shows any relationship to a vote for Perot. Pro-choice voters were more likely to vote for Perot than were pro-life voters (though pro-choice voters still strongly favored Clinton over Perot).

The absence of a relationship between issues and voting for Perot demonstrates in part how difficult it is for candidates to convey to the public information about themselves. Perot spent a great deal of time and money presenting his positions on issues, but to the end of the campaign many voters, including a good number who voted for him, never clearly grasped his issue stands. Given his support from voters with very different issue positions, clarifying matters might have cost Perot votes. It is very likely his supporters did not care about issues so much as casting a vote against "politics as usual."

Figure 8-4 looks at vote choice in a somewhat different manner by illustrating the electorate's perceptions of the ideological positions of Bush, Clinton, and Perot as well as the relationship between the voters' own ideological positions and their vote choices among the three candidates. In the 1992 NES survey, voters were asked to locate each candidate on a seven-point scale ranging from "extremely liberal" to "extremely conservative." In Figure 8-4 the frequency distributions in the lower half of the chart illustrate the voters' perceptions of the three candidates' ideological positions. For example, 7 percent of the respondents labeled Clinton as extremely liberal, and only 2 percent labeled him extremely conservative. Eleven percent placed Bush in the most

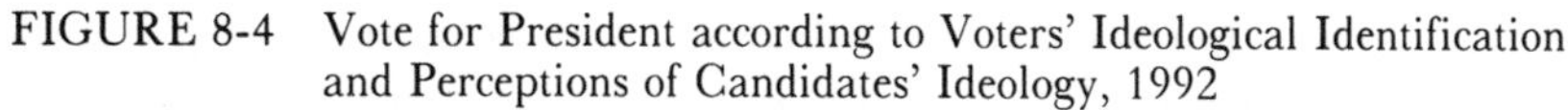

FIGURE 8-4 Vote for President according to Voters' Ideological Identification and Perceptions of Candidates' Ideology, 1992

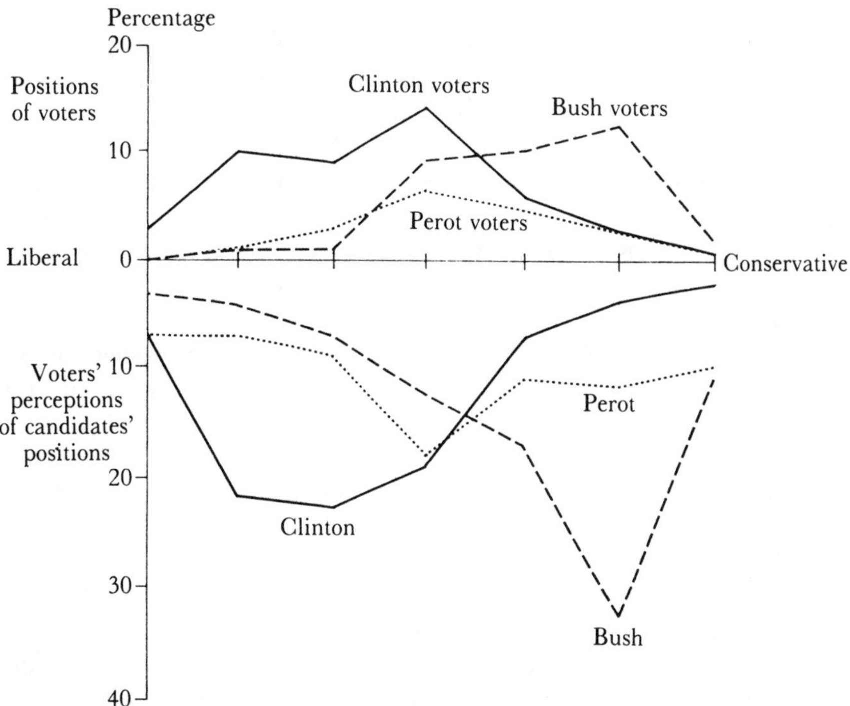

SOURCE: Center for Political Studies 1992 National Election Study. Data provided by the Inter-university Consortium for Political and Social Research.

NOTE: In the top half of the figure, the percentages represented by points along the three lines sum to 100 percent, that is, all percentages are calculated over the total number of voters. In the bottom half of the figure, the points along each line sum to 100 percent, that is, the perceptions about each candidate are calculated separately over the total number of respondents.

extreme conservative position. Most voters placed Clinton on the liberal end of the scale and placed Bush on the conservative side. More voters (18 percent) put Perot in the middle category than in any other. (Another 25 percent, not shown in the figure, did not attempt to locate Perot on the scale.)

Voters were also asked about their own ideological position using the same seven-point scale. The distributions in the upper half of Figure 8-4 indicate Bush, Clinton, and Perot voters' self-placements. They show that Bush drew most of his support from conservative voters, while Clinton received most of the liberal vote. It is significant that Clinton also gained the lion's share of the votes of those in the middle of the ideological spectrum. Perot's support is spread across the ideological spectrum as it was across the range of issues.

A number of factors must be present for issues to have an impact on vote choice: first, voters must be informed and concerned about an issue; second, candidates must take distinguishable stands on an issue; and third, voters must perceive the candidates' stands in relation to their own. As we have seen, these conditions often are not achieved. Voters may be unable to locate themselves or the candidates on one or more issues. In 1992, 18 percent of the electorate had no opinion on government spending versus cutting government services. An additional 11 percent were unable to locate the candidates' positions on this issue. Similar proportions of the electorate could not locate themselves or the candidates on the issue of defense spending. Voters may misperceive the candidates' positions. For example, some voters viewed Clinton as an extreme conservative or Bush as an extreme liberal. If candidates take the same positions—both Perot and Clinton took pro-choice positions—a voter wishing to vote on that basis could choose either one.

It also has been suggested that the lack of a strong relationship between an individual's issue positions and vote choice results from the fact that the analyst chooses the issues for analysis, issues that are not necessarily important to the individual. If the voter is allowed to define what he or she sees as the most important issue, a somewhat stronger relationship between his or her position on issues and voting decisions is found.[7]

Others have argued that a rational and issue-oriented voter judges the past performance of the candidates rather than simply comparing the candidates' promises for the future.[8] For example, in 1980 Carter was widely perceived as unable to govern effectively, and for many voters this was a more prominent concern than their relative proximity to the candidates on the issues. In 1992 Bush was viewed as having mishandled the economy. That fact dominated other issue considerations.

Furthermore, this analysis does not tell us what causes these relationships. Perception of issues may cause an individual's vote choice; alternatively, a preference for a candidate on other grounds may lead individuals to adjust their perceptions of issues in support of their vote choice. No data are available that would conclusively resolve this question. Regardless of the causal relationship, it is significant that, although many voters lack opinions on issues or on the candidates' positions, those who do have opinions show considerable consistency between issue positions and vote choice.

Determinants of Vote Choice

The preceding sections considered candidate images, party images, and issues as short-term forces that either reinforce or deflect voters from their long-term party loyalty. An interesting, but far more difficult, question is the relative impact of these various factors on vote choice. Since all these factors are strongly interrelated and almost certainly all influence each other, it is virtually impossible to disentangle their effects with the kind of data available in nationwide surveys. If one assumes that issues are all-important in determining vote choice, most voting behavior can be accounted for by issues alone, ignoring other factors. On the other hand, if one assumes that party identification and a few social characteristics are all-important, most voting behavior can be accounted for with these variables, ignoring issues. The conflicting conclusions that are reached are largely a matter of the theoretical assumptions with which one starts.

In light of these difficulties, some analysis of the impact of short-term forces has focused on the unique impact of each element in the presence of others. One of the best examples of this mode of analysis is Donald Stokes's effort to measure attitudinal forces influencing presidential vote choices.[9] Following Stokes's method, Arthur Miller and Martin Wattenberg have analyzed the nine presidential elections from 1952 to 1984 (see Table 8-5).[10] Negative values indicate a factor that helped the Democratic candidate; positive values indicate a benefit to the Republican candidate. The perception of group benefits is a consistently large pro-Democratic element in all nine elections. Foreign policy matters have almost always helped the Republican candidate, with the exception of Goldwater in 1964 and Reagan in 1984. The impact of foreign affairs and domestic policies was unusually strong and pro-Republican in 1980. This reflected the strongly unfavorable reactions to Carter's handling of the economy and the Iranian hostage crisis. In contrast, the candidates' personalities had an unusually weak influence on vote choice in 1980. Evidence presented by Shanks and Miller also suggests that personalities played a small role in voting for president in that year.[11] In contrast, in 1984 foreign and domestic policy considerations had declined in importance, but the personalities of the candidates had become significantly pro-Republican factors.

Almost all discussion of vote choice in the United States has understandably focused on just two candidates. A rich, complex tradition of analysis has developed over the years. Unfortunately for this tradition, the 1992 presidential election was a three-candidate race, and the usual

TABLE 8-5 Net Impact of Six Attitudinal Components in Determining Vote Choice, 1952-1984

	1952	1956	1960	1964	1968	1972	1976	1980	1984
Domestic policy	−1.3	−0.9	−0.5	−2.4	1.1	1.4	−0.7	3.1	1.5
Foreign policy	3.3	2.5	1.8	−0.3	1.0	3.2	0.4	2.8	−0.3
Party management	5.4	1.2	1.2	−0.3	1.5	0.0	0.2	0.6	0.5
Group benefits	−4.3	−5.5	−4.0	−2.6	−3.6	−4.6	−4.5	−4.5	−5.6
Democratic candidate	−1.2	0.2	−2.0	−4.0	0.9	4.3	−0.1	−0.4	1.3
Republican candidate	4.4	7.6	5.7	−2.6	1.6	4.0	2.2	−0.5	1.5

SOURCES: For 1952-1980, Arthur H. Miller and Martin P. Wattenberg, "Policy and Performance Voting in the 1980 Election," cited in *Controversies in Voting Behavior,* 2d ed., ed. Richard Niemi and Herbert Weisberg (Washington, D.C.: CQ Press, 1984), 91; for 1984, Martin P. Wattenberg (personal communication).

NOTE: Positive values are pro-Republican effects; negative values indicate a Democratic advantage. The values can be interpreted as the percentage of the vote moved in one partisan direction or the other.

forms of analysis are not usable. Table 8-6 presents data that analyze presidential vote choice in 1992 in two ways. The first three columns report analysis of the factors influencing vote choice as if the election were a series of two-candidate races. The choices between candidates are analyzed two at a time, with the third candidate ignored. In the last three columns, each candidate is pitted against the combination of the other two. The larger the absolute value of the coefficient, the more influence that factor had on vote choice in that contest. The R^2 at the bottom of the column indicates how well all the factors, taken together, account for the choice made.

By treating the 1992 presidential election as if it involved six different races, we can draw certain general conclusions. Regardless of how we view the separate candidate choices, party identification appears a major determinant of the vote. This may seem odd with Perot, a candidate without a party, among the choices, but the relationship of partisanship to the choice of Bush or Clinton is strong enough to dominate the presence of Perot. (In the analysis of Perot versus the field in the last column, we compared independents with partisans of both parties. Party identification was related to the Perot vote insofar as he was disproportionately supported by independents rather than partisans.)

It should also be noted that the retrospective evaluation of President Bush as measured by his approval ratings was strongly related to a vote for or against him but irrelevant, naturally, to the choice between Clinton and Perot. Retrospective evaluation of Bush—more disapproval than approval—was the strongest factor influencing voters for or against him.

Ideology had a relatively modest impact on vote choice in 1992, but it tends to be more important than the various issues presented in Table 8-6. Across the various "races" in the table, government guarantees of a job, a New Deal-style issue, generally had the most impact on voting. In some comparisons, the abortion issue appears to have a slight effect, but foreign policy rarely does.

As with most previous analysis of presidential elections, party identification and retrospective evaluation appear to be most strongly related to vote choice—even when the analysis is complicated by a third candidate. While not as potent as those two elements, ideology is also important and should not be ignored. Issue impact is part of the overall process of vote choice but a distinctly minor part.

During the conventions and the brief period of the campaign, political parties cannot do much about the basic strength each party

TABLE 8-6 Determinants of Presidential Vote Choice, 1992

Vote determinants	Bush versus Clinton	Bush versus Perot	Clinton versus Perot	Bush versus the field	Clinton versus the field	Perot versus the field
Party identification	.30	.10	−.36	.24	−.36	.22 [a]
Ideology	.15	.13	−.12	.12	−.15	.05 [b]
Bush approval rating	−.41	−.43	.09	−.42	.25	.08
Domestic policy						
Government job guarantee	.08	.06	−.07	.06	−.08	.06
Abortion	−.03	−.08	−.03	−.05	−.00	.03
Foreign policy						
Bush approval rating in foreign affairs	−.02	.02	.01	−.00	.02	−.03
Keeping the United States out of war	−.02	−.01	.07	−.02	.04	−.05
R^2	.63	.33	.25	.50	.48	.07
(*N*)	(1,006)	(688)	(798)	(1,246)	(1,246)	(1,246)

SOURCE: Center for Political Studies 1992 National Election Study. Data provided by the Inter-university Consortium for Political and Social Research.

NOTE: Entries are standardized partial regression coefficients.

[a] Party identification "folded over" so that "strong partisans" were coded 1, "weak partisans," 2, and so forth.

[b] Ideology "folded over" so that "strong ideologues" were coded 1, "weak ideologues," 2, and so forth.

commands; therefore, they concentrate on presenting candidate images and issue positions calculated to have greatest appeal to the uncommitted voters. Even if the outcome of an election is not substantially affected by party strategies, the content of the campaign and the meaning the election comes to have for leaders and the public are created by these strategies. The information in Tables 8-5 and 8-6 can be viewed as measures of the content of the campaign and its meaning for voters.

Vote Choice in Other Types of Elections

We have suggested that vote choice can be thought of as the product of a voter's long-term partisanship and the impact of the campaign's short-term forces of candidate characteristics, issue positions, and evaluation of the party's performance. In presidential elections, in which information about the candidates and issues is widespread and easily available, short-term forces often overcome partisanship and cause substantial numbers of voters to defect from a party. As we consider less prominent races, voters make choices with less information and fewer factors influence their decisions.

Voting for the U.S. House of Representatives

In voting for members of Congress, most of the electorate has relatively little information about the candidates, especially candidates challenging incumbents. One of the results of this is a greater partisan stability from year to year in voting for Congress. This greater stability can be seen by looking at the aggregate vote for Congress since 1868, as shown in Figure 8-5. If one compares the congressional voting patterns in Figure 8-5 with the presidential vote in Figure 3-1, it is immediately clear that the congressional vote is considerably more stable in its partisan division than the vote for president. In addition, presidential elections show an increasing amount of variability since the end of the nineteenth century, whereas the congressional vote evidences, if anything, somewhat greater stability in the twentieth century. The higher visibility of presidential candidates and the greater availability of information about them through mass communication have led to a higher rate of defection from party lines in presidential voting. It is well established that party-line voting becomes stronger for less visible offices, since issues and personal attributes of the candidates are less likely to have an impact on the voter in less publicized races.

FIGURE 8-5 Partisan Division of the Nationwide Vote for Congress, 1868-1992

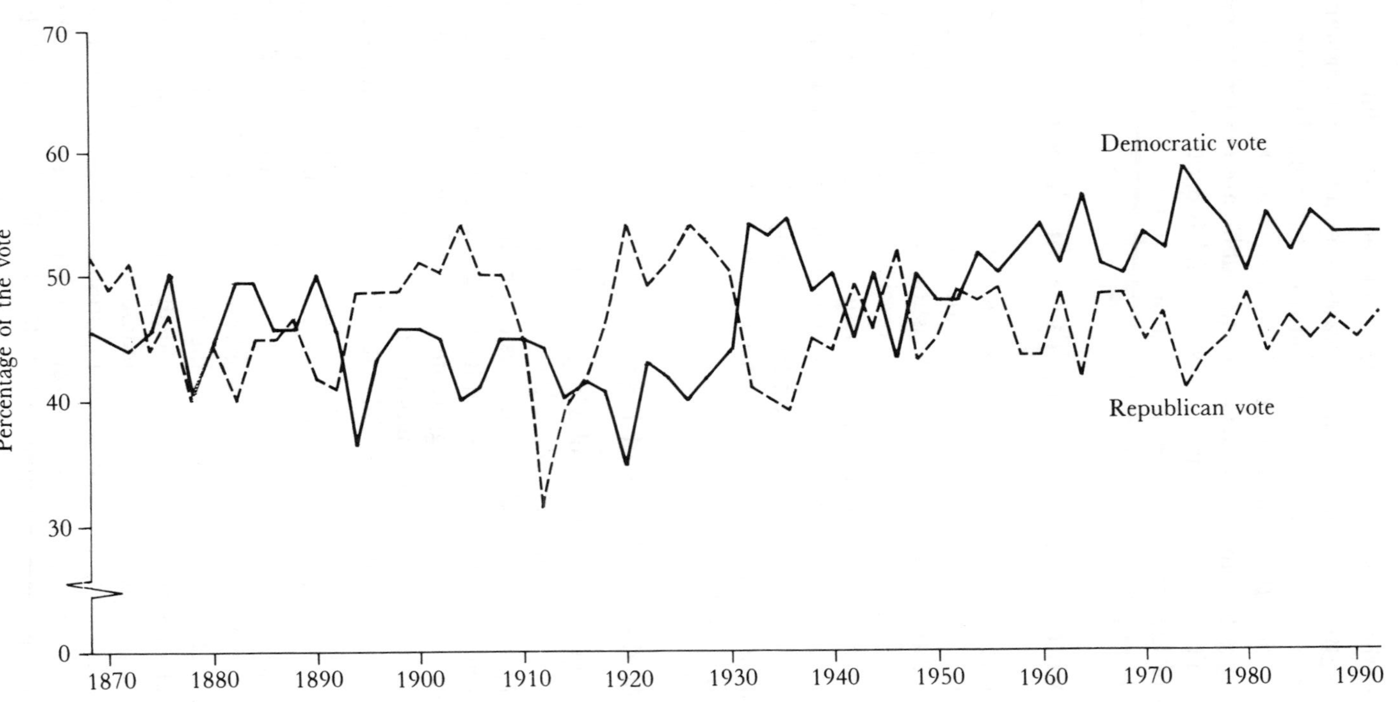

SOURCES: U.S. Bureau of the Census, *Statistical Abstract of the United States, 1992*, 112th ed. (Washington D.C.: U.S. Government Printing Office, 1992), 257; Inter-university Consortium for Political and Social Research.

Another very significant factor in congressional elections is incumbency. Studies have shown that voters are about twice as likely to be able to identify the incumbent as the challenger in congressional races, and almost all the defections from partisanship are in favor of the more familiar incumbent.[12] Both Republicans and Democrats seem strongly susceptible to voting for incumbents, with more than one-third typically abandoning their usual party for an incumbent representative of the other party. Strong partisans of both parties frequently defect to incumbents of the other party but on balance support the challengers from their own party more often than not. Both Democratic and Republican weak partisans, on the other hand, are more likely to defect for incumbents than to vote for challengers from their own party.

In recent decades more than 90 percent of the members of the House of Representatives have sought reelection, and all but a few have survived the occasional challenges for nomination or endorsement.[13] In 1992 this changed dramatically. Sixty-five of the 435 members of the House decided not to run for reelection. Another 19 incumbent members were defeated in primary elections, the largest number of such defeats in many years. The House bank scandal and the redrawing of district boundaries took a further toll on those incumbents who ran in the November general election, when another 24 were defeated. Through resignations and defeats, 110 freshman members of the House took office in January 1993, the largest group of new members since 1948. Nevertheless, the advantages of incumbency still operated to a significant degree. Of those who sought reelection, 88 percent were successful. For all the changes in membership, the partisan composition of the House was barely affected, with the Democrats retaining their comfortable majority.

The advantage that incumbents have does not mean that congressional districts are invariably safe for one party, though many are. Rather, it suggests that even in those districts where the outcome is virtually a toss-up when two nonincumbents face each other, the representatives who manage to survive their first few terms soon find reelection almost assured. This tendency becomes accentuated as the opposition party finds it increasingly difficult to field an attractive candidate to challenge a secure incumbent. Thus, many incumbent representatives are elected again and again by safe margins from districts that may easily fall to the other party once the incumbent no longer seeks reelection. Put another way, the existence of a safe incumbent in a district may say little about the underlying partisan division in that district. It may simply reflect short-term forces that were at work in the last election in which two nonincumbents faced each other. Basically, though, the bias in favor of incumbents means that changes in public sentiments are unlikely to be reflected quickly in changes in the composition of the House.

It is this fact as much as anything else that has led to the demand for term limits. The lack of turnover in Congress as a whole creates an image of unresponsive governance. Actually, most voters believe their own representative is doing a good job; it is Congress as a whole they object to. Perhaps if there were a way to express this preference, most people would impose term limits on everyone else's representative but not on their own.

Voting for the U.S. Senate

U.S. senators are in a somewhat different position than members of the House. In the past, incumbency was as potent an advantage for senators as for representatives, with about 85 percent of the incumbents reelected in an average year.[14] From the mid-1970s throughout the 1980s, however, senators were much more vulnerable, with up to a third of incumbent senators being defeated in some years. In 1990 and 1992 incumbency again appeared to almost guarantee victory. In 1992, for all the talk of change, once again 85 percent of the incumbent senators running in the general election were returned. One additional senator was defeated in a primary. The party division was unchanged in the Senate in 1992, and all in all the election appeared quite typical.

A number of factors suggest that incumbent senators may be more vulnerable to defeat than incumbent representatives. A Senate election has relatively high visibility and, unlike a congressional race, is amenable to a mass media campaign utilizing television. As more information about the election gets through to the voters, the less they rely on either partisanship or the familiarity of the incumbent's name. Indeed, the visibility of a race makes an incumbent senator vulnerable to a well-financed campaign by an attractive opponent; incumbency may, in fact, become a disadvantage in such circumstances since the incumbent has a voting record to defend.

Voting in Primaries

Another particularly important type of election, party primaries, where choices are made among candidates within a political party, eliminates the usual influence of partisanship and party images. Primary elections occur in many races, but most attention and analysis have been focused on presidential primaries in recent decades.

Primary elections are unusual in a number of ways. Not only are the candidates from the same political party, but they also frequently will not differ much from each other on major issues and ideology. The political similarity of the candidates in a primary contest may lead to great emphasis on the candidates' personalities. It has been argued, in fact, that candidates and their campaign organizations learn to emphasize candidate imagery during the primaries, and they carry this style into the general election even though it may be less appropriate.

Additionally, some factors become relevant in primary vote choice that do not appear in general elections. First, voters in a primary (who are likely to be fairly strong partisans) may be concerned with assessing how well each candidate would represent the party in the general election. In particular, some voters may support the primary candidate they perceive as having the best chance of winning the general election, even if that candidate is not their personal favorite.

A similar effect, the "bandwagon effect," is the tendency to support a candidate because of the perception that he or she will win the party's nomination. This is a specific form of *momentum,* or the tendency to support a candidate because that candidate appears to be gaining support.[15] Media commentary often attributes this to a psychological desire to "vote for a winner." Since this phenomenon, often alluded to in primary elections, rarely occurs in general elections, a better explanation is probably the recognition by partisans that a candidate rapidly gaining popular support represents the best chance to beat the opposing party in the general election.

The Meaning of an Election

Politicians and news commentators spend much time and energy interpreting and explaining the outcome of an election. The difficulties in assigning meaning to election results are easy to exaggerate; the most important element is usually quite clear—the winner. Elections are primarily a mechanism for selecting certain governmental leaders and, just as important, for removing leaders from office and preventing others from gaining office. Nevertheless, an effort is often made to discover the policy implications of patterns of voting and to read meaning into the outcome of elections. This effort raises two problems for analysis: first, the policy implications of the winning and losing candidates' issue stands and, second, the issue content of the voters' decisions.

In both 1980 and 1984 Reagan articulated an unusually clear set of ideological and policy alternatives. Not all elections offer voters a clear choice between a conservative and a liberal candidate, but the 1980 and 1984 races between Reagan and Carter and Reagan and Mondale were widely perceived as doing so. Since Reagan won both elections by wide margins, his administration understandably claimed a popular mandate for a wide range of policies.

It is perfectly appropriate to attribute policy significance to an election on the basis of the policy preference of the winning candidates, so long as it is not implied that the voters had these policy implications in mind when they voted. In other words, it is appropriate to observe, particularly in presidential elections, that the election outcome means lower taxes or an expanded program because the victor has pledged to implement lower taxes or to expand a program. But it is very difficult to establish that the voters' preferences have certain policy meaning or that the votes for a particular candidate provide a policy mandate. Several obstacles lie in the way of stating simply what policies are implied by the behavior of the voters. In many elections, the voters are unaware of the stands of candidates on issues, and sometimes the voters are mistaken in their perception of candidates' stands.

Furthermore, many voters are not concerned with issues as such in a campaign but vote according to their party loyalty or a candidate's personality. Their vote has no particular policy significance but reflects a general preference for one candidate. Voters who supported Reagan in 1980 had an unfavorable view of Carter's performance as president, especially his handling of the Iranian hostage crisis. The dissatisfaction with Carter was clear enough; however, the expectations about Reagan were quite vague and perhaps limited to the hope that he would strengthen national defense and balance the budget. In 1992 many voters cast a ballot against Bush because of dissatisfaction over the state of the economy, though not for any particular policies. This characteristic of the vote, added to Clinton's low percentage (well below 50 percent) of the overall vote, have made it difficult for him to claim any clear mandate. Instead, he has made the more vague claim that the repudiation of Bush by both the Clinton and Perot voters represented a mandate for change.

Occasionally in a congressional election an incumbent's loss can be traced to a position or action at odds with majority sentiment among the district's constituents. More commonly, election victories say more about the incumbent's attention to constituent service and the advantages of incumbency than about the policy views of the candidates or voters.

A candidate has considerable freedom under most circumstances to interpret a victory with respect to the issues. Obviously, President Reagan felt free to interpret his mandate as requiring a massive tax cut but not dictating a balanced budget. There was no more basis for this distinction in public opinion than a mandate to reduce social programs drastically. Most election outcomes are just this vague and conflicting with respect to most issues. This partially explains the failure of the American political system to impose policy stands on elected officials. This illustrates as well the opportunities for leadership afforded to electoral victors. If they are perceived as successful in handling their job, political leaders can convert their following to support their policies, and subsequently it will appear as if the public had demanded the policies in the first place.

It is also true that the supporters of a candidate usually do not intensely or widely oppose his or her stands. Voters will often vote for candidates who hold views they do not share, but these views are on matters of little interest to the voters. Presumably, voters seldom support candidates who hold views with which they disagree intensely.

American elections are hardly a classic model of democracy with rational, well-informed voters making dispassionate decisions. On the other hand, American elections provide an acceptable opportunity for parties and candidates to attempt to win or hold public office. Although the electorate is capable upon occasion of responding to issue appeals both positively and negatively, the electorate does not appear easily moved by most appeals. The electorate offers the parties modest opportunities to gain voters without offering extreme temptations to reckless appeals.

Notes

1. Some good research on the media and politics is available. See, for example, Doris Graber, *Media Power in Politics,* 2d ed. (Washington, D.C.: CQ Press, 1990); and Doris Graber, *Mass Media and American Politics,* 3d ed. (Washington, D.C.: CQ Press, 1989). For a scholarly survey of campaign techniques, see Dan Nimmo, *The Political Persuaders* (Englewood Cliffs, N.J.: Prentice-Hall, 1970).
2. Morris P. Fiorina, *Retrospective Voting in American National Elections* (New Haven, Conn.: Yale University Press, 1981).
3. Warren E. Miller and J. Merrill Shanks, "Alternative Interpretations of the 1988 Election: Policy Direction, Current Conditions, Presidential Performance,

and Candidate Traits" (Paper presented at the annual meeting of the American Political Science Association, Atlanta, 1989).

4. A good discussion of this topic in a single source is the collection of articles and commentary by Gerald Pomper, Richard Boyd, Richard Brody, Benjamin Page, and John Kessel in *American Political Science Review* 66 (June 1972): 415-470. See also Benjamin I. Page, *Choices and Echoes in Presidential Elections* (Chicago: University of Chicago Press, 1978).
5. Norman H. Nie, Sidney Verba, and John R. Petrocik, *The Changing American Voter* (Cambridge, Mass.: Harvard University Press, 1976), chap. 10.
6. J. Merrill Shanks and Warren E. Miller, "Policy Direction and Performance Evaluation: Complementary Explanations of the Reagan Elections" (Paper presented at the annual meeting of the American Political Science Association, New Orleans, 1985); Miller and Shanks, "Alternative Interpretations of the 1988 Election"; and Shanks and Miller, "Performance, Policy, Partisanship—and Perot: Complementary Interpretations of the 1992 Election" (Paper presented at the annual meeting of the American Political Science Association, Washington, D.C., 1993).
7. David RePass, "Issue Salience and Party Choice," *American Political Science Review* 65 (June 1971): 368-400.
8. Fiorina, *Retrospective Voting in American National Elections.*
9. Angus Campbell, Philip E. Converse, Warren E. Miller, and Donald E. Stokes, *The American Voter* (New York: John Wiley & Sons, 1960), 524-531; and Donald E. Stokes, "Some Dynamic Elements of Contests for the Presidency," *American Political Science Review* 62 (1966): 19-28.
10. Arthur H. Miller and Martin P. Wattenberg, "Policy and Performance Voting in the 1980 Election" (Paper presented at the annual meeting of the American Political Science Association, New York, 1981), cited in *Controversies in Voting Behavior,* 2d ed., ed. Richard Niemi and Herbert Weisberg (Washington, D.C.: CQ Press, 1984), 91.
11. Shanks and Miller, "Policy Direction and Performance Evaluation."
12. Donald E. Stokes and Warren E. Miller, "Party Government and the Saliency of Congress," *Public Opinion Quarterly* 26 (Winter 1962): 531-546.
13. Gary Jacobson, "Congress: A Singular Continuity," in *The Elections of 1988,* ed. Michael Nelson (Washington, D.C.: CQ Press, 1989), 127-152.
14. Barbara Hinckley, "Incumbency and the Presidential Vote in Senate Elections: Defining Parameters of Subpresidential Voting," *American Political Science Review* 64 (September 1970): 837.
15. For an excellent analysis of primary elections, see Larry M. Bartels, *Presidential Primaries and the Dynamics of Public Choice* (Princeton, N.J.: Princeton University Press, 1988).

Suggested Readings

Abramowitz, Alan I., and Jeffrey A. Segal. *Senate Elections.* Ann Arbor: University of Michigan Press, 1992. An extensive analysis of the factors contributing to election outcomes in Senate races.

Bartels, Larry M. *Presidential Primaries and the Dynamics of Public Choice.* Princeton, N.J.: Princeton University Press, 1988. The best available analysis of public opinion and vote choice during presidential primaries.

Fiorina, Morris P. *Retrospective Voting in American National Elections.* New

Haven, Conn.: Yale University Press, 1981. An important conceptual argument for viewing vote choice as judgments about the past.

Jacobson, Gary C. *The Politics of Congressional Elections.* 3d ed. New York: HarperCollins, 1992. An authoritative survey of a broad topic and the literature surrounding it.

Niemi, Richard G., and Herbert F. Weisberg. *Classics in Voting Behavior.* Washington, D.C.: CQ Press, 1993. Niemi and Weisberg. *Controversies in Voting Behavior.* 3d ed. Washington, D.C.: CQ Press, 1993. These two collections offer the best readings from decades of research on public opinion and voting behavior.

a p p e n d i x

Survey Research Methods

MANY OF THE data in this book have come from survey research, and most of the analysis reported has been based on findings from survey research. For more than thirty years the data from the National Election Studies of the Survey Research Center and the Center for Political Studies, as well as from other major survey projects in political science, have been available through the Inter-university Consortium for Political and Social Research and have formed the basis for countless research projects in many fields by scholars, graduate students, and undergraduates. Given this widespread use of survey data, it is appropriate to give some description of the data collection methods that underlie them.

During the last sixty years, social scientists have developed an impressive array of techniques for discovering and measuring individual attitudes and behavior. Basically, survey research relies on giving a standard questionnaire to the individuals to be studied. In most major studies of the national electorate, trained interviewers ask the questions and record the responses in a face-to-face interview with each respondent. A few studies depend on the respondents themselves filling out the questionnaires. Recently, the rising costs of survey research, the pressure for quick results, and the availability of random digit dialing have led commercial pollsters to rely increasingly on telephone interviewing.

There are four data-collection phases of survey research: (1) sampling, (2) questionnaire constructing, (3) interviewing, and (4) coding. In most instances, the methods of the Survey Research Center at the University of Michigan will be described.

Sampling

It may seem inappropriate to analyze the entire American electorate using studies composed of fewer than two thousand individuals, which is about the average number of respondents in the studies used in this book. But it would be prohibitively expensive to interview the entire electorate, and the only way to study public opinion nationally is by interviewing relatively few individuals who accurately represent the entire electorate. Probability sampling is the method used to assure that the individuals selected for interviewing will be representative of the total population. Probability sampling attempts to select respondents in such a way that every individual in the population has an equal chance of being selected for interviewing. If the respondents are selected in this way, the analyst can be confident that the characteristics of the sample are approximately the same as those of the whole population. It would be impossible to make a list of every adult in the United States and then draw names from the list randomly, so the Survey Research Center departs from such strict random procedures in three basic ways: the sample is stratified, clustered, and of households.

Stratification means that random selection occurs within subpopulations; in the United States the sample is customarily selected within regions to guarantee that all sections are represented and within communities of different sizes as well. *Clustering* means that relatively small geographical areas, called "primary sampling units," are randomly selected within the stratified categories so that many interviews are concentrated within a small area to reduce the costs and inconvenience for interviewers. Finally, the Survey Research Center samples *households* rather than individuals (although within households individuals are sampled and interviewed); this means that within sampling areas households are enumerated and selected at random. (This sampling procedure means that no respondents are selected on military bases, in hospitals, hotels, and prisons, or in other places where people do not live in households. However, after the enfranchisement of eighteen-year-olds the Survey Research Center began to include college dormitories as residences to be sampled.)

An alternative procedure for selecting respondents is quota sampling. The area where interviews are to be made may be picked by stratified sampling procedures, but at the last stage of selection the interviewer is given discretion to choose respondents according to quotas. Quotas usually cover several social characteristics, but the intention is to create a collection of respondents with proportions of quota-controlled characteristics identical to those in the population. For example, the quota might call for half the respondents to be men, half to be women; for one-third to be grade-school educated, one-third high-school educated, and one-third college educated; and so forth. The advantage of this procedure is that it is much faster and less expensive than probability sampling, but the disadvantages are severe. With quota sampling, the analyst cannot have confidence that respondents are representative of the total population because the interviewers introduce conscious or unconscious biases when selecting respondents. In the past, commercial polling organizations used quota sampling, which allowed the interviewer to have discretion over whom to interview. As a result, easily contacted people—like retired persons or young women at home with small children—were likely to be overrepresented in the sample.

Both methods of sampling depend heavily on the ability and integrity of the interviewers, but probability sampling does not permit interviewers to introduce biases. Most statistical techniques assume that probability sampling has been used in collecting the data.

Increasingly, the commercial polling organizations have turned to telephone interviewing as a faster and cheaper alternative to field interviewing. Random digit-dialing is typically used by these polling operations to select both listed and unlisted numbers and to give each number the same chance of being called. Obviously, this practice ignores individuals without telephones, but there are no major obstacles to drawing an excellent sample of telephone numbers. The problems begin at that point. Success in finding someone at home and completing a telephone interview is uneven and failures may run as high as 50 percent. Some polling organizations make repeated callbacks, and of course the chances of getting an answer increase with the number of callbacks.

Once the phone is answered, it is necessary to select a respondent from the household. Some randomizing procedure is typically used to select the respondent. If the respondent selected is not at home, either an appointment is arranged for a callback or the household is dropped. The more often respondents are lost in this way or refuse to be interviewed, the more the sample departs from its original design. These procedures are likely to generate a sample that is biased toward women, so all the polling organizations take steps to counter this tendency. These organizations differ in the degree to which they weight the results to compensate for other demographic biases.[1]

Probability sampling also can result in unrepresentative samples. Of particular concern is the *nonresponse rate,* that is, the number of respondents originally selected who refuse to be interviewed and thus do not appear in the sample.[2] Should these nonrespondents share some characteristic disproportionately, the resulting sample will underrepresent that type of person. For example, if residents of high crime neighborhoods, the elderly, or alienated people refuse to be interviewed at higher rates than others, the sample will have fewer of these people than occur in the population and thus the sample will be biased. Currently, survey organizations have the greatest difficulty getting interviews in the inner cities of the largest metropolitan areas. The likelihood is high that the people who consent to be interviewed in these areas are different from, and therefore not representative of, those who refuse.

Questionnaire Constructing

In survey questionnaires, several types of questions will ordinarily be used. Public opinion surveys began years ago with forced-choice questions that a respondent was asked to answer by choosing among a set of offered alternatives. For example, forced-choice questions frequently take the form of stating a position on public policy and asking the respondent to "agree" or "disagree" with the statement. The analysis in Chapter 6 was based in part on the answers to forced-choice questions on public policy that were used in Survey Research Center and Center for Political Studies questionnaires in which respondents were asked to "agree strongly," "agree," "disagree," or "disagree strongly." Some respondents either gave qualified answers that did not fit into these prearranged categories or had no opinions.

A major innovation associated with the Survey Research Center is the use of open-ended questioning. Open-ended questions give respondents the opportunity to express their opinions in their own way without being forced to select among categories provided by the questionnaire. Questions such as "Is there anything in particular you like about the Democratic party?" or "What are the most important problems facing the country today?" permit the respondents to answer in their own terms. Interviewers encourage respondents to answer such questions as fully as they can with neutral "probes" such as "Could you tell me more about that?" "Anything else?" and similar queries that draw forth more discussion. There is no doubt that open-ended questions are a superior method of eliciting accurate expressions of opinion.

There are two major disadvantages to open-ended questioning: (1) it places more of a burden on interviewers to record the responses; and (2) the burden of reducing the many responses to a dimension that can be analyzed is left for the coders. For example, if Americans are asked, "Do you think of yourself as a Democrat, a Republican, or an independent?" almost all the responses will fit usefully into the designated categories:

1. Democrat
2. Independent
3. Republican
4. Other party
5. I'm nothing; apolitical
6. Don't know
7. Refused to say
8. Not ascertained

If a relatively unstructured, open-ended question is used, however, such as "How do you think of yourself politically?" some people would answer with "Democrat," "Republican," and so forth, but many others might give answers that were quite different, such as "liberal," "conservative," "radical," "moderate," "pragmatic"—and these could not easily be compared with the partisan categories. Analysts often intend to force responses into a single dimension, such as partisanship, whether the respondents would have volunteered an answer along that dimension or not. This is essential if they are to develop single dimensions for analytic purposes. Modern survey research includes questions and techniques considerably more complex than these examples for establishing dimensions.

Interviewing

The selection of the sample depends in part on the interviewer, but even more important is the role of the interviewer in asking questions of the respondent and in recording the answers. Motivated, well-trained interviewers are crucial to the success of survey research. The interviewer has several major responsibilities. First, the interviewer must select the respondent according to sampling instructions. Second, the interviewer must develop rapport with the respondent so that he or she will be willing to go through with the interview, which may last an hour or more. Third, the interviewer must ask the questions in a friendly way and encourage the respondent to answer fully without distorting the answers. Finally, the interviewer must record the answers of the respondent fully and accurately. To accomplish these tasks with a high level of proficiency, a permanent staff of interviewers is trained and retrained by survey organizations.

Coding

Once the interviewers administer the questionnaires to respondents, the coders take over and reduce the verbal information to a numerical form, according to a code. Numeric information, unlike verbal information, can be processed and manipulated by high-speed, data-processing equipment. The coder's task may be simple or complex. For example, to code the respondent's sex requires a simple code: 1 = male, 2 = female. A data card or magnetic tape that contains information on the respondent will have a location designated for indicating the respondent's sex. A value of 1 will indicate male, and a value of 2 will indicate female. The code shown above in the list of partisan categories gives the numbers that would stand for various responses.

Some coding is very complicated, with elaborate arrays of categories. For example, coding the responses to a question such as "Is there anything in particular you like about the Democratic party?" might include fifty or one hundred categories covering such details as "I like the party's farm policies," "I like the party's tax program," and "I've just always been a Democrat." Some codes require the coders to make judgments about the respondents' answers; in political surveys these codes have included judgments on the level of sophistication of the respondents' answers and judgments as to the main reason for respondents' vote choices.

After the coders have converted the verbal information into numbers according to the coding instructions, the numbers are entered into the computer and readied for analysis. At this point, the survey research process ends; the political analysts take over to make what use of the data they can.

Validity of Survey Questions

A frequent set of criticisms directed at public opinion research questions the validity of the responses to survey items. Validity simply means the extent to which there is correspondence between the verbal response to a question and the actual attitude or behavior of the respondent that the question is designed to measure. There is no one answer to

Table A-1 Recalled Vote for President in 1960, 1962, and 1964

Recalled vote	1960	1962	1964
Kennedy	49%	56%	64%
Nixon	51	43	36
Other	[a]	[a]	[a]
Total	100%	99%	100%
(*N*)	(1,428)	(940)	1,124)

SOURCE: Survey Research Center National Election Studies. Data provided by the Inter-university Consortium for Political and Social Research.

[a] Less than 0.5 percent.

doubts about validity, since each item has a validity applicable to it alone. Some items are notoriously invalid; others have nearly perfect validity. Many survey items have not been independently tested for their validity, and for practical purposes, the researcher is forced to say that he or she is interested in analyzing the responses, whatever they mean to the respondent. In other instances the sample result can be compared with the known population value.

The items with the most questionable validity in political studies come from those situations in which respondents have some incentive to misrepresent the facts or when their memories may not be accurate. Questions about voter turnout or level of income are noteworthy in this regard; validity checks reveal that respondents are about as likely to underestimate their income as overestimate it and a noticeable percentage of respondents claim to have voted when they did not.[3]

Recall of past voting behavior falls victim to failing memories and intervening events. Changes in party identification, past votes cast, the party identification of one's parents—all may contain substantial error. For example, during November and December immediately after the 1960 election, respondents were asked how they had voted for president. Most remembered voting for either John Kennedy or Richard Nixon, and, as shown in Table A-1, they were divided about evenly between the two. (The slight deviation of 1 percent from the actual results is within sampling error by any reasonable standards.) The 1962 and 1964 sample estimates of the 1960 vote reveal increasing departures from the actual outcome. Granting that some change in the population over four years may affect vote-choice percentages, a substantial proportion of the 1964 sample gave responses to the question of 1960 presidential vote choice that misrepresented their actual vote. The validity of this item always declines over a four-year period, but President Kennedy's assassination in the intervening years created an unusually large distortion in recalled vote.

Validity vs. Continuity

One of the important features of the National Election Studies is their continuity over a forty-year time span. Samples of the American population have been asked the same questions during every national election campaign throughout this period, offering an extraordinary opportunity for studying trends in the attitudes of the American electorate. The development of this valuable, continuous series does have one unfortunate aspect, however. Since the value of the series depends on the comparability of the questions, researchers are reluctant to alter questions, even when doubts about their validity arise. Improving the questions undermines comparability. Therefore, a choice between continuity and validity must be made.

The National Election Studies' questions concerning religious preference provide a recent example where validity was chosen over continuity. For years, respondents were simply asked, "What is your religious preference?" Although a small percentage in each survey answered "None," it was clear that a significant number of those answering "Protestant," and fewer numbers citing other religions, had in fact no meaningful religious affiliation. In the 1992 survey, the NES began asking the question differently. Respondents were first asked, "Do you ever attend religious services, apart from occasional weddings, baptisms and funerals?" Those who answered "no" were asked an additional question about their religious preference: "Regardless of whether you now attend any religious services, do you ever think of yourself as part of a particular church or denomination?" Those who did not answer "yes" to one of these two screening questions were not asked the traditional question about religious affiliation that then followed. As a result, the percentage of the population categorized as having no religious affiliation increased dramatically. This new question more validly reflects the religious sentiments of the American public, but it is now impossible to compare these later results with those of previous years. We cannot infer a large drop in religious affiliation on the basis of the responses to these new and different questions. In this instance, continuity has been sacrificed in favor of validity.

Despite inevitable concerns about validity, survey research provides the best means of investigating the attitudes and behavior of large populations of individuals such as the American electorate.

Notes

1. *Public Opinion* 4, (1) (February/March 1981): 20.
2. See John Brehm, *The Phantom Respondents* (Ann Arbor, Mich.: University of Michigan. Press, 1993).
3. Paul Abramson and William Claggett, "Race-Related Differences in Self-Reported and Validated Turnout," *Journal of Politics* 46 (August 1984): 719-738.

Suggested Readings

Asher, Herbert. *Polling and the Public.* Washington, D.C.: CQ Press, 1987. A good discussion of how polls are conducted and how they are used.

Backstrom, Charles H., and Gerald D. Hursh-César. *Survey Research,* 2d ed. New York: John Wiley & Sons, 1981. A good introduction to survey research methods.

Kish, Leslie. *Survey Sampling.* New York: John Wiley & Sons, 1965. By far the most authoritative work on sampling.

Mann, Thomas E., and Gary R. Orren, eds. *Media Polls in American Politics* (Washington, D.C.: The Brookings Institution, 1992). An excellent collection of essays on the use of polls in contemporary media analysis.

Survey Research Center. *Manual for Interviewers* and *Manual for Coders.* Ann Arbor, Mich.: Survey Research Center, University of Michigan. A simple, thorough introduction to the interviewing and coding processes.

Weisberg, Herbert F., Jon Krosnick, and Bruce D. Bowen. *An Introduction to Survey Research and Data Analysis.* San Francisco: W. H. Freeman and Co., 1989. A good methodological text on survey research and the interpretation of statistical analysis.

Index

NOV 1 8 1994

JAN 0 3 1995

JUL 1 8 2000